NEW ENGLAND

GETTING STARTED GARDEN GUIDE

Grow the Best Flowers, Shrubs, Trees, Vines & Groundcovers

First published in 2014 by Cool Springs Press, an imprint of the Quarto Publishing Group USA Inc., 400 First Avenue North, Suite 400, Minneapolis, MN 55401

Cool Springs Press titles are also available at discounts in bulk quantity for industrial or sales-promotional use. For details write to Special Sales Manager at Quarto Publishing Group USA Inc., 400 First Avenue North, Suite 400, Minneapolis, MN 55401 USA. To find out more about our books, visit us online at www.coolspringspress.com.

Library of Congress Cataloging-in-Publication Data

Nardozzi, Charlie.
  New England getting started garden guide : grow the best flowers, shrubs, trees, vines & groundcovers / Charlie Nardozzi.
     pages cm
  Includes index.
  ISBN 978-1-59186-610-7 (sc)
  1. Gardening--New England. 2. Plants, Ornamental--New England. I. Title.

SB453.2.N3N37 2014
635.90974--dc23

                    2014014508

Acquisitions Editor: Billie Brownell
Senior Art Director: Brad Springer
Layout: Kim Winscher

Printed in China
10 9 8 7 6 5 4 3 2 1

NEW ENGLAND

GETTING STARTED GARDEN GUIDE

Grow the Best Flowers, Shrubs, Trees, Vines & Groundcovers

Charlie Nardozzi

COOL SPRINGS PRESS
Home and Garden Experts™

MINNEAPOLIS, MINNESOTA

DEDICATION

To my mom, who still grows geraniums in her window boxes and who still likes to tell me the right way to do it.

CONTENTS

WELCOME TO GARDENING

IN NEW ENGLAND

We New Englanders have always appreciated a beautiful garden and landscape. We are blessed to live in a unique part of the world that gives us such natural beauty. From the plethora of wildflowers in spring to the amazing fall foliage that people from around the world come to admire, New England is a colorful place. We've added to that beauty with amazing landscapes and gardens. Each spring, yards burst forth with spring flowering bulbs. Many homeowners (and businesses) adorn their landscapes with annual and perennial flowerbeds along with islands of attractive trees and shrubs. Even in cities and small space areas, you'll find pots filled with geraniums, marigolds, and salvia adding bright touches to the landscape. As much as we love flowers and beautiful landscapes, we're also an eclectic bunch with influences from around the world. Our gardens and landscapes reflect that diversity. English gardens were the first to make a statement on our soils, introducing bright colors and perennial flowers to mix and match with smaller trees and shrubs. But we also have influences from

Potted mums can bring color to the fall landscape.

Asia, with simpler, less complex gardens. More recently, the native plant movement, favoring plants that have adapted well to our climate, has gained lots of attention.

Whatever the influence, growing gardens around your home or yard is a wonderful way to increase its value and increase your enjoyment of living there. It's estimated a well-landscaped yard will increase the value of your home by as much as 15 percent. But more important, a beautiful yard is a reflection of the gardener who tends it. The joy of working the soil, matching plant flower colors, dreaming of hedges and trees, and adding landscape features far outweighs the monetary value of those projects.

Whether you're just starting out with a new home, inheriting a landscape of an older home, or have a smaller space, this book is all about helping you create your own beautiful yard. Even if you don't have a whole yard to work with, there are still options of using outdoor containers to brighten up an apartment or condo. I'll offer a plethora of annual flower, perennial flower, bulb, perennial vine, tree, and shrub ideas that will grow well in our climate and soil to help you landscape your own paradise.

Blueberry bushes provide delicious fruits in the summer and brilliant red color in the fall.

New England Climates and Seasons

The first step to planning a garden is to understand where we live. New England is a great place for plants that like humid, cool, moist conditions. That's why many English garden plants grow well here. Our climate keeps us on our toes too. Each season is unique and the transitions from one to the other can seemingly happen overnight. Spring can be long and luxurious or short and quick. Some springs I'll watch my flowering bulbs slowly emerge over a period of a month or two, while other springs I remember seeing them flower and be done in a matter of a few weeks. Summer can be hot and humid, especially if you live along the Massachusetts, Rhode Island, and Connecticut coast. But the coast has the advantage of the moderating effect of the ocean. Winters are shorter, springs progress slowly, and falls can last forever.

Cooler mountain areas, such as in Vermont, Maine, and New Hampshire, offer a respite from the heat and humidity. Cool-loving flowers and plants grow well here. But the winters can be long and harsh, challenging some plants survival.

Fall is a special time in New England. Our forests light up with the bright autumn colors from native maples, oaks, ash, and many other trees. The short days and cool nights bring out a rainbow of colors, such as red, orange, yellow, purple, and gold, on tree and shrub leaves. Adding some of these trees and shrubs to your yard helps bolster us for the cold, bleak winter ahead.

Winters have traditionally been long, cold, and snowy. We're famous for our Nor'easter storms that ride up the East Coast bringing moisture from the ocean to combine with cold air from Canada. The meeting happens right above us, resulting in heavy rain or snowstorms and lots of wind. But having lived in New England my whole life, I also have noticed things are changing. I can say that springs are coming a little earlier, and falls seem to be lasting a little longer. Mostly the weather variability has gone up a notch. We can have a huge snowstorm one week, followed by 60 degree Fahrenheit temperatures the next. For our yards, this means we really need to choose our plants wisely to be able to withstand these quick changes in the weather.

Hardiness Zones

One of the tools for helping select plants that are well adapted to our climate is the hardiness zone map (page 23). This map is a standard tool for anyone growing perennial flowers, vines, trees, and shrubs. The United States Department of Agriculture's (USDA) map is split into 13 zones. The lower the zone number, the colder the *average* winter minimum temperatures will be in that zone. For New England, we are mostly in USDA hardiness zones 3 to 6. And there will be locations along the southern coast that even touch into zone 7. Our winter minimum temperature averages range from -30 degrees F in zone 3 to 0 degrees Fahrenheit in zone 6. The map even breaks the zones into "a" and "b" levels to give you further detail. You should always purchase a plant that is rated at or lower than the zone you live in. For example, in my zone 5 garden I can plant a spirea rated to zone 3 or 4, but not one rated to zone 6. I give the hardiness zones for each perennial vine, flower, tree, and shrub listed in this book or sometimes I'll simply note it's hardy throughout New England.

While the hardiness zone map is an important tool for deciding which plant to buy, it's not the only factor. Hardiness zones are just average annual winter minimum temperatures over a thirty-year period. As I mentioned, the variability of our weather has made it harder to predict what plant will survive your location long-term. I know some gardeners who have been lulled into a sense of false security thinking they were living in a warmer hardiness zone due to some mild winters, only to lose plants when a bitterly cold winter came around.

Where you plant your perennial flower, tree, or shrub makes a difference too. Each yard is unique. Many yards will have natural warm spots that may literally be a zone warmer than the rest of the yard. These warm spots are called "microclimates." These microclimates could be in a south-facing alcove, along an east-facing building, or in front of a south-facing stone wall. The plants are protected from cold winds, and being near a structure, the locations often are warmer than in more exposed ones. Look for microclimates in your yard, or create them with structures if you want to try growing plants that might be on the edge of your hardiness range.

Another deciding factor in the hardiness of your plants is natural and manmade protections. I often would have a hard time growing a certain perennial flower in my zone 5 climate only to have friends in zone 3 areas have no problem at all. What was the difference? Snow cover. Often in mountainous areas of zone 3 and 4, there is consistent snow cover all winter. Snow is an excellent insulator and will protect perennial flowers buried underneath it. In my zone 5 yard it doesn't get as cold in winter, but the snow comes and goes, not offering consistent protection.

My solution is manmade protection. Covering low-growing plants that are marginally hardy with bark mulch helps insulate their roots. I try to avoid burying them with grass clippings or fallen leaves because these tend to mat and accumulate moisture, keeping the soil too wet around the plant. For taller shrubs, creating a wind barrier with burlap often will help the plant survive. Many times it's the drying winds in winter, not the absolute cold, that cause winter damage.

Site Assessment

Before you go selecting plants based on your hardiness zone, perform a site assessment. On a piece of paper, roughly sketch out where the permanent features are in your yard. These might include buildings, power lines, underground gas lines, the mailbox, driveway, walkways, sidewalks, rocks, walls, fences, and large trees. Don't worry about the accuracy or scale of the drawing. You're just trying to get a sense of what you have now that probably won't change. Indicate where the north, south, east, and west directions are.

Then dream a little. Create circles or bubbles where you'd like to plant different types of plants based on the sun exposure. For example, draw bubbles near your house for sun- or shade-loving perennials. Draw one near the mailbox for perennial vines. Perhaps you want an annual flower garden along the driveway. Whatever thoughts you have, place these bubbles on the drawing so that you can start to see how the yard will look when you're finished. Then assess the "business" of the yard before finally deciding what trees, shrubs, flowers, and vines will be planted. This assessment will help you determine if some of your plans need scaling back or some planting just won't work in your yard. You can also enlist the help of a garden coach or landscape designer to help draw up the plan and offer suggestions for the best plants.

The Right Plant Rule

Another important factor to a successful landscape is the health of your plant. A healthy tree, shrub, vine, or perennial flower will be hardier and tougher than one that is struggling to survive. A sure way to have success is growing the right plant in the right place. You'll see me referring to this rule throughout the book. I think it's the number one reason why many plants don't survive in people's yards.

The first criterion is to find a plant that will fit in that location when it's mature. This isn't as much an issue for annual and perennial flowers (although I've seen some huge perennials misplaced in gardens), as it is for vines, trees, and shrubs. We've all seen many yards where the shrubs are chopped back because they started to block a window or walkway. Large trees can grow into power lines and buildings. The solution is to know the plant you're growing, its growth habit, and what to expect. All that information is included for the plants described in this book.

Selecting the right location also concerns the sun, soil, and wind

Hardy geraniums

exposure. Some flowers and shrubs, such as ferns and hostas, *love* shade and can burn up in the summer sun. Many other trees, shrubs, and perennial flowers need the sun to thrive. How windy and exposed your site is will factor into what you're going to be growing. Evergreen shrubs, such as mountain laurel and pieris, hold their broad leaves in winter and benefit from a more protected spot away from winter's winds. Some shrubs, such as cotoneaster and hydrangeas, are tolerant to salt spray and make good choices for coastal gardens. While most plants like a well-drained soil, some trees and shrubs like the soil consistently moist, whereas others like it to dry out a bit.

New England Soils

This leads us to soils. New England isn't known for its fertile, deep soils like some areas of the country. Sure, we have rich soil in the river valley areas where periodic flooding has dropped loads of fertile silt on the land over time. But mostly we're dealing with rocky, gravelly, sandy, and clayey soils. When I was growing up on a farm in Connecticut I'd help my grandfather pick rocks out of his fields each spring. No matter how many we picked up each spring, there would always be more next year. It seemed as if his land produced a better crop of rocks than any other crop.

Soil types around many homes can be variable. That's mostly because we've lived here for so long. Over the years, the use of the land where you lived has changed. Perhaps it was forest originally with its shallow, rich soils. It could have been farmland for a while with grass growing and animals grazing the land. It may have been an industrial site, which has the possibility of contamination of the soil. Previous homeowners may have brought in soil to level the land or grow gardens.

Your first order of business before you start planting anything is to know what type of soil you have. Soils are usually a mix of clay, silt, and sand. Certain plants prefer certain types of soils. Sycamores and cottonwood trees thrive in deep, silty soils near rivers. Crabapples and tamaracks grow well in rocky, clay soils on hillsides. Knowing what type of soil you have to start with will help you determine which plant to grow.

Let's start with a little "Soil 101." Clay soil is made up of small-sized particles. These particles hold onto water and nutrients well. Clay-dominated soils are very fertile, but warm up and dry out slowly. There's little space between the particles, so air and water doesn't drain well through clay soils.

Sandy soils are just the opposite. Sand is made up of large-sized particles. These particles have lots of room between one another for air and water to move freely. But the particles don't hold water and nutrients well, so sandy soils tend to be dry and not very fertile.

Silty soils are in between the two. Their moderate-sized particles have fair water drainage and moderate fertility.

A quick way to determine which type of soil particle dominates your soil is to do some fun, easy home tests. The first is the feel test. Dig a small hole and take a sample of soil about 4 inches below the soil line. Rub it between your fingers. If it feels gritty, then it is mostly sandy. If it feels sticky, then it has mostly clay. If it feels slick, then it's mostly silt. Next, try the ball test. Roll the soil between your hands forming a small ball. If the ball falls apart easily, then it's mostly sand. If it stays together, but changes shape easily, then it's mostly silt. If it stays together and doesn't change shape readily, then it's mostly clay. A final test is the ribbon test. Take a small handful of soil and roll it between your hands forming a ribbon. If the ribbon doesn't form, it's mostly sandy soil. If the ribbon is only 1 to 2 inches long when it's made to stand up, then it's mostly silt. If the ribbon is more than 2 inches long when it's made to stand up, then

Your soil type may be completely different from your neighbor's; gardens close in proximity often have vastly different soil types, with different color and textures from the outset.

it's mostly clay. Check around your yard in different locations for different types of soil. It's not at all uncommon for the front yard to have one type of soil and the back yard to have another.

Your soil type may be completely different from your neighbor's; gardens close in proximity often have vastly different soil types, with different colors and textures from the outset.

In urban areas another concern may be contaminated soils. For example, soils in old industrial sites may have petrochemicals or other contaminants still in them. These may affect the growth of your gardens. In the resource section, I mention soil-testing labs where you can submit soil samples to be tested for any suspected contaminants.

By knowing what type of soil you have, you can get a good idea of how the water will drain through it. Most plants need well-drained soil to survive. Some, such as ferns or silver maples, can tolerate waterlogged soils better than others. In our climate, soils can stay cool and moist for much of the growing season. If the soil doesn't drain water well, it can lead to root and crown rot and eventually to plant death. If you have mostly sandy soil, the other extreme can happen. Water will drain away so fast you'll be watering very often, or the plant will be wilting daily. Knowing the soil type will help you know how well a soil drains, but there is also a percolation test you can do at home. Dig a one-foot-diameter hole one foot deep. Fill it with water, and let it drain. Then fill it up again. If it takes more than 4 hours to drain the water a second time, that site is poorly drained. If it takes less than 10 minutes to drain, then it might be too well drained. You can look for another site for your plants, or you can amend the soil. In poorly drained soils, consider building a raised bed and amending it with compost to help the soil drain faster. In too well-drained soils, amend it with compost to hold more water. You can see compost is the key to healthy soils. Let's talk more about this magic ingredient next.

Soil Test, Compost, Mulch, Fertilizer, and Water

Whatever soil you have can be made better by adding organic matter. Organic matter makes sandy soils hold water and nutrients better, clay soils to drain water better, and any soil to be more fertile. The most common form of organic matter we can add to a soil is compost.

There has been a compost revolution happening across our region in the last twenty years. Many municipalities and private companies are making compost from fallen leaves, grass clippings, and other organic waste. In Vermont it's now illegal to send organic materials to the landfill. You have to compost them or send them to someone who does. Not only is this reducing the amount of waste going to landfills, this organic matter makes a great soil additive for our yards and gardens.

Compost is food for microbes in the soil. The more food, the more soil microbes. As these microbes die off they help make nutrients more available to plants. You really notice the results of high-fertility soils in annual flowerbeds. We often turn the soil in annual beds in the spring, which introduces more oxygen. Oxygen and organic matter make a great haven for bacterial microbes in particular. These microbes release nutrients quickly as they live and die a fast life. Our annual flowers respond with quick growth.

For trees and shrubs a different type of process is happening. These plants grow best in garden soils that mimic the forest. They like a thick layer of slow-to-decompose organic matter, such as bark or wood. This material creates the perfect environment for fungal microbes to proliferate. That's why trees and shrubs really benefit from mulching with bark and wood chips. It creates the perfect conditions for the right type of microbes to live in the soil for those plants.

So, adding compost and mulching are great ways to naturally build your soil. Certainly adding fertilizer can help as well. The first step, though, should always be a soil test. A soil test will give you a snapshot view of the nutrient levels and acidity and alkalinity of your soil. It won't be the last word, but will be a good indication if any major nutrients are way out of balance. It's often easier to amend the soil before planting to correct a problem than to try to correct it later. Check the back part of this book where I list soil labs in our region where you can have your soil tested. You can also purchase soil test kits and do your own test.

I usually recommend using an organic granular fertilizer. It's easy to use and the nutrients are released slowly into the soil. This makes them more available to the plants over time, giving them a consistent supply of nutrients. But there isn't "just one" fertilizer for every plant. Certain plants, such as rhododendrons, hydrangeas, and azaleas, like a more acidic soil, so look for fertilizers recommended for these plants. Evergreen trees and shrubs or bulbs have special formulations for their needs. Often fertilizer bags will list the types of plants that will benefit from that product.

Making sure your plants have enough water is also important. Young plants have small root systems, so they need more pampering. Annual flowers will need watering every few days, especially during hot spells, until their roots get established. Perennial flowers, trees, and shrubs will need a different type of watering. For these plants, you want to encourage the roots to grow deep into the soil. Infrequent but deep watering is the best way to water. This allows the water to soak deeply into the soil. The roots follow the water and grow deeper. Then when a dry spell happens, the roots are in a better position to tap into the natural soil water.

The Container Condition

While most gardeners will be planting in the ground, many urban or small-space gardeners will have no choice but to grow their favorite plants in containers. Container gardening is booming and, in fact, even gardeners with space to grow in the soil also grow in containers. There are many benefits to growing your favorite flowers in containers. Containers are

Lemons planted in a container can be moved inside during the cold winter months.

smaller, more portable, and easy to care for. New self-watering designs reduce the amount of watering you'll have to do to keep your plants alive in the summer. No longer will you be a slave to your container every summer weekend. The smaller soil mass means you'll have to do less weeding. Containers can be moved to just the right location. You can move them to protect against late spring or early fall frosts, winds, or even heavy rain. You can move containers to get more or less sun, depending on what you're growing. Another advantage is to move containers just because you want to change the look on your deck or patio. Flowers in containers can be switched out a number of times during the growing season. You can plant cool-loving pansies and violas in spring, heat-loving lantana and

Japanese barberry can be an invasive plant in the Northeast.

salvia in summer, then fall mums and snapdragons in autumn. Plant breeders have been developing smaller-sized varieties to fit in containers. You can now grow dwarf zinnias, sunflowers, and coneflowers that fit nicely in a pot.

There are a few points on the downside. Container plants will need more frequent fertilizing and care. The smaller soil mass holds fewer nutrients than locations in the ground, and they will need to be replenished regularly. Even with self-watering pots, container plants will need more water than their in-ground cousins. A few insects in a garden probably won't cause much harm, but in a small container they can be devastating. Larger containers can be harder to move.

Annual flowers and bulbs thrive in containers and many of those I mention in these chapters grow well in containers. Perennial flowers can be mixed and matched with annuals and bulbs or grown on their own. Even dwarf trees, shrubs, and vines can grow well in containers. I've seen many a rooftop garden in New England adorned with these plants. However, as with any perennial plant, they will need protection during our cold New England winter to survive. Often it will mean moving the container with perennial flowers, vines, trees, and shrubs in an unheated garage or basement for winter.

Invasive Plants

While many plants are opportunists, spreading themselves around the landscape, some go too far. Plants that are nonnatives can quickly become invasive in our yards and natural areas. Invasive plants are different from weeds. Weeds are just the wrong plant in the wrong place. Invasive plants spread and disrupt the whole habitat. Some exotic invasive species were accidentally introduced, and others were intentionally brought here for ornamental purposes before anyone knew their tendency to spread.

New England is not immune to invasive species. All you have to do is drive on one of the interstate highways in our region in summer and you'll see some of these invasive plants crowding out the natural growth on the roadsides. For example, I'm always amazed when I see an oriental bittersweet vine literally growing up and covering large trees, eventually killing them.

While invasive species are a big problem, only a minority of plants growing in our region is invasive. Mass Nature, a nonprofit group based in Massachusetts, estimates that only one-third of wild plants in Massachusetts are nonnative and only 7 percent of those are invasive. But the few that are invasive often grow unabated because they lack the disease or insect predators that would naturally help keep them in check in their native land. They can take over a habitat, crowding and killing off native species, reducing biodiversity, and changing ecosystems, making them less habitable for animals and birds. Their presence even can reduce the value of your home.

Many of these invasive plants are not of ornamental quality. But some were introduced into New England for their attractive properties and have been sold in nurseries for years. Many states now have laws about purchasing and planting invasive species in your yard, and the states encourage homeowners to remove any invasive exotics to reduce their spread. Invasive species mostly spread by seeds and roots. While rampant growth of plants, such as oriental bittersweet and Japanese knotweed, is a concern, a bigger problem is when their seeds are spread throughout the environment by birds, creating new seedlings in previously pristine areas. Invasive plants that spread rapidly by seed include some familiar characters, such as purple loosestrife (perennial flower), Japanese barberry, and burning bush.

Some invasive plants spread by their roots. Japanese knotweed, common reed grass, and multiflora rose have aggressive root systems that will spread throughout an area out-competing other plants.

To reduce the destruction caused by invasive plants, don't purchase any plants that are considered invasive. In the resource section, I note websites with lists of invasive plants in our region. Some states, such as Connecticut and Massachusetts, are very aggressive about reducing invasive plants in the landscape and have banned the sale of some invasive, yet very familiar plants, such as burning bush. Look at these lists carefully. Often one species within a plant group may be invasive and should be avoided, but there may be a noninvasive alternative in that same plant family. For example, Norway maple is considered an invasive species, but red, sugar, and silver maples are not. In this book I indicate the noninvasive selections for different plant groups. Double-check your choices for your yard against these lists to be sure you're not inadvertently spreading invasive species just by planting them in your yard.

If you do have invasive plants in your yard, and it's hard not to anymore, there are some means of control to help reduce or eliminate them. Plant researchers have introduced pests of some of these invasive plants collected from their natural homeland

Daylily and yarrow

to help control the plant in our environment. A good example is a small beetle imported to control the perennial flower purple loosestrife. There's ongoing research to find other similar diseases or insects that will help control other invasive species.

You can spray herbicides to kill many invasive plants, but you'll have to be very careful not to kill native and landscape plants. Also, many times you'll have to reapply the herbicide repeatedly to kill the aggressive plant. This runs the risk of inadvertently damaging the ecosystem. The best way to reduce the amount of invasive plants in your yard is to cut down or dig out the plants and kill them. Buckthorn, oriental bittersweet, and tree of heaven (*Ailanthus altissima*) are some of the shrubs and vines that will need to be aggressively dug up or repeatedly cut back to the ground in order to kill them. It's best to do this in fall or winter when birds aren't nesting in the trees or vines. For lower-growing, seed-spreading invasive species, such as garlic mustard, try to cut these plants down to prevent them from flowering and setting seed. This will slowly reduce the amount of seed in the environment.

Once you've done the hard work of removing an invasive species from your yard, don't stop there. You'll need to replace that plant with a noninvasive alternative. If you don't, the invasive plant may show up again in the near future. Below are some common invasive species in our region and some possible alternatives to them.

Many of the best alternatives to invasive species are native plants. Native plants have been growing successfully in our environment for long periods and have evolved slowly with other species, insects, and wildlife to create an ecological balance. Research has shown that native species of trees, shrubs, perennial flowers, and vines create a more diverse habitat by encouraging a broad range of insects, birds, and animals to live there. Many gardeners are trying to introduce native species into their landscape.

Invasive Species	Alternative Plants
Burning bush (*Euonymous alatus*)	Gray dogwood, blueberry, sumac
Japanese barberry (*Berberis thunbergii*)	Winterberry, summersweet, smooth-leafed hydrangea
Multiflora rose (*Rosa multiflora*)	Raspberry, winterberry, summersweet
Autumn olive (*Elaeagnus umbellata*)	American cranberry viburnum, winterberry, beach plum
Tree of Heaven (*Ailanthus altissima*)	Redbud, flowering dogwood, serviceberry
Oriental bittersweet (*Celastus orbiculatus*)	Trumpet honeysuckle, Virginia creeper
Japanese knotweed (*Polygonum cuspidatum*)	Elderberry, pussy willow
Purple loosestrife (*Lythrum salicaria*)	Bee balm, purple coneflower, butterfly weed

Adapted from Connecticut River Coastal Conservation District, Inc.

The native species are usually tough plants that are easy to grow. They can be beautiful in themselves, and there are often improved versions of natives that make excellent plants. One of my favorites is the serviceberry (*Amelanchier*). This native grows into a 15- to 30-foot tall, multistemmed tree. It has bright white flowers in spring, blue berries in summer, and orange-red fall foliage color. Insects love the flowers, birds love the berries, and the fall color is outstanding in the landscape. Newer selections feature better fruit production (the edibles are tasty for us too) and better fall color.

When shopping in garden centers or nurseries, look for plants identified as native and try to include some of those in your plant lists.

Controlling Pests

Growing the right plant in the right place, growing natives, and growing plants adapted to your climate and soils are important ways to avoid having to deal with pests. Insects, diseases, and animals seem to know when a plant is stressed and will often attack that plant before healthy ones. Just like us, if your plant stays healthy, it is less likely to get sick.

That being said, even the best New England gardener with the healthiest plants will have to deal with pests at some time or another. Here are some ways to control pests using sprays only as a last resort.

When selecting plants look for disease- or insect-resistant varieties. It's a lot easier to prevent powdery mildew on bee balm by growing a resistant variety than having to spray for it each summer. Avoid having problems with the red lily leaf beetles by planting more resistant varieties, such as *Lilium* 'Black Beauty'. Deer is a *huge* problem in our region. Deer herds have adapted well to our building into their habitat, and they enjoy munching on their newfound food source—our gardens. Based on regional research, I indicate in this book the plants that are more deer *resistant*, but know that no plant is totally deer resistant. If they're hungry enough, deer will eat anything. However, some plants are less likely to be damaged than others.

This leads me to a second way to prevent damage: barriers. Keep rabbits, deer, and woodchucks out of your yard and garden with a fence. The fence can protect individual plants or a whole area. Make sure it's the right size so that deer can't jump over it or bunnies tunnel under. You can use barriers also to block insects, such as leaf miners, from attacking plants such as columbine. Remove the lightweight row covers when the flowers start to emerge. Copper stripping can be used to keep slugs and snails away from hostas and other perennials grown in containers or raised beds. Slugs and snails don't like crossing copper barriers, so attaching copper strips on the lip of containers or along the edge of raised beds can save you a lot of headaches.

You can also create a habitat that certain insects or diseases don't like. Keep foliage dry to slow down diseases such as rust and blackspot. Space plants farther apart and keep areas weed-free to help keep leaves dry. Remove mulch and cultivate regularly to keep the top layers of the soil dry. This removes places for slugs and snails to hide. Taste- and smell-based repellent animal sprays contain lovely ingredients such as putrescent eggs and cayenne pepper. If applied regularly these can work to keep animals away from prized plants.

Traps, such as Japanese beetle traps, can help reduce pest populations. To work most effectively, locate traps away from the plants you are trying to protect. If you must resort to pesticide sprays, use those that are specific to that pest. For example, *Bacillus thuriengensis* (Bt, thuricide, dipel) kills caterpillars in the butterfly family such as tent caterpillars on crabapples trees. But, try to spray when bees and other insects aren't as active, such as in the evening, to reduce harm to them.

Time to Get Started!

So with your plant list and yard assessment in hand, it's time to explore all the possible plants that you can grow and make your yard a beautiful oasis for your family. Happy gardening!

Clematis

How to Use *New England Getting Started Garden Guide*

The main section of this book is an extensive garden guide of annual flowers, perennial flowers, perennial vines, bulbs, shrubs, and trees. Each entry includes the botanical name and pronunciation, common name, maximum height and width of the plant, sun preferences, bloom season and seasonal color, and growing information. The growing information is geared toward New England and includes planting, watering, fertilizing, pruning, and general care of that plant.

There is also a section titled "Companion Planting and Design" that offers some tips on where to grow this plant in the landscape and which plants are good partners for it. In the "Try These" section I suggest new and old varieties that grow well in our region.

Sun Preferences

While each entry is mostly a narrative about that plant, there are symbols that are used to give more information. The sun preferences for each entry have symbols that represent the primary sun need or a range of sun conditions suitable for that plant. "Full Sun" means at least 6 hours of direct sun a day. "Part Sun" means 4 to 6 hours of direct sun a day. "Part Shade" means 2 to 4 hours of direct sun. "Full Shade" means less than 2 hours of direct sun. You'll often see more than one sun exposure listed for a particular plant. This means that plant can grow well under a number of different conditions.

Full Sun   Part Sun   Part Shade   Shade

Additional Benefits

Many plants offer benefits beyond their obvious flowers or stature. These are symbols that represent these benefits.

 Attracts Beneficials - Butterflies, bees, and birds are attracted to this plant.

 Edible - This plant produces edible fruits, flowers, leaves, or seeds for us to eat.

 Attracts Hummingbirds - Hummingbirds like to feed on the flowers of this plant.

 Fall/Seasonal Color - This plant produces beautiful fall leaf color.

 Drought Tolerant - This plant can withstand dry periods and still thrive.

 Native - This plant is native to our region making it more likely to survive our climate and conditions.

 Deer Resistant - Although no plant is totally deer resistant, this plant is less likely to be harmed by browsing deer.

USDA Hardiness Zone Map

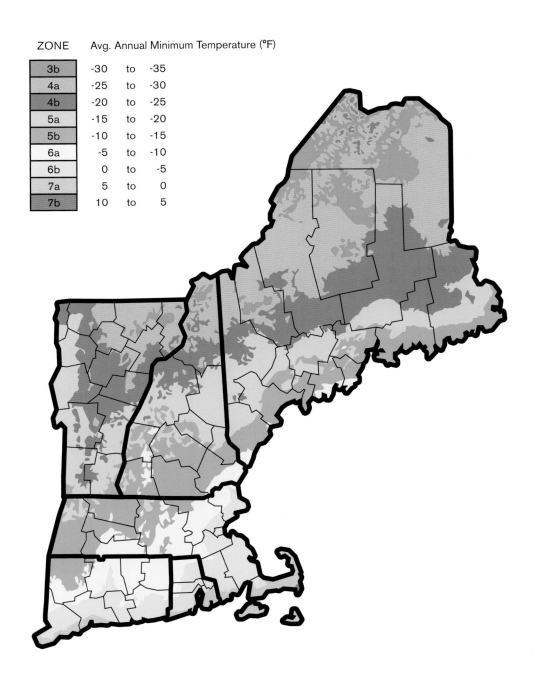

ZONE	Avg. Annual Minimum Temperature (°F)		
3b	-30	to	-35
4a	-25	to	-30
4b	-20	to	-25
5a	-15	to	-20
5b	-10	to	-15
6a	-5	to	-10
6b	0	to	-5
7a	5	to	0
7b	10	to	5

USDA Plant Hardiness Zone Map, 2012. Agricultural Research Service, U.S. Department of Agriculture. Accessed from http://planthardiness.ars.usda.gov.

ANNUALS
FOR NEW ENGLAND

Annual flowers are the workhorses in the garden. They are bred to grow quickly to the flowering stage in spring or early summer and then it's the "petal to the metal," blooming until frost. There aren't a lot of surprises with annuals. They are the "what you see is what you get" flowers.

You Know Where You Stand with Annuals

Perennial flower gardens are a bit of a guessing game. You never know how flower combinations will look until they bloom. Annuals are not that subtle. You'll often find annual flowers in bloom in garden centers in pots. This makes it easier to select annual flower varieties. That's a good thing because some annuals, such as petunias and geraniums, have *hundreds* of varieties to choose from. Without seeing the flower in bloom, it would be tough to know the difference between colors just based on a name. So, although it's usually best to select flowers in a garden center that aren't in flower, you'll be more satisfied with what you get.

Remember your color schemes when planting annual flowers. If you're planting a bed that will be primarily viewed from a distance, like the road, plant bright colors such as red, orange, and yellow. For beds of annual flowers that will be viewed close up,

A colorful flower garden with zinnias, crocosmia, daylilies, and boxwood.

along a walkway or a deck, plant more pastel colored flowers such as lavender, white, and pink. Pastel colors are easier on the eyes and you can notice the subtleties of the flower patterns better. Loud colors close up are too much on the eyes, while pastel colors viewed from far away just get lost in the landscape.

More than Just Bedding Plants

Annuals are more than bedding plants. They work great with perennial flowers or around shrubs to provide color when your garden is transitioning from spring to summer or summer to fall bloomers. Annuals provide beauty during those in-between times when there's little color.

Impatiens, geranium and begonia

Annuals work great in small spaces. Window boxes, railing planters, containers, and hanging baskets are perfect places for cascading or mounding annuals. Mix and match different-sized annuals in larger containers using the "thrillers, fillers, and spillers" rule. Plant tall annuals, such as larkspur and cleome, in the center of the container as your thriller plant. Around that centerpiece, plant shorter filler plants such as Profusion zinnias, marigolds, and salvia. Then along the edge of the container add spiller plants that cascade, such as calibrochoa, scaevola, lobelia, and ivy geraniums. This makes your container seem larger as you fill spaces above and below the rim.

While annuals can be grown in many locations, you do have to keep them fueled so they stay blooming all summer. Annuals are like teenage boys. The refrigerator is always empty trying to keep up with all their energy. But first, plant annuals in the right spots. Shade lovers, such as torenia, begonia, and impatiens, should be kept out of hot afternoon sun. It's better to plant the sun and heat lovers, such as moss rose and lantana, in those places. Keep all annuals watered and fed regularly, especially in containers. During hot periods you may be watering daily and feeding every few weeks.

While annuals are bred to grow, bloom, and die in fall, some just won't go away, even in our cold New England climate. Some annuals, such as cleome, nicotiana, poppies, and calendula, will form seedpods and drop hundreds of seeds around your garden in summer. These seeds will overwinter and start growing in spring. This could mean free plants next year, but you'll have to be diligent about weeding them out so they aren't overcrowded. Plus, sometimes the quality of the resulting flower is not as good as the original. If you don't want your annuals to self-sow, select sterile seeded varieties or weed well in spring. Some annuals, such as violas and snapdragons, might even overwinter under our snow cover and provide an early spring surprise of color.

African Daisy

Osteospermum spp.

Botanical Pronunciation
oss-tee-oh-SPUR-mum

Other Name
Cape daisy

Bloom Period and Seasonal Color
All summer; purple, pink, yellow, rose, and white, with blue centers

Mature Height × Spread
1 to 3 feet × 1 to 2 feet

This South African native looks like a Shasta daisy or zinnia, but the flower centers are blue, and the plants are more drought tolerant. Although botanically they're perennial in warmer climates, in New England we grow them as an annual flower. I love how they give the garden a burst of color. The lance-shaped leaves grow on short, bushy plants that produce a wide range of flower colors depending on the variety. Many mixes have multiple-colored flowers in one mix. The flower petals can be smooth or tube-shaped. They will bloom all summer, but may temporarily stop during hot spells. In Northern parts of New England where the summers are cooler, they may bloom nonstop all summer.

When, Where, and How to Plant

African daisies grow best in slightly acidic soil with a pH around 5.5. Amend your soil accordingly before planting. Although they can be grown from seeds started indoors, most are purchased as transplants in spring and planted out after all danger of frost has passed. You can start seedlings indoors, but they need light to germinate and cool temperatures, so grow them under lights but *don't* grow them on a heating mat. Sow seeds directly into the garden, but don't cover them with soil so they get light to germinate. Plant individual seedlings or thin seeds to 1 foot apart in beds or containers.

Growing Tips

Although drought tolerant once established, keep plants well watered the first few weeks. African daisies bloom best with cool nights. During hot, dry periods in summer, they will go dormant. Cut back foliage during hot spells once the flowering stops, and the new growth will produce more flowers once the weather cools. Feed every few weeks with a complete liquid fertilizer to keep them blooming. Most varieties have sterile seeds so deadheading isn't necessary to prevent self-sowing, but it does make the plant look tidier.

Regional Advice and Care

Pinch back the center of young plants to stimulate branching and a bushier, more floriferous plant. During hot, humid summers, remove mulch around plants to increase airflow and reduce fungal diseases. Watch for whiteflies and aphids on new growth and spray insecticidal soap to kill them.

Companion Planting and Design

African daises can go dormant in summer heat, so it's good to pair them with other annuals or midsummer blooming perennials, such as moss rose, salvia, and veronica. The blue flower centers look particularly attractive when paired with blue flowers. They can be planted together on banks for more of a wildflower look or grown in containers and paired with other annuals such as stocks, alyssum, and lobelia.

Try These

The 'Soprano Mix' features more heat-tolerant plants that will bloom longer in hot spells and the plants are more compact. 'Passion Mix' is quick to bloom and easy to grow from seed.

Ageratum

Ageratum houstonianum

Botanical Pronunciation
ah-jer-AY-tum hous-tone-ee-AN-um

Other Name
Floss flower

Bloom Period and Seasonal Color
Summer to frost; blue, white, violet, and pink

Mature Height × Spread
6 to 24 inches × 6 to 12 inches

Ageratum is a workhorse annual flower in many New England gardens. It's a low-growing, low-maintenance annual that blooms all summer in sun or part sun with little care. The small mounding plants tolerate dry, infertile soil once established. The small, buttonlike flowers are produced in clusters. Although various shades of blue are the most common colors of ageratum, pink and white selections are now available to broaden the color scheme and allow gardeners to mix and match ageratum with a wider variety of plants. They look particularly attractive used along the front edge of a border of annual or perennial plants or in a container with taller annuals. In my garden, butterflies *love* to alight on patches of ageratums.

When, Where, and How to Plant
Ageratums are not fussy about soil as long as it's well drained. Purchase transplants from your garden center and set them out into the garden 6 inches apart in spring after all danger of frost has passed. To produce a larger quantity of ageratum for less cost, start seeds indoors 8 to 10 weeks before the last frost date in your area. Barely cover the seed with potting soil, as they need light to germinate. Plant in full sun in cooler parts of New England. Plant in part shade in warmer regions, or if grown in a warm microclimate, such as near a south-facing stone wall.

Growing Tips
Keep plants well watered and weeded once transplanted. Although they can tolerate dry conditions, young plants need moist soil to get established. Pinch back the growing tips of young plants to stimulate them to branch out and form a bushier plant. This will lead to more flowers. Deadhead the flowers to keep them blooming all summer and for a tidier appearance.

Regional Advice and Care
During hot, dry spells spider mites can attack ageratum causing them to dieback. To prevent spider mite infestations, mist the plants during dry spells with water; spider mites don't like humid conditions. Cut back damaged plants if you miss the infestation, and they should regrow and flower again.

Companion Planting and Design
Ageratums are best grown in front of walkways or flowerbeds. They look great planted in masses of one color. They also are attractive paired with silver foliaged plants such as artemesia. Petunias and another low-growing annual look great next to ageratum. Plant contrasting colored flowers, such as rudbeckia or tall marigolds, behind ageratum to create a nice color combination.

Try These
The 'Hawaii Series' of ageratum features white, pink, and blue selections that only grow 6 inches tall. 'Hawaiian Royal' is particularly attractive for its true blue color. 'Blue Horizon' is a taller growing ageratum that can reach 2 feet tall. 'Red Top' is another tall grower that features burgundy-colored flowers. 'Southern Cross' features bicolored flowers on compact plants.

Alyssum

Lobularia maritima

Botanical Pronunciation
lob-you-LAIR-ee-uh muh-RIT-ih-muh

Other Name
Sweet alyssum

Bloom Period and Seasonal Color
Blooms all summer; white, lavender, and pink

Mature Height × Spread
4 to 6 inches × 6 to 12 inches

Alyssum is a low-growing annual that is known for its carpet of sweet smelling white-, violet-, or purple-colored flowers. It grows and flowers best during the coolest parts of the summer in New England, but in northern and coastal areas it can be in flower all summer long. The narrow hairy leaves are inconspicuous when alyssum is in full flower. Bees, butterflies, and other insects love alyssum, making it a good plant in a pollinator garden. In my garden it will self-sow readily and become a permanent fixture each year. However, I still like to replant new varieties each spring for added color and to grow more vigorous plants.

When, Where, and How to Plant

Alyssum grows best in well-drained, humusy soil that holds moisture well in summer. Hot, dry spells cause alyssum to stop flowering and potentially die back. Alyssum needs at least 4 to 6 hours of direct sun to flower well. Alyssum grows well planted directly in the garden from seed, started as seedlings indoors 8 to 10 weeks before the last frost date or purchased as a transplant. Alyssum seeded directly in the garden will bloom later than those started or purchased as transplants. Sow seeds or plant transplants in spring after all danger of frost has passed. Simply sprinkle seeds in the soil bed and lightly press them into the soil. Keep the soil evenly moist, and seeds will germinate within one week. Plant alyssum tightly together in groups spaced only 6 inches apart to create a quicker flowering carpet effect.

Growing Tips

Keep alyssum well watered during hot, dry weather. It has few pests and diseases. To stimulate more growth and flowering, in midsummer shear alyssum by one-third. Afterward fertilize with a balanced product and water; they will regrow for a late summer flower show. When grown in containers or small spaces with little soil, fertilize monthly to keep them growing strong.

Regional Advice and Care

Alyssum will self-sow readily in our climate. However, the seedlings tend to have poorer quality flowers so it's best to remove them and start with fresh seed or transplants yearly.

Companion Planting and Design

Sweet alyssum grows best where it can be showcased. Plant or sow seeds in front of flower borders, in containers with other taller-growing annuals, such as salvia and Profusion zinnias, and in walls or rock gardens among other low-growing perennials and wildflowers, such as columbine.

Try These

Newer varieties have sterile flowers so they don't self-sow readily. 'Easter Bonnet Mix' has flowers with white, purple, and pink colors on plants that hold their mounded shape well in summer. 'Aphrodite Mix' has unusual apricot, salmon, and red flowers. 'Clear Crystals Mix' has more traditional white and pink flowers that are larger and more clear colored.

Bachelor's Buttons

Centaurea cyanus

Botanical Pronunciation
sen-TAR-ee-a sy-AN-us

Other Name
Cornflower

Bloom Period and Seasonal Color
Summer until frost; blue, pink, crimson, white, and bicolors

Mature Height × Spread
1 to 3 feet × 4 to 8 inches

Traditional bachelor's buttons are true blue-colored annual flowers with attractive double flowers that can be grown in gardens or containers, used as cut or dried flowers in arrangements, or even eaten in salads. They look like mini-carnations and were once worn in the lapels of bachelors, hence its common name. These easy-to-grow, lightly fragrant flowers now come in a broad range of flower colors, such as pink, purple, crimson, white, and bicolors. Mixes look great planted together producing a riot of color or planted in groups of individual flower colors to harvest for flower arrangements. Keep them healthy and these carefree plants will reward you with flowers all summer long in our climate.

When, Where, and How to Plant

Bachleor's buttons grow easily directly sown in the garden. A frugal way to have a mass of these flowers is to sow seeds after all danger of frost has passed in spring in a sunny, well-drained location. Keep the seedbed moist, and the plants will emerge in about 10 days. If you only need a few bachelor's buttons, buy transplants from the local garden center or start seeds indoors under grow lights 8 weeks before your last frost date to transplant into the garden. Transplants will flower sooner than plants sown directly in the soil. Space transplants 8 to 12 inches apart for best flowering.

Growing Tips

Thin directly sown transplants after the second set of leaves emerge. Keep plants well weeded and watered. Mature plants are drought tolerant. Fertilize monthly with a complete, organic fertilizer. To keep the plants from flopping over, plant them closer together so they support each other or stake them. Deadhead spent flowers to keep the flower show coming all summer.

Regional Advice and Care

Bachelor's buttons self-sow readily and the offspring are just as colorful as their parents. Plant bachelor's buttons where you can enjoy them each year, or save the seed from the brown seedpods and sow the seeds in new locations each spring. Once established, you'll have bachelor's buttons for *years* in your yard.

Companion Planting and Design

Plant bachelor's buttons in the garden with complementary-colored flowers, such as orange Profusion zinnias or yellow marigolds. Consider planting several in a cutting garden for a continual crop of flowers for the house or in a meadow setting to grow them more like a wildflower.

Try These

'Blue Boy' is a traditional variety with double, fringed, thistlelike, sky blue flowers on 2- to 3-foot-tall plants. 'Polka Dot Mix' offers a unique range of colors from pink, blue, lavender, red, white, and unusual bicolors. 'Black Ball' is a unique, dark crimson-colored bachelor's button that makes a great cut flower.

Begonia

Begonia spp.

Botanical Pronunciation
buh-GO-nya

Other Name
Wax begonia

Bloom Period and Seasonal Color
Summer until frost; white, pink, coral, salmon, and red

Mature Height × Spread
6 to 24 inches × 12 to 18 inches

Begonias are a broad group of shade-loving flowers. The wax leaf begonia is probably the most popular annual for shade gardens and container growing. They're one of the few annual plants that flower well in part shade. Not only are the flowers attractive in shades of white, pink, and red, but some varieties have red or bronze-tinged, glossy leaves making them an attractive plant even when they aren't in flower. This low-growing plant will flower right up to frost and can be brought indoors to continue flowering in a sunny window. Another popular type of begonia for gardens is the tuberous begonia. I'll cover those in the bulb section of this book.

When, Where, and How to Plant

While you can grow wax begonias from seed started indoors 12 weeks before your last frost date, most home gardeners prefer to buy transplants from the local garden center. Although they grow well in shade, too much shade will inhibit flowering. Ideally they will get a few hours of morning sun to flower best. Plant seedlings in well-drained, moist soil in a part sun or part shade location after all danger of frost has passed. Space plants 8 inches apart in beds and closer together in containers.

Growing Tips

Keep the plants well watered, but be careful not to overwater. During our humid, sometimes rainy summers, overwatered begonia stems and roots often rot. Water more frequently when it's grown in hanging baskets or containers. Fertilize monthly with an organic plant food.

Regional Advice and Care

Deadhead spent flowers on your begonia plants, and remove any rotting stems if they get overwatered. Watch for slugs and snails on the foliage during wet weather and set up traps or spread iron phosphate organic baits to protect your plants if needed.

Companion Planting and Design

Wax begonias are often seen as the classic hanging basket or container plant. The small plants flower quickly and never get too large for their container. Hang the baskets where they get some sun and away from the roof edge where they might get drown in water during a storm. In the garden, plant wax begonias under trees or in front of shady flower or shrub borders to brighten up a dark area. They look best planted together in masses to create a flowering groundcover effect.

Try These

The 'Ambassador Series' begonia features a compact, early flowering mix of red-, pink-, and white-flowering plants. The 'Big Series' features larger flowers and plants with bronze or green leaves. 'Whopper Series' is a new sun-tolerant wax begonia that blooms as well in full sun as shade in our region and can grow to 24 inches tall.

Calendula

Calendula officinalis

Botanical Pronunciation
kuh-LEN-dew-luh uh-fiss-ih-NAY-liss

Other Name
Pot marigold

Bloom Period and Seasonal Color
Early summer to fall; white, orange, gold, and yellow

Mature Height × Spread
12 to 30 inches × 12 to 18 inches

Calendula is a bright, cheery addition to any annual garden. The small plants produce vibrant white-, yellow-, or orange-colored flowers, depending on the variety, from early summer through fall; some are even bicolor. The plants can even withstand a light frost in fall. The flowers come with single or double petals. Not only are the flowers showy, but the petals are edible. I love sprinkling a small handful of calendula petals on my summer salads or in soups. The petals can also be used to make a yellow pigment similar to saffron. Calendula craves full sun. They will survive less than ideal light conditions, but won't bloom as vigorously. Calendula grows equally well in containers as they do in the ground.

When, Where, and How to Plant
Sow calendula seeds in the spring in a full or part sun location in the garden as soon as the soil can be worked. To get a faster start, sow seeds indoors under grow lights 6 weeks before your last frost date. Transplant seedlings or thin direct sown seeds to 6 to 12 inches apart in beds amended with compost. Calendula grows best in well-drained compost-rich soils.

Growing Tips
Calendula flowers best during the cooler parts of early and late summer. Deadhead spent flowers to keep the plant looking tidy and to encourage more flowering. During hot weather the plants may stop flowering and the foliage looks ragged. Cut back the plants to about 3 inches tall to encourage more new growth, and they should start to flower again

soon afterward. Fertilize calendula with an organic plant food monthly to encourage blooms.

Regional Advice and Care
Calendula are easy-to-grow annuals that suffer few pests. During periods of wet, humid summer weather, some varieties can develop powdery mildew disease and should be cut back and sprayed with an organic fungicide to control it. Harvest newly opened flowers in the morning after the dew has dried if you're going to eat them. Single-petaled varieties have a less bitter taste than double-petaled flowers. You can also dry petals for later use. Calendula self-sow readily in our climate, so don't be surprised to see some seedlings next spring. Thin these to 6 inches apart and enjoy the flower show.

Companion Planting and Design
Calendula look best grouped together in a flowerbed or container. You can also mix and match this annual with the blue flowers of lobelia and salvia. Many gardeners grow calendula near vegetables as companion plants to aid the vegetables growth and brighten up the veggie garden.

Try These
'Calypso Series' features pompomlike flowers in orange or yellow with dark-colored centers. The plants are dense growers making them great for container growing. 'Pacific Beauty Mix' are heat-tolerant plants with long-stemmed orange- or golden-colored flowers. 'Kablouna Series' has gold-, lemon-, orange-, or apricot-colored flowers on powdery mildew-resistant plants.

Celosia

Celosia argentea var. *cristata*

Botanical Pronunciation
sel-O-see-a ar-JEN-tee-a cris-TAY-ta

Other Name
Cockscomb

Bloom Period and Seasonal Color
Summer until fall; red, pink, yellow, apricot, gold, and cream

Mature Height × Spread
6 to 24 inches × 8 to 12 inches

Whether you grow the feather-shaped or coral-like-shaped celosia, you'll be able to enjoy this annual flower with its multitude of colors from early summer until frost. Celosia is a classic bedding plant, meaning it looks best planted in groups in the ground where the color show can really be highlighted. The vibrant colors definitely put on a show when grown together making them great for a bed that's viewed from a distance. And some varieties have bronze-colored foliage too, making for an even better color contrast. The feathery types are more delicate, while the coral-shaped varieties look more like a brain (but in a good way). Taller types are great for use as cut flowers, lasting up to 3 weeks indoors, or dried flowers.

When, Where, and How to Plant

Although you can direct sow celosia seed into the garden in spring, they will take so long to get to the flowering stage that it's better in our climate either to sow seeds indoors under grow lights 6 weeks before your last frost date or purchase seedlings from a local garden center. Plant celosia seedlings in full sun for best flowering, in compost amended soil after the last frost, spacing plants about 6 to 12 inches apart. Celosia seedlings like the heat, so don't rush them into the ground in early or mid-May when the soil may still be cool.

Growing Tips

Poorly drained soils can lead to root rot, so grow celosia in raised beds or in sandy loam soils. Group tall varieties together or stake them to prevent strong winds from breaking their stems. Don't worry if the stems break; the side shoots will form and soon you'll have more, but smaller, flowers. Fertilize monthly with a complete organic plant food to keep them flowering. Keep the plants well watered.

Regional Advice and Care

With our sometimes rainy springs, celosia is prone to needing some extra nitrogen fertilizer to get growing. A dose of fish emulsion fertilizer right after planting may also help if young plants are looking yellow.

Companion Planting and Design

Different varieties of celosia look great planted *en masse* in a bed varying the heights and flower colors. Celosia also pairs well with other annual flowers, such as zinnia, marigold, and amaranth. You can plant the tall varieties in a cutting garden for use in arrangements and grow some celosia in pots to bring indoors in fall. After a few weeks they will start looking ratty, but will be nice fall accents in a sunny window.

Try These

The 'Fresh Look Series' has won awards for the vivid yellow- or red-colored feathered blossoms that don't fade and compact plants that are drought and heat tolerant. They look equally good in the ground as in containers. 'Bombay Series' features coral-like, brightly colored heads in red, yellow, and even purple.

Chrysanthemum

Chrysanthemum indicum

Botanical Pronunciation
kris-AN-thee-mum-In-dee-kum

Other Name
Garden mum

Bloom Period and Seasonal Color
Late summer into fall; white, yellow, pink, burgundy, red, and lavender

Mature Height × Spread
1 to 3 feet × 1 to 2 feet

No flower says fall in New England like the chrysanthemum. The garden mum is just one type of chrysanthemum that we can grow in our gardens. Although it's botanically a perennial, most gardeners grow these as annual flowers. They can be coaxed to come back in warmer parts of New England. The colors are diverse and vivid. The flower shapes can be almost as varied including pompon, spider, button, and daisy shapes. Mums provide a splash of fall color when few other perennials or annual flowers are still thriving. They can take a frost and keep flowering, sometimes right up to Thanksgiving, depending on the autumn weather.

When, Where, and How to Plant
Look for garden mums in garden centers starting in September. These plants are grown in greenhouses from cuttings, so growing your own from seed isn't really possible. Plant in full sun, in well-drained, compost-amended soil. Plant them in a protected spot if you intend on trying to overwinter your garden mum. Planting in early fall will increase the chances of a chrysanthemum surviving the winter because it will have more time to establish its root system in the native soil. Planting in containers or in late fall is best for chrysanthemums that you plan on growing only as an annual and composting after it's done flowering.

Growing Tips
Keep plants well watered, especially if the fall is dry. Don't fertilize fall-planted chrysanthemums since you don't want to encourage new growth. If

you can successfully overwinter your garden mum, fertilizer in spring with an all-purpose, granular, organic plant food.

Regional Advice and Care
Plant garden mums in a protected location, such as along a foundation, in well-drained soil if you intend on overwintering the plant. Garden mums grown as annuals don't need deadheading or pinching. However, overwintered plants should be pinched back in early summer for a bushier plant. Don't crowd chrysanthemums in a bed as you may get leaf spots and fungal diseases developing, especially during wet falls.

Companion Planting and Design
Chrysanthemums look great planted together in different colors in beds. You can mix and match them in containers with other fall annuals, such as flowering kale. They look great in a harvest scene paired with pumpkins, stalks of corn, and sunflowers. Mix chrysanthemums in with perennials, such as ornamental grasses, sedums, and low-growing evergreens.

Try These
Most garden mums in garden centers don't have specific variety names. Look for colors that are attractive for your yard, especially when only growing these annuals for fall. Some named varieties that a little hardier than the average garden mum and available as perennials include the single, pink-flowered 'Clara Curtis' and the single, apricot-colored 'Mary Stoker'.

Cleome

Cleome hasslerana

Botanical Pronunciation
klay-O-mee has-ler-i-AN-a

Other Name
Spider flower

Bloom Period and Seasonal Color
Early summer until fall; white, pink, lavender, and rose

Mature Height × Spread
3 to 6 feet × 12 to 18 inches

Cleome, or spider flower, is often overlooked as a seedling in garden centers because of its nondescript, almost weedy appearance. However, once established in the flower garden, cleome puts on a dazzling summer flower show until frost. It's a tall, thorny-stalked annual with spiderlike flower heads. When planted in groups it gives the impression of a flowering shrub. The flowers can have a musky odor, but that doesn't stop hummingbirds and butterflies from flocking to this flower all summer. Once the flowers have passed the seedpods drop cleome seed on the ground so you'll have a patch of them, for better or for worse, next year as well.

When, Where, and How to Plant

Plant cleome seed on fertile beds in spring after all danger of frost has passed. Don't bury the seed as it needs light to germinate. Simply press the seed into the soil and keep it well watered. You can also purchase cleome transplants from garden centers or start them indoors under grow lights 6 weeks before your last frost date. Direct seeded cleome will start blooming later than transplants, but if you're growing many plants this is a less expensive way to grow them. Plant in full sun, thinning or spacing individual plants to 1 foot apart. Plant where you won't have to brush against the stems since many varieties have thorns. Look for newer hybrid thornless varieties if that becomes an issue.

Growing Tips

Cleome don't usually require extra feeding so if you have fertile soil, no additional fertilizing

will be needed. Plants not thinned properly and grown too close together will be shorter, with smaller flowers and may be yellow due to lack of nitrogen from the competition. Keep seedlings well watered. Once it's established, cleome is drought tolerant.

Regional Advice and Care

Cleome have a strong propensity to self-sow. It's not unusual to see hundreds of baby cleomes growing in your garden the following spring. If you want to limit the amount of seed being sown, deadhead spent flowers before the seedpods brown and mature. You can also grow newer hybrids that produce sterile seeds.

Companion Planting and Design

Grow cleome in masses for drifts of colors. Cleome pairs well with shorter-growing annuals and perennials, such as sedum and mounding zinnias, since the bottom cleome leaves often yellow by late summer. The flowers will still look good in the back of the flower border, but the foliage from other low-growing plants will hide the bare cleome stalks.

Try These

'Senorita Rosalita' and 'Senorita Blanca' are two new hybrids that are thornless and produce sterile seed. The 'Queen Series' features tall, sturdy plants with flower colors, such as white, rose, and violet. It self-sows readily. The 'Sparkler Series' has short, bushy plants that perform well in containers.

Clown Flower

Torenia fournieri

Botanical Pronunciation
tour-E-EN-ah four-knee-ER-e

Other Name
Wishbone flower

Bloom Period and Seasonal Color
Early summer to fall; red, violet, purple, white, and bicolors

Mature Height × Spread
6 to 12 inches × 6 to 9 inches

If you want an annual to flower in the shade in New England, this is one most gardeners overlook. Torenia, also called clown flower, is a low-growing, mounded annual flower that produces tubular blooms in a variety of colors. Often the blossoms will be bicolored with contrasting colored throats. The flowers tend to be in the cool pastel color range making them seem relaxing when viewed in the hot summer. Because it's a small plant that doesn't get out of hand, clown flower is a perfect plant for window boxes, hanging baskets, and containers. It doesn't require much light to bloom, so you can also bring pots of clown flowers indoors to place in a sunny window to enjoy for weeks after the last frost.

When, Where, and How to Plant
Because *Torenia* seed are small and slow to germinate, it's best to start them indoors under grow lights 8 to 10 weeks before your last frost date. Garden centers often carry a few varieties of clown flowers as well, but you'll be able to enjoy a wider range of colors if you start your own from seed. Plant seedlings in compost-amended soil that is well drained, about 6 to 8 inches apart. Wishbone flowers bloom best with some morning sun and won't flower well in deep shade, such as under an evergreen.

Growing Tips
Keep the plants well watered, especially during hot, windy spells. Feed plants every three weeks with a balanced organic plant food. Torenia will self-sow, but not as readily as cleome and calendula. Look for seedlings to keep or remove the following spring.

Regional Advice and Care
You can deadhead clown flowers to encourage more flowering. However, the seedpods are attractive too, and some gardeners like to leave them on the plants. During cool, rainy summer periods, slugs and snails are attracted to the clown flower plants. Spread iron phosphate bait or use beer traps to thwart them. Humid weather can also cause fungal rots to kill plants so plant clown flowers in well-drained soil. Remove diseased plants so they don't spread to healthy plants. Avoid using mulch around the plants during wet weather to slow the onset of diseases.

Companion Planting and Design
Grow clown flowers in front of and with other shade-loving flowers, such as hostas, ferns, and astilbe. Clown flowers can add much needed color to a shade and woodland garden area. Grow them in containers with begonias, impatiens, and other shade-loving annuals.

Try These
The 'Summer Wave Series' comes in a variety of colors, such as blue and violet, and can tolerate heat and humidity better than other clown flower varieties. 'Duchess Mix' features white, blue, and pink colors on each flower on well-branched, dwarf plants.

Coleus

Solenostemon scutellariodes

Botanical Pronunciation
so-len-o-STE-mon sku-te-lay-ri-OID-es

Other Name Painted leaf

Bloom Period and Seasonal Color
Summer; grown for colorful foliage in shades and combinations of cream, green, burgundy, pink, white, and yellow

Mature Height × Spread
6 to 24 inches × 12 to 18 inches

Coleus have become the darlings of the annual shade gardens. Since they're grown mostly for the colorful leaves, there's no need to wait for the inconspicuous flowers to get a color show. Varieties range in size from 6 inches tall to 2 to 3 feet tall and are multi-branching. I planted one coleus once that grew so quickly it filled a one-half whiskey barrel all by itself. While they're traditionally grown in shady areas to brighten up a garden, newer varieties are more sun tolerant. In our northern climate they can be grown in full sun and not fade or be harmed. Look for red-foliaged plants for the best sun-tolerant varieties.

When, Where, and How to Plant
While you can sow seeds directly in the garden in spring, it's easier to purchase seedlings or grow your own under grow lights 6 to 8 weeks before your last frost. Don't cover the seeds as they need light to germinate. You can also take cuttings from a friend's plant and root them in potting soil. Plant in part to full shade areas unless you're growing the sun-tolerant varieties. Plant in well-drained, fertile soil that's been amended with compost after all danger of frost has passed. Space seedlings 1 to 2 feet apart depending on the ultimate size of the variety.

Growing Tips
Coleus should be pinched back at a young age to encourage bushy growth. Also, pinch out any flower stalks that form so the plants send more energy into leaf production. Keep plants well watered and feed every three weeks with a complete organic plant food.

Regional Advice and Care
Coleus are very frost sensitive so protect them when temperatures dip into the 30s F. Another way to preserve coleus is to take stem cuttings and root them. Take a 3- to 5-inch-long section of the stem end, dip the cut end in rooting hormone powder, and stick the cutting in a pot filled with moistened potting soil. Keep it away from direct light and keep it moist. It should root within 2 weeks. Rooted cuttings can be grown as houseplants in a sunny winter window and then transplanted back into the garden in spring.

Companion Planting and Design
Plant coleus in shady areas with other flowers with attractive foliage, such as hostas, ferns, perilla, and canna lilies. Mix and match different varieties of coleus in containers and try pairing them with other shade-loving annuals, such as impatiens.

Try These
'Wizard Mix' features heart-shaped leaves with a variety of leaf colors in yellow, bronze, red, and pink combinations. It's well branched and dwarf so it doesn't need pinching. The 'Kong Series' is known for its large, colorful leaves. The 'Solar Series' is a mix of sun-tolerant coleus types.

Cosmos

Cosmos bipinnatus

Botanical Pronunciation
KOZ-mose bye-pin-ATE-uss

Other Name
Mexican aster

Bloom Period and Seasonal Color
Midsummer to fall; red, violet, orange, white, and pink

Mature Height × Spread
1 to 5 feet × 2 feet

Cosmos are easy to grow, tall annual flowers that feature airy foliage and cup-shaped flowers that flow in the breeze. The foliage almost resembles asparagus while the flowers can be single or double petaled. Cosmos look great planted in groups, are tolerant of many types of soils, self-sow, and have few pests. They are a common ingredient in Northeast wildflower and meadow mixes for these reasons, but also can be used in cottage gardens since they're very attractive to butterflies. The tall plants have sturdy stalks so they make excellent cut flowers. They only need staking if they're grown in high wind areas. Some newer varieties are dwarf and bushy, making them perfect for containers.

When, Where, and How to Plant

Direct sow cosmos seeds in spring around the last frost date for your area. Even if the soil isn't warm enough for seed germination, cosmos seed will wait for the ideal conditions to grow. Don't pamper the seedbed. Other than having well-drained soil, high fertility is not critical for cosmos growth. Plant them in full sun. Plants grown in part sun will flower, but may be more prone to blowing over in the wind due to weaker stems. Thin seedlings so plants are spaced 1 foot apart. For faster flowering in summer consider buying transplants from a local garden center or starting seeds indoors under grow lights 4 to 6 weeks before the last frost dates in your area.

Growing Tips

Pinch the tops of plants when they're 2 feet tall to encourage branching and more flowers. Pinch the tops of side branches the same way after they develop. Don't fertilize cosmos unless you have very poor soil conditions. Too much nitrogen fertilizer will encourage lots of leaf growth with little flowering. Water well when seed is germinating, but cut back on watering once established since the plants are drought tolerant.

Regional Advice and Care

Cosmos self-sow readily so don't deadhead flowers if you want more cosmos in that area next year. Birds particularly like the seedpods and it's fun to watch them feast on them in fall.

Companion Planting and Design

Plant cosmos in a meadow area with other wildflowers such as rudbeckia and daisies. In a cottage garden, plant them to add color next to Shasta daisies and salvia. Plant cosmos in butterfly gardens with butterfly weed and other butterfly-attracting plants. Grow cosmos in cutting gardens to use as cut flowers indoors. Try dwarf varieties in containers to add a splash of color.

Try These

'Sonata Mix' features heavy-blooming plants on 2-foot-tall stalks with colors such as white, pink, and red. 'Seashells Mix' has fluted flower petals in pastel colors. 'Ladybird Mix' is a dwarf selection with semidouble flowers that only grows 12 inches tall. 'Versailles Mix' features strong-stemmed flowers that are perfect for cutting.

Fan Flower

Scaevola aemula

Botanical Pronunciation
skay-VO-lah EYE-mew-lah

Other Name
Fairy fan flower

Bloom Period and Seasonal Color
Summer to fall in colors of blue, pink, white and purple

Mature Height × Spread
8 to 18 inches × 1 to 2 feet

Fan flower is a relative newcomer to New England. It hails from "Down Under" (Australia) so it loves hot, humid conditions with lots of sun. It's a tough plant that will grow well in part sun as well. The sprawling plant is perfect for containers, hanging baskets, and rock wall edges since it can spread across the ground and not grow too tall. In sun, it will flower nonstop all summer until frost. The thick stems and dandelion-shaped leaves produce blue-, white-, or pink-colored flowers that look like five-fingered, palm-shaped fans. The flower consists of a semicircle or colored petals with a yellow dot in the center.

When, Where, and How to Plant
Plant fan flowers in full to part sun after all danger of frost has passed in your area. It's easiest to purchase fan flower as transplants from garden centers. However, to grow many flowers for a reduced cost, consider starting them from seed indoors 6 to 8 weeks before your last frost date. Harden off transplants (acclimate to the outdoors) before planting in containers, window boxes, hanging baskets, or garden beds. Plant in well-drained soil.

Growing Tips
Although they're drought tolerant once established, keep transplants and seedlings well watered for the first few weeks. Feed plants monthly with an organic plant food and more often if it's being grown in a container or hanging basket. Overwatered fan flowers or those allowed to sit in waterlogged soil can rot. There's no need to deadhead fan flowers. You can try to overwinter fan flowers indoors either taking the whole container indoors and cutting plants back, or taking a stem cutting in summer and rooting it. Keep the plant in a sunny south-facing window, cut back on watering, and it should survive until spring.

Regional Advice and Care
This easy-to-grow annual flower requires little care. Pinch back fan flowers in midsummer if they get long and leggy to stimulate more growth and keep the plant tidy and a manageable size. After pinching back stems to just above a side branch, fertilize, and water well.

Companion Planting and Design
Fan flowers look great planted alone in a garden or hanging container of all one color or mixed with other fan flower colors. Try pairing blue fan flowers with yellow-colored taller flowers, such as marigolds, calendula, and African daisy. The complementary colors play well off each other. Consider creating an all-blue container with blue salvia, fan flowers, and ageratum.

Try These
'Blue Lagoon' and 'Blue Wonder' feature long stems with dark blue flowers. 'Pink Fanfare' has vigorous growth and pink-colored flowers. The 'Whirlwind' Series has blue or white flowers.

Four-O-Clocks

Mirabilis jalapa

Botanical Pronunciation
mih-RAB-ih-liss juh-LAY-puh

Other Name
Marvel of Peru

Bloom Period and Seasonal Color
Midsummer until frost; yellow, pink, rose, salmon, white, red, and striped

Mature Height × Spread
2 to 3 feet × 1 to 2 feet

Four-o-clocks are bushy annuals with colorful flowers and a sweet lemon or orange fragrance. They grow equally well in part shade as well as full sun. They begin flowering in midsummer when sown directly as seed, but will flower earlier if grown as transplants. The individual flowers open in late afternoon, usually between 4 p.m. to 8 p.m. (hence the common name). I won't set my watch by them though. They often will stay open until the following morning, then close and die. This makes them great flowers to enjoy after work or first thing in the morning. Flowers may remain open all day on cloudy days. A single plant may contain different colored flowers depending on the mix.

When, Where, and How to Plant
Plant seeds directly into the soil after all danger of frost has passed in spring, around the time you plant tomatoes. Soak seeds overnight in warm water the night before planting to hasten germination. Start seedlings indoors under grow lights 6 to 8 weeks before your last frost date and transplant seedlings into the garden as well. Transplants will bloom earlier than direct seeded plants. Plant in a full sun or part shade location in well-drained, compost-amended soil. Sow seeds or transplant seedlings 1 to 2 feet apart. You can also plant four-o-clocks in 1- to 5-gallon-sized pots, growing 2 to 5 plants per pot depending on the pot's size. Keep the containers well watered and fertilize monthly.

Growing Tips
Keep plants well watered and weeded. Fertilize in midsummer with an organic plant food to spur more growth and flowering. Fertilize more often for plants growing in containers.

Regional Advice and Care
Pinch back the main shoot when the transplant is young to promote a bushier plant and more flowering. Four-o-clocks are perennial flowers in warmer climates and produce underground tubers that will overwinter. In New England the tubers die with winter's cold, but the seeds that drop from spent flowers will survive in the ground and sprout in your garden next year. Collect the black seeds after the flowers have faded in fall to sow in your garden next spring or thin out self-sown seedlings the following year.

Companion Planting and Design
Plant in flower gardens, along walkways, and in containers in decks and patios to enjoy their fragrance. Four-o-clocks add color to the part shade garden and can get quite bushy by fall. They are a good choice to add color to a partly shaded hosta bed and a low-growing shrub border.

Try These
While you can buy four-o-clock varieties in single colors, I like the 'Marbles Mix' with an assortment of striped flower colors. Another favorite is the eye-catching 'Limelight' featuring lime green leaves and fuchsia-colored flowers.

Fuchsia

Fuchsia spp.

Botanical Pronunciation
FEW-she-uh

Other Name
Ladies eardrop

Bloom Period and Seasonal Color
Summer until frost; red, pink, white, blue, lavender, and many bicolors

Mature Height × Spread
1 to 6 feet × 1 to 5 feet

Fuchsia is a large group of flowers that are grouped either as trailing plants often seen in hanging baskets or upright plants that can be featured in a container or the garden equally as well. Upright fuchsias tend to have smaller flowers. They are a perennial in warmer climates, but are grown in New England as an annual. Some gardeners, like me, have overwintered them indoors as houseplants and kept the plants for a number of years. The downward-facing flowers come in an amazing array of color combinations. While some varieties are all one color, most varieties have at least two colors paired together making these great showpieces grouped together or standing alone. Hummingbirds also love fuchsias.

When, Where, and How to Plant

The easiest way to grow fuchsias is to purchase seedlings at your local garden centers. Fuchsia seed is not readily available. Plant trailing fuchsia varieties in containers, hanging baskets, and window boxes. Plant upright varieties in garden beds or large containers. Plant fuchsias after all danger of frost has passed in well-drained soil, in a part sun or shade location They're well adapted to our sometimes cool summers; fuchsias don't like high heat, humidity, or drought.

Growing Tips

Keep plants well watered, especially if they're growing in sun or in containers. Fuchsia roots don't like to dry out. The more sun they get, the more water they will need. Fertilize monthly with an organic plant food. Pinch back the growing tips to stimulate new flowers if the plant stems grow leggy.

Regional Advice and Care

Watch for whiteflies on fuchsia plants. Check under the leaves periodically for infestations and spray with insecticidal soap if you start seeing clouds of white insects flying off the leaves when they're jostled. To overwinter favorite varieties, bring plants indoors in winter, cut them back, reduce the watering, and place in a sunny window until spring.

Companion Planting and Design

Fuchsias are so showy by themselves they often don't need any other flower in the container or ground near them. However, they do look attractive when paired with shade-loving foliage plants such as coleus or ferns. Grow fuchsias near other part shade-loving flowers such as begonias and torenia as well.

Try These

Some colorful trailing varieties to try include 'Dark Eyes', with its purple flowers and red sepals (petals) and 'Trailblazer' with double pink flowers. The 'Diva Series' has white-, pink-, or coral-colored flowers, and 'Marinka' has red- and pink-colored flowers. Some good upright varieties to try include 'Gartenmeister Bonstedt' with orange-colored flowers on a 3-foot-tall plant. It also has greenish purple leaves. 'Black Prince' has dark violet and red flowers on a compact 2-foot-tall plant.

Geranium

Pelargonium hybrids

Botanical Pronunciation
pell-ar-GO-nee-um

Bloom Period and Seasonal Color
Spring until fall; pink, red, white, salmon, and bicolors

Mature Height × Spread
1 to 2 feet × 1 to 2 feet

These are not only my mother's flower, but also a joy for everyone. Potted geraniums are one of the classic annual flowers seen in many window boxes throughout New England. (There is also a perennial flower also called geranium that I cover in that section.) They're most often grown in containers, window boxes, or planters close to the house. The large, circular, bright-colored flowers bloom from spring until frost. Given plenty of sun and warmth they're an easy-to-grow flower. There are many different types of geraniums. Zonal and Martha Washington geraniums can have bi- or tricolored leaves. Ivy-leafed geraniums are a cascading plant with smaller flowers and grow best in hanging baskets. Scented geraniums have small flowers, but possess deliciously scented leaves.

When, Where, and How to Plant
Geraniums can be grown from seed, but are slow to germinate and take up to 4 months of indoor growing before they can be planted outdoors. It's much easier to purchase your favorite varieties from garden centers in spring and then propagate and store them for the future. Plant in full to part sun in a warm area. Don't rush to plant geraniums outdoors since they love the heat. Wait until you plant other warm-season crops, such as tomatoes and corn. Plant in well-drained containers, such as clay pots that breathe, allowing the water to drain faster. Geraniums don't grow well in soggy soils.

Growing Tips
Pinch the new growth of young geraniums to promote bushier plants, especially if you have overwintered plants and the stems are tall and leggy. In sunny, hot weather, water well, but otherwise let the soil dry out a bit. Feed plants monthly with an organic plant food.

Regional Advice and Care
Deadhead geraniums to increase flowering and tidy them. Cut stems back twice during summer to promote branching. Bottom watering and keeping the leaves dry avoids soilborne fungal leaf spot diseases. Bring geraniums indoors once outdoor temperatures dip below 40 degrees Fahrenheit. To overwinter, cut back plants by one-third, reduce watering to once a week, and place in a sunny, south-facing window. Or, cut them back to 8- to 10-inch-tall stems, remove the soil around the roots, and place the roots in perforated plastic bags filled with slightly moistened peat moss. Store in a dark, cool basement or garage where plants won't freeze. In spring, with signs of new growth, pot the plants, and bring them up to a sunny window to grow.

Companion Planting and Design
Geraniums look great grouped as all one color or in combinations of white, orange-pink, and red. Grow them in containers with trailing companions, such as fan flower, or with silver-colored foliage such as dusty miller.

Try These
'Apple Blossom Rosebud' has pink and white flowers while 'Black Velvet Rose' has chocolate brown leaves with rose-pink flowers. 'Tornado' is a good ivy geranium. Scented geraniums include "flavors" like lemon and rose.

Heliotrope

Heliotropium arborescens

Botanical Pronunciation
hel-ee-oh-TROH-pee-em ar-bo-RES-enz

Other Name
Cherry pie plant

Bloom Period and Seasonal Color
Summer until fall; white, blue, and lavender

Mature Height × Spread
1 to 2 feet × 1 to 2 feet

If you're looking for a fragrant annual that will perfume a container or bed, look no further than the heliotrope. It's called the cherry pie plant because some think the fragrance resembles that fruity dessert. I think it smells more like vanilla, but to each his own. Even without the scent, heliotrope would be a popular annual to grow. It features blue-, white-, or purple-colored flower clusters on a bushy dwarf plant that's perfect in a low-growing flowerbed, container, or window box. It's best to plant them near a window or doorway and at waist height or higher so you can enjoy the fragrance that much more. The foliage is dark green and pleated, giving this plant another attractive feature.

When, Where, and How to Plant
Start heliotrope seed indoors under grow lights 10 to 12 weeks before your last frost date. You can also buy heliotrope seedlings from garden centers in spring. Plant seedlings or transplants outdoors after all danger of frost has passed in a full to part sun location in well-drained fertile soil. Plant in containers or in the ground, spaced about 1 foot apart. Important Note: Despite its common name of cherry pie plant, all parts of heliotropes are poisonous and should not be ingested.

Growing Tips
Keep heliotrope plants well watered. Fertilize monthly with an organic plant food.

Regional Advice and Care
Pinch back the young plants to stimulate more branching early in the season. Deadhead the plants regularly to keep them flowering. The flowers actually move with the sun, like a sunflower, and will follow the sun's path throughout the day. So place heliotropes where you can enjoy this movement. To increase the fragrance, plant heliotrope in groups and in a location with hot, afternoon sun. The heat will help release more fragrance. If powdery mildew disease causes the leaves to turn white, then yellow and die, consider spacing the plants farther apart to increase air circulation to dry out the leaves and spray with an organic fungicide. Keep an eye out for whiteflies and aphids and spray insecticidal soap to kill them. Heliotropes can also be brought indoors and grown as houseplants in winter. Cut back the plants, reduce watering, and grow them in a sunny south-facing window.

Companion Planting and Design
Grow heliotropes in containers or in the ground close to the house to enjoy their fragrance. Companion plant them with low-growing, colorful annuals such as nasturtiums and calendula. Mix them with silver-foliaged plants, such as dusty miller or cascading, pastel-colored trailers such as lobelia or alyssum.

Try These
'Marine' heliotrope features dark purple flowers while a 'Mini Marine' version grows only 8 to 10 inches tall; it's perfect for window boxes. 'White Queen' features fragrant white flowers.

Impatiens

Impatiens walleriana

Botanical Pronunciation
im-PAY-shunz wall-ur-ee-AY-nuh

Other Name
Busy Lizzie

Bloom Period and Seasonal Color
Spring until frost; white, pink, red, orange,
purple, and bicolors

Mature Height × Spread
6 to 24 inches × 6 to 24 inches

Impatiens is the classic shade-loving annual flower that brightens up dark areas with its colorful flowers. You'll often see garden centers loaded with a rainbow of impatiens flower colors in spring. This plant can be low trailing or tall depending on the variety. The New Guinea impatiens tend to be taller versions of this popular flower while the garden impatiens are the low-growing counterparts. Their succulent stems produce single or double flowers (some even look like miniature roses) that bloom nonstop throughout the summer in shade, if given adequate moisture and not too hot conditions. Some varieties even have burgundy-colored leaves. Impatiens are commonly seen growing under trees or shrubs, in containers, in hanging baskets, and in front of shady perennial gardens.

When, Where, and How to Plant
Although you can start impatiens indoors from seed 8 to 10 weeks before the last frost date, it's easier to buy inexpensive starts in garden centers in spring. Impatiens are very frost sensitive, so wait until it's time to plant basil and other warm-season loving plants to transplant. Plant in part sun to part shade, but not full shade if you want full flowering. New varieties of impatiens can tolerate more sun and still grow well. Plant trailing impatiens 6 to 10 inches apart in beds in well-drained soil. Give taller impatiens 1 foot spacing.

Growing Tips
Keep plants well watered, especially if you're growing in part sun, to keep them flowering. However, poorly drained soils can lead to stem rot diseases. Space plants farther apart if diseases such as mildew are an issue in your landscape. Fertilize monthly with an organic plant food. Pinch back leggy stems in midseason to encourage more flowering.

Regional Advice and Care
Unfortunately, the trailing type has been devastated in New England recently by a new strain of downy mildew disease. This disease causes leaves to yellow and drop, leaving bare stems behind. Once established in your soil it can infect future impatiens plantings. Consider New Guinea impatiens, or new varieties, such as 'Sunpatiens', that are resistant to this disease. Slugs and snails can also attack impatiens. Consider using traps or organic baits, such as iron phosphate, to thwart this pest.

Companion Planting and Design
Plant impatiens in multicolored groups, in containers for a kaleidoscope effect, or pair them with attractive foliage plants, such as Japanese painted ferns, hostas, and astilbe, to add color to a shade garden area.

Try These
'Super Elfin Series' features low-growing small plants. 'African Queen' is a tall yellow-flowered variety. The 'Divine Series' of New Guinea impatiens grows 12 to 16 inches tall with a wide variety of colored flowers. 'Sunpatiens Series' is a cross between a New Guinea and trailing impatiens. It features 18- to 24-inch-tall plants and colorful selections that tolerate sun and heat and resist downy mildew disease.

Lantana

Lantana camara

Botanical Pronunciation
lan-TAY-na ca-MA-ra

Other Name
Shrub verbena

Bloom Period and Seasonal Color
Midsummer until fall; red, orange, yellow, violet, white, pink, and many bi- and tricolors

Mature Height × Spread
1 to 2 feet × 1 to 4 feet

If you're looking for the beach baby of the annual world, consider lantana. This shrubby plant is a perennial in warmer climates, but an annual in New England. Because of our short growing season, lantana never reaches shrublike proportions. It loves the sun and heat, producing verbena-like flowers all summer until frost. The color selections of the flowers have expanded in a range of many colors from white to red. However, the most striking varieties have two or even three colors on each flower. They're drought resistant so they can be planted in containers or in garden hot spots to add color in tough-to-grow locations. There are also weeping types that grow well in hanging baskets and containers.

When, Where, and How to Plant

Since lantana seed are hard to germinate and can take more than 3 months to grow indoors before transplanting, it's easiest to purchase transplants from a local garden center. Plant seedlings outdoors after all danger of frost has passed, about the same time you'd plant basil. Lantana grows best in full sun and can have disease problems if grown in part shade. Plant in compost-amended, well-drained soil or containers filled with potting soil. Space plants 1 to 2 feet apart depending on the variety.

Growing Tips

Lantana is drought tolerant once established, but needs adequate moisture for the first few weeks to get established. Keep plants well watered and mulched when they're young. Fertilize monthly with a complete organic fertilizer to keep the flowers producing.

Regional Advice and Care

Cut back leggy plants, especially on the weeping types, in midsummer to encourage a bushier plant and more blooms. Plants grown in part shade can develop powdery mildew disease so plant in full sun beds or containers. Since lantana is a heat lover, plant in microclimates, such as next to south-facing stone walls or a building, to get the most growth in one season.

Companion Planting and Design

While the flowers are colorful, the green foliage can have a pungent aroma when rubbed. Plant lantana in containers or beds where the foliage won't be frequently brushed up against. These showy flowers are best planted together in a group of multiple varieties to create a rainbow effect of color. Because they're so brightly colored, lantana also looks good paired with dark-foliaged plants, such as sweet potato vine and scented geraniums. They also are butterfly magnets, so plant where they are easy to view.

Try These

The 'Lucky' Series features yellow, orange, red, and bicolored varieties on dwarf plants that only grow 1 foot wide and tall. They're perfect for small containers and window boxes. 'Ham and Eggs' is a shrubby, older variety of lantana that has pink, fading to yellow and orange, colored flowers. 'Samantha' has variegated white-and-green leaves to go with its yellow flowers.

Larkspur

Consolida ambigua

Botanical Pronunciation
kun-SOLL-ih-duh am-BIG-you-uh

Other Name
Rocket larkspur

Bloom Period and Seasonal Color
Midsummer to fall; blue, pink, rose, white, and lavender

Mature Height × Spread
2 to 4 feet × 1 to 2 feet

If you love the colorful flower spikes of delphiniums, but have a hard time getting them to grow and flower well, consider trying larkspur. This annual flower is related to delphinium, grows and produces similar flower stalks as delphinium, but it blooms in the first year, even if it's planted from seed. The 2- to 4-foot-tall hollow flower stalks have single or double blooms in colors from white to lavender. They're perfect to use as cut flowers, or they can add color to the back of a flower border. Unlike the densely packed delphinium flower stalks, larkspur blooms tend to have a looser configuration of flowers all along the stem. The dark green, fernlike leaves contrast well with the colorful flowers.

When, Where, and How to Plant
Sow larkspur seeds directly into the soil in spring after the danger of a heavy freeze is past or in early fall. Larkspur can also be purchased as seedlings from a garden center, but they don't like to be transplanted. You'll get the best results from direct seeding. Thin plants to 6 inches apart. Grow plants in full sun on compost-amended, well-drained, fertile soil in a location out of the wind.

Growing Tips
Grow larkspur plants together so they can support one another from the wind. In very windy locations, consider staking or caging the flower stalks. Mulch the plants well to maintain even soil moisture and keep plants well watered. Fertilize monthly with an organic plant food.

Regional Advice and Care
Larkspur tends to bloom in midsummer from a spring planting in our climate. They will, however, self-sow, and you may get larkspur seedlings the following year in the same area. Thin those new seedlings in spring so they aren't overcrowded. If you don't want new larkspur seedlings, deadhead the spent flower stalks as soon as they are done flowering in summer. All parts of the larkspur plant are toxic if ingested, so keep children and pets away from them. Larkspur plants can get powdery mildew. If mildew is a concern, space plants farther apart or plant in a location with good airflow to keep the dry leaves dry.

Companion Planting and Design
The bottom foliage of larkspur plants can thin out, so plant larkspur with annuals and perennials, such as peonies, daylilies, and salvia. These have attractive foliage to cover the bottom of the larkspur flower stalks. They can be planted in a cutting garden to produce blossoms for indoors. Cut the flower stalks when one-half of the flowers are open for indoor use. They are also good dried flowers as well.

Try These
The 'Sublime Series' features 4-foot-tall, brightly colored flower stalks that hold their color well for drying. The Giant Imperial Series has large flower stalks and flowers, and the Cannes Series features pastel-colored flowers.

Lobelia

Lobelia erinus

Botanical Pronunciation
loe-BEEL-yuh ur-EYE-nus

Other Name
Edging lobelia

Bloom Period and Seasonal Color
Early summer until fall; blue, violet, pink, and red

Mature Height × Spread
4 to 6 inches × 4 to 12 inches

Lobelia is a widely popular, low-growing, bushy or trailing annual flower that often is matched with alyssum in containers and garden beds. It can just litter the ground or a container in color. The traditional variety has electric blue- or violet-colored flowers, but newer varieties stretch the color range to pink and red, too. The foliage and flowers are delicate, but lobelia flowers in abundance, blooming all summer right until frost. In spring and fall lobelias grow well in full sun, but in summer the sun may be too strong for this plant; some shade will help keep it in bloom. Bushy plants grow well grouped in beds, while trailing varieties are perfect for containers, window boxes, and hanging baskets.

When, Where, and How to Plant

Lobelia seedlings take up to 10 weeks to start indoors when sown from seed. The seed can be difficult to germinate, and plants are widely available, so most gardeners purchase seedlings from local garden centers in spring. Plant in full to part sun after all danger of frost has passed in well-drained, compost-amended soil or in containers filled with potting soil. If the bed or container is in a warm area, grow in part sun since the midsummer heat can cause lobelia to stop flowering and dieback. Plant bushy varieties 6 inches apart and plant trailing varieties up to 12 inches apart.

Growing Tips

Keep plants well watered, especially during hot spells in midsummer. Fertilize every 3 weeks with a complete organic plant food to keep plants blooming. Lobelias are stunning plants that attract butterflies and beneficial insects. If the plant stops flowering or even dies back in midsummer, simply keep it well watered and fertilized and it will bounce back with the cooler weather of late summer.

Regional Advice and Care

Cut back plants after the early summer blush of flowers to promote more branching and flowering later in summer and fall. In northern regions of New England, it often continues flowering nonstop all summer long.

Companion Planting and Design

Bushy lobelia varieties look great in front of a flower border or mixed with other annuals in containers. Trailing types are perfect in containers to cascade over the edge, and they pair well with alyssum to give a blue-and-white color combination. Other flowers that look good with lobelia include petunias, fuchsias, and love-in-a-mist. They are often used as the "spiller" in containers paired with tall zinnias, salvia, and other annuals.

Try These

The 'Cascade Series' featured trailing lobelia varieties of various colors. The Rainbow Series is a bush-type that is great planted in flower borders or edges. 'Crystal Palace' is a stunning, blue heirloom variety. 'Bed O' Roses' features different shades of pink- and rose-colored selections.

Love-in-a-Mist

Nigella damascena

Botanical Pronunciation
ni-GEL-a dam-a-SKAY-na

Other Name
Devil in the bush

Bloom Period and Seasonal Color
Midsummer until fall; blue, rose, and white

Mature Height × Spread
1 to 2 feet × 6 to 12 inches

It's hard to miss love-in-a-mist. The blue, rose, or white flowers are surrounded by airy bracts and ferny, delicate foliage. You can see by its flowers and foliage where gardeners got the common name for this plant. The pastel-colored flowers are puffy and even the egg-shaped, horned seedpods are attractive. They can be used as a cut flower, and the seedpods are often dried and used in arrangements. In fact, I sometimes like the seedpods more than the flowers for arranging. Love-in-a-mist is a great cottage garden plant providing interest and complimenting other annual and perennial flowers. This annual flower likes the cool weather and can be short-lived even during the summer. However, it self-sows freely, creating nigella seedlings for years to come.

When, Where, and How to Plant

Love-in-a-mist can be directly sown in gardens in spring in full to part sun as soon as the soil has warmed and can be worked—about the time you'd be sowing radish seeds. Love-in-a-mist doesn't like to be transplanted. Even though you can start seeds indoors 6 to 8 weeks before your last frost date, the success rate of transplanting those seedlings may be disappointing. Thin seedlings or plant transplants to 1 foot apart in the garden. Love-in-a-mist isn't particular about the soil fertility and will grow in any moderately fertile soil.

Growing Tips

Keep plants well watered. Love-in-a-mist seeds need consistent moisture to germinate well, but don't like soggy soils. Mulch around the base of flowers to keep the soil cool and moist and to extend flowering.

Regional Advice and Care

Original plants may die off after their flush of flowers, so sow seeds every month into midsummer to keep the flowers coming into fall. Love-in-a-mist will self-sow, so to prevent them from becoming a weed, remove the seedpods even if you aren't using them as cut or dried flowers. You can also deadhead spent flowers to extend the plant's life, but you'll be sacrificing the equally attractive seedpods. To dry the seedpods, cut the pods while they are still green, bundle them together, and hang them upside down in an airy, warm room out of direct sun.

Companion Planting and Design

Love-in-a-mist grows well mixed with other cottage garden plants, such as salvia, bachelor's button, sweet William, and dwarf cosmos. Consider planting in the front of a border or near a deck or patio to enjoy the interesting flowers and seedpods. Love-in-a-mist also grows well in containers and in a cutting garden.

Try These

'Miss Jekyll' is a popular series with blue-, rose-, and white-colored variations. 'Blue Midget' is a dwarf variety that only grows 10 inches tall. 'Cambridge Blue' is a long-stemmed variety that's good for cutting and for drying the seedpods. 'Mulberry Rose' features large, double, rose-colored flowers.

Mandevilla

Mandevilla × amabilis

Botanical Pronunciation
man-de-VIL-le-a a-MAB-a-lis

Other Name
Chilean jasmine

Bloom Period and Seasonal Color
Mid- to late summer to fall; pink, red, white, and yellow

Mature Height × Spread
5 to 10 feet × 1 foot

This climbing tropical vine is native to South America and a perennial in warmer climates. In New England it's mostly grown as an annual and/or houseplant since it will die with the first frost. In warmer climates the vine can reach up to 20 feet tall, but in our colder climate, it more likely grows 5 feet tall. When it does bloom in late summer, the large, trumpet-shaped, tropical flowers are outstanding with their bright pink, red, and yellow colors. If they're grown in a container, mandevilla vines can be cut back and brought indoors as a houseplant to grow in a sunny window all winter. Even though it won't flower indoors in winter, it can survive to be moved back outdoors next summer.

When, Where, and How to Plant
Mandevilla vines are best purchased as potted plants from a local garden center. Wait until warm weather is well established, even into early June, before planting it outdoors. This tropical plant does *not* grow well in cool conditions. Grow mandevilla in a full to part sun location, protected from cold breezes. You can grow mandevilla in hanging baskets or a container on the ground. One plant per 12- to 14-inch container works best.

Growing Tips
Keep plants well watered and fertilized to stimulate lots of vining growth and flowering during our short summers. Mandevilla will grow fast during hot weather so don't let the pots dry out. Fertilize every few weeks with an organic plant food.

Regional Advice and Care
Since mandevilla flowers best in the heat, grow plants in containers in a microclimate near a south-facing wall or building. It will be easier to protect them from an early frost in fall by laying a sheet or row cover across them when temperatures dip. Train plants, using wire or string, to climb up pillars or trellises. Cut back the vines in fall and bring plants indoors before a killing frost to overwinter in a sunny window. Keep plants barely moist indoors and watch for insects, such as whiteflies, scale, and aphids on the leaves. Spray with Neem oil to protect your plants from these pests. Your plant won't grow much in winter, but should be ready to be moved outside in late spring.

Companion Planting and Design
Mandevilla vines look great trained to a trellis, a lamppost, arbor, or fence. They are a showy flower so place them where they're protected from cold winds and weather, but keeping them visible. Consider planting colorful, warm-weather loving flowers, such as lantana, tropical hibiscus, and coleus, near this vine.

Try These
'Alice du Pont' is a popular pink-flowered variety. The 'Parfait Series' offers pink and white varieties with double flowers. 'Red Riding Hood' has deep pink flowers.

Marigold

Tagetes species and hybrids

Botanical Pronunciation
TAH-get-ee

Other Name
French marigold

Bloom Period and Seasonal Color
Midsummer to fall; yellow, orange, white, burgundy, maroon, and bicolors

Mature Height × Spread
6 inches to 2 feet × 6 inches to 2 feet

What would our annual and vegetable gardens be without marigolds? They are one of the most common and popular annual flowers to grow in any garden. There is a wide range of plant sizes and shapes of flowers, as well as colors ranging from white to maroon. This tough flower comes into its own in midsummer and blooms right to frost. The two most common types are the French or signet marigold, with its small plants, and the taller African marigold. Both types have varieties with small or large flowers. Some flowers can be as large as 3 inches across and come as single or double blooms depending on the variety. They flower quickly from transplants or even when directly sown in the garden.

When, Where, and How to Plant

Direct sow marigold seed in spring in a full to part sun location into compost-amended soil after all danger of frost has passed, or start seeds indoors under grow lights 4 to 6 weeks before the last frost date. Direct seeded marigolds will bloom later than transplants. Transplant home-grown or store-bought seedlings in the soil spaced 6 inches to 2 feet apart depending on the variety. Thin directly sown plants to a similar spacing.

Growing Tips

Keep plants well watered when young. Once established, they can be drought tolerant. Mulch around plants to maintain soil moisture and deter weeds. Fertilize every 3 weeks with an organic plant food.

Regional Advice and Care

Deadhead flowers to keep the plants blooming and cut back leggy plants to stimulate more blooms. During hot, dry weather watch for spider mite infestations. Spray plants with insecticidal soap when you notice stippling on the leaves and insect webbing. Stake tall African marigolds if grown in a windy location.

Companion Planting and Design

Plant the diminutive French or signet marigolds in containers with cascading annuals, such as lobelia, and tall plants, such as salvia. Marigold flowers are edible and are a great garnish in salads. Interplant marigolds with other annuals, around perennials, and in vegetable gardens to add color. The wide variety of flower colors makes them good companions with many other colored flowers. Tall African marigolds make great cut flowers. Some gardeners grow marigolds to ward off insects in the vegetable garden. However, only African marigolds have been scientifically proven to keep away nematodes and then only if the plants are tilled under the soil.

Try These

'Jubilee Series' and 'Inca Series' grow 2 feet tall with double flowers. 'Sunburst Mix' and 'Zenith Series' are crosses between the French and African marigolds producing large flowers on 14-inch-tall plants that don't need deadheading. 'French Vanilla' has creamy white flowers on 1- to 2-foot-tall plants. 'Bonanza Series' produces golden- to red-colored flowers on 12-inch-tall plants. 'Gem Series' produce lemon-, red-, and tangerine-colored dainty flowers that are good for salads.

Million Bells

Calibrachoa hybrids

Botanical Pronunciation
CAL-ih-bra-ko-a

Other Name
Trailing petunia

Bloom Period and Seasonal Color
Early summer to fall; blue, pink, red, yellow, white, lilac, purple, orange, striped, and bicolors

Mature Height × Spread
6 to 8 inches × 1 to 2 feet

Calibrachoa is a mini version of the traditional petunia that has really caught on as an annual flower in the last 10 years. Like petunias, there is a wide range of flower colors of this cascading plant. The flowers often have contrasting throat colors or stripes, making them an attractive choice for containers, hanging baskets, and annual groundcovers. The flowers are single or double petaled, smaller than regular petunias, and *don't need deadheading*. The plants tend to get less spindly and need less cutting back. For me, they seem more manageable than petunias. They will bloom their heads off in full sun and less so in part sun. Once established, they are drought tolerant, and butterflies and hummingbirds are attracted to their colorful flowers.

When, Where, and How to Plant
Million bells are only available as transplants from local garden centers. Plant in spring after all danger of frost has past in containers or the ground. To make a full container, plant 2 to 3 plants per 12-inch pot. In the ground, space them 12 to 18 inches apart to allow for spreading. Million bells flowers best in full sun in well-drained, compost-amended, fertile soil.

Growing Tips
Since these are hybrid plants that are bred to bloom, keep them well fed by fertilizing every 2 weeks with an organic liquid fertilizer, such as fish emulsion. This will help keep them in flower. Keep plants well watered and mulch around plants in the ground to maintain the soil moisture levels and keep weeds away.

Regional Advice and Care
Million bells are great container plants. They need little care other than water and fertilizing. They start blooming early in the season, which is great in our short summer climate. Keep plant foliage misted during dry periods to prevent spider mite infestations. Spray plants with insecticidal soap if you notice leaf stippling and webbing from these mites.

Companion Planting and Design
Plant different varieties of million bells together in the ground or in containers, mixing and matching contrasting and complementary colors. Match million bells with tall annuals, such as salvia and geraniums, in containers. Since there is such a variety of flower colors, there's often a variety that blends well with almost any annual and perennial flower.

Try These
'Superbells Series' features strong trailing plants in a wide variety of colors including striped and bicolors. One of the most striking is 'Lemon Slice' with its combination of white and yellow stripes. Cabaret and MiniFamous are two series that feature early blooming plants in a wide range of colors. 'Can-Can Mocha' in the Cabaret Series features creamy flowers with a chocolate-purple throat. The MiniFamous series also has double flowered blooms in colors such as blush, blue, pink, and yellow.

Morning Glory

Ipomoea tricolor

Botanical Pronunciation
ip-uh-MEE-uh TRYE-kol-or

Other Name
Common morning glory

Bloom Period and Seasonal Color
Midsummer until fall; blue, pink, red, white,
purple, and bicolors

Mature Height × Spread
6 to 15 feet × 1 to 2 feet

Morning glories are popular annual vines for growing up a fence, arbor, trellis, or arch. There are also selections that grow well in containers on a deck or patio. The heart-shaped leaves form on quick-growing stems reaching up to 15 feet tall. They can become a mass of leaves and flowers by late summer. The flowers, in colors from white to purple, begin forming in midsummer and continue until frost. As the name implies, morning glory flowers open in the morning and close in the afternoon. The large, colorful flowers attract butterflies and hummingbirds. Morning glories also self-sow readily so they will surprise you each year as new plants pop up in different parts of the garden.

When, Where, and How to Plant
The easiest way to plant morning glories is to direct sow seeds into well-drained soil after the last frost date. To ensure quick germination, nick the seeds with a nail file and soak them in warm water the night before sowing. The seeds will absorb water quickly and germinate faster in the ground. You can also buy transplants in garden centers if you're only growing a few plants. Plant in a full sun location only a few inches from a place where your morning glory vines can climb. In a container, erect a trellis or grow them near a railing so they can be supported.

Growing Tips
Keep young seedlings well watered. Although morning glories grow best on fertile soil, don't overfertilize your plants or you'll get mostly leaves, fewer flowers, and they will bloom later in the season.

Regional Advice and Care
Train morning glory vines to climb up a trellis, fence, or arch, removing or redirecting errant vines. Morning glories twine around a support and don't cling like a grapevine, so they grow quickest around narrow diameter fences, poles, and trellises. Protect morning glory vines from a frost and they will continue to bloom into fall. Keep the plants weeded.

Companion Planting and Design
Morning glory vines are best planted together with different colored varieties. You can grow a trellis of red, white, and blue morning glories if you're feeling patriotic. They don't partner well with other annual or perennial flowers since their growth can overwhelm those plants. However, they can grow well with evergreen shrubs, such as junipers and yews, providing a pleasant surprise of color against the green foliage.

Try These
'Heavenly Blue' is a popular baby blue-colored morning glory with large flowers. 'Scarlett O'Hara' is a common bright red variety. 'Grandpa Otts' is one of my favorites. This heirloom variety has deep purple flowers with rose star patterns on the petals with a pink throat. 'Red Picotee' is a newer variety with white edges on the petals and a double flower. It only grows 6 feet tall.

Moss Rose

Portulaca grandiflora

Botanical Pronunciation
por-too-LAK-a gran-di-FLOR-a

Other Name
Flowering purslane

Bloom Period and Seasonal Color
Midsummer until fall; yellow, orange, white, pink, red, and bicolors

Mature Height × Spread
6 to 10 inches × 6 to 12 inches

The name "moss rose" describes this annual beautifully. The plant is a low-growing spreader, like moss, with succulent leaves that remind you of a plant in the cactus family. The flowers do look like miniature roses, especially when growing double-flowered varieties. Moss roses feature bright, vividly colored flowers so they shine in a container or garden bed. Moss rose is drought tolerant and loves the heat, so it's perfect for small pots; sunny, dry areas in the yard; and specialty gardens such as rock gardens. In New England, the more sun and heat the better it is for these plants. They aren't an aggressive spreader so they grow well in small spaces without overwhelming other flowers.

When, Where, and How to Plant
Plant moss rose seeds directly into well-drained soil in a full sun location. Don't rush getting your moss rose plants or seeds into the garden. Let the soil warm and plant in early June. Moss roses don't grow well on heavy, clay soils or soils with poor water drainage. Barely cover the small seeds as they need light to germinate. You can also start seeds indoors 8 weeks before your last frost date or buy transplants locally and transplant seedlings outdoors. Try to space plants about 6 to 12 inches apart so they aren't overcrowded. Overcrowded plants won't flower as well.

Growing Tips
Moss roses have shallow root systems, so keep plants well watered the first few weeks until established. Once established, they are drought tolerant. However, too much water will cause the plants to rot, so be sure you have good drainage. Moss roses don't require fertile soils and rarely need extra fertilizer to thrive. In fact, fertilizer can cause a delay or lack of flowering.

Regional Advice and Care
Come midsummer, the plants may get leggy and have few flowers. Pinch back the stems to a side shoot, add a small dose of fertilizer, and they should regrow and flower more for late summer and fall. Moss roses also don't compete well with weeds or other flowers, so give them plenty of space and keep the bed well weeded. Moss roses self-sow readily so don't be surprised if you see seedlings in the same areas the following spring.

Companion Planting and Design
Plant moss roses in containers, railing planters, or window boxes. They look great in the shallow soils of a rock garden, in front of a flower border, or even trailing out of a hanging basket or over a wall. They look good paired in a container with taller annuals with contrasting flowers and foliage such as salvia.

Try These
The Sundial series features 6-inch, trailing plants with brightly colored, roselike blooms. The Happy Hour series flowers a few weeks earlier than most moss rose varieties with mounding, 1-foot-wide plants.

Nasturtium

Tropaeolum majus

Botanical Pronunciation
troe-pay-OH-lum MAY-jus

Other Name
Indian cress

Bloom Period and Seasonal Color
Summer to fall; orange, yellow, red, cream, and bicolors

Mature Height × Spread
1 to 4 feet × 12 to 18 inches

Nasturtiums are a fast-growing and fast-flowering annual that can give your garden a tropical touch. There are two types of nasturtiums: bush and trailing. The bush types stay in a 1- to 2-foot mound and are perfect for small spaces and containers. Trailing varieties can grow 4 to 5 feet tall and have to be trained up a fence, trellis, or down a wall. They don't attach themselves to a structure like a morning glory or grapevine. The round, waterlily-like leaves are green or sometimes variegated. The trumpet-shaped flowers come in bright colors such as red, orange, and yellow. Nasturtium flowers and leaves are edible with a peppery flavor. I love adding them to salads, soups, and stir-frys.

When, Where, and How to Plant

Plant nasturtium seeds directly into well-drained soil in a full to part sun location after all danger of frost has passed. Nasturtiums don't like being transplanted so if you start seeds indoors or buy seedlings, be sure to use a biodegradable pot so you won't disturb the roots. Consider nicking seeds and soaking them in warm water the night before sowing to hasten germination. Plant bush types a foot apart. Plant trailing types near a fence, trellis, wall, or structure where they can be trained vertically, or off a railing where they can cascade. Nasturtiums will create a mass of foliage so give them some room apart from other low-growing flowers.

Growing Tips

Keep plants well watered and don't overfertilize. Too much fertilizer will produce lush, large leaves but fewer flowers, and they will be later blooming. Keep plants well weeded until they get established.

Regional Advice and Care

Nasturtiums need little care once established. Aphids can sometimes be a problem on young leaves. Spray insecticidal soap to reduce the damage. During hot, dry summers, nasturtium leaves may get ratty-looking. Either cut back the plant so it grows healthier leaves for fall or consider planting a new crop of nasturtiums in midsummer for autumn flowers.

Companion Planting and Design

Train trailing varieties by tying up the stems to a trellis or wire. Mounding varieties look great in containers, window boxes, or in front of flower borders. Since they're edible, consider planting nasturtiums in the vegetable and herb gardens to remind you to eat the tasty foliage and flowers. Trailing varieties can also be trained to climb among shrubs, such as junipers and yews, offering some unexpected flower color in summer.

Try These

The Alaska series features dwarf, bushy plants with variegated foliage. The Whirlybird series has large, double flowers on bushy plants. The 'Empress of India' has vivid scarlet-colored flowers on blue-green-colored leaves. 'Moonlight' is a yellow-flowered trailing variety; it pairs well with blue morning glories.

Nicotiana

Nicotiana spp. and hybrids

Botanical Pronunciation
knee-co-she-ANNA

Other Name
Flowering tobacco

Bloom Period and Seasonal Color
Midsummer until fall; blue, white, red, and pale green

Mature Height × Spread
1 to 5 feet × 1 to 2 feet

This relative of the nightshade family (tobacco, tomato, petunia, and deadly nightshade plants) features sometimes fragrant, trumpet-shaped flowers on plants ranging from 1 to 5 feet tall. These sturdy plants are reliable bloomers in a flower border with their colorful flowers that hummingbirds and butterflies love. While newer varieties are compact and bloom almost right in the container, older heirlooms are taller, later blooming, and have more fragrant flowers. Nicotiana are great plants to give your garden bed a midsummer boost since they bloom so profusely, and you can grow varieties with varying heights to match your needs. Nicotiana will self-sow readily so watch for seedlings in spring the following year.

When, Where, and How to Plant
Start seeds indoors 4 to 6 weeks before your last frost date or purchase seedlings from a local garden center. When buying seedlings, avoid plants with flowers or yellowing leaves. These may be slow-growing in the garden. Plant in the ground or containers after the last frost date for your area, in a full to part sun location in well-drained soil. The more sun nicotiana receives, the better it will flower. Space shorter varieties 6 to 12 inches apart and tall varieties up to 3 feet apart.

Growing Tips
Keep plants well watered and fertilize monthly with an organic plant food. Keep plants weeded and remove or thin out any self-sown seedlings from previous years. Self-sown seedlings from hybrid varieties tend not to flower as well as new plants. Remove these seedlings each spring.

Regional Advice and Care
Newer varieties of nicotiana are self-cleaning, meaning the flowers don't have to be deadheaded. However, older, taller varieties benefit from removing the spent blossoms. Support taller varieties with a stake or cage or plant in groups so they can support one another. Control aphids and spider mites on plants by spraying insecticidal soap. Tobacco hornworm will eat the leaves of nicotiana. Spray *Bacillus thuringiensis* to control that pest.

Companion Planting and Design
Plant fragrant, tall heirloom varieties close to a window, deck, or porch where you can enjoy the fragrance and see the butterflies and hummingbirds visiting the blooms. Group newer hybrid varieties with other annual and perennial flowers, such as foxglove, hollyhocks, and zinnias, or with other nicotiana varieties of various colors.

Try These
The Saratoga series and Domino series feature short plants that flower in pink, white, or red, while the 'Sensation Mix' have plants that grow to 3-feet tall. 'Lime Green' has unusual pale green-colored flowers. 'Nicki Red' is an award-winning compact variety with good weather tolerance. 'Sylvestris' is an heirloom that grows up to 5 feet tall with fragrant flowers.

Pansy

Viola × wittrockiana

Botanical Pronunciation
VYE-oh-luh ex wit-rok-ee-AH-na

Other Name
Viola

Bloom Period and Seasonal Color
Spring and fall; blue, red, yellow, pink, orange, rose, purple, black, white, and bicolors

Mature Height × Spread
6 to 10 inches × 8 to 12 inches

This cool-season-loving flower is a common sight in garden centers in spring and increasingly in late summer as a fall crop. Both pansies and violas are terms that are used interchangeably for the same plants. The flowers are large with "faces" or dainty and small depending on the variety. These low-growing spring beauties offer a shot of color after a long New England winter. The summer heat forces plants to die back or to just stop flowering. But those that survive often can be revived for a fall flower show. Some of the small-flowered varieties tend to be hardier, and I've had many a 'Johnny Jump Up' overwinter in my Vermont garden. The flowers are edible and are great in salads.

When, Where, and How to Plant

While you can start pansies from seed indoors under grow lights 10 to 12 weeks before your last frost date, their seeds are small and germination is sometimes problematic. It's easier to purchase transplants in spring from a local garden center. Plant pansies in well-drained, fertile soil as soon as the ground can be worked in spring, about the time you plant peas. Although they can survive a frost, protect plants from prolonged freezing temperatures with a row cover. Pansies grow best in full to part sun. Space plants 6 to 8 inches apart in beds or containers. Plant a fall crop of pansies in late summer to bloom into autumn. Protect plants from freezes and you can get your plants to flower into November in New England.

Growing Tips

Keep plants well watered. Pansies will flower longer into the summer if planted in part shade. Feed pansies monthly with an organic plant food. Some varieties self-sow readily. Thin self-sown seedlings in spring to proper spacing for best flowering.

Regional Advice and Care

Protect pansies in fall by covering them with a mound of bark mulch applied after a few hard freezes. This will protect them from cold and help them overwinter. In spring, remove the mulch once the temperatures warm. In summer, cut back struggling plants, fertilize, and water. They will revive with cooler temperatures. Control slugs with organic baits, traps, and barriers. Pansies planted in containers can be grown indoors as houseplants to overwinter in a sunny window. Indoors, cut back leggy plants to promote bushy growth.

Companion Planting and Design

Plant pansies in containers on a deck or patio for early spring and fall color. Mix different varieties to have a rainbow of colors. In the garden combine pansies with other cool-weather lovers, such as calendula and snapdragons.

Try These

The Joker series has very pronounced faces. The Bingo series are early bloomers and the Majestic series features large-sized flowers. For hardier varieties try the Icicle series. 'Johnny Jump Ups' are small-flowered pansies that self-sow readily and spread throughout the garden.

Pentas

Pentas lanceolata

Botanical Pronunciation
PEN-tas lan-see-o-LAY-ta

Other Name
Egyptian star cluster

Bloom Period and Seasonal Color
Summer to fall; red, pink, white, and purple

Mature Height × Spread
1 to 2 feet × 1 to 2 feet

Considered a subtropical perennial, pentas are grown as annuals in New England. These medium-sized plants produce clusters of star-shaped red, pink, white, or purple flowers that butterflies and hummingbirds love. When they're in full bloom they are a showstopper in the garden. They love the heat and will bloom from summer to fall, making a nice addition to an annual flower garden and adding color to a perennial flower border. There are even smaller varieties that grow well in containers. I've found container growing a good trick to attract butterflies close to the house on a deck or patio, which makes them easier to view. These plants love full sun and will get leggy and not flower well in part shade.

When, Where, and How to Plant

Because pentas will need about 16 weeks of indoor growing under lights when started from seed, most gardeners prefer to purchase pentas transplants from a local garden center. Plant transplants in fertile, slightly acidic, well-drained soil in full sun after all danger of frost has passed, about the time you'd plant tomatoes. Plant seedlings about 1 to 2 feet apart. Pinch back the tops of newly transplanted seedlings to promote side branching and more flowering.

Growing Tips

Pentas grow best with consistent soil moisture. Plants that dry out have poor foliage color and flowering. During hot periods you may have to water daily. It's best to bottom water pentas, since overhead watering can cause unsightly brown spots on the leaves. Mulch pentas to help keep the soil evenly moist and prevent weed growth. Fertilize monthly with an organic plant food.

Regional Advice and Care

Pentas love the sun and heat so grow them in a warm microclimate area, such as in front of a south-facing building or wall or in containers. Keep the plants deadheaded to promote more blooms and keep them well weeded. During dry periods spider mites may attack the plants. Spray pentas with insecticidal soap to ward them off.

Companion Planting and Design

Pair pentas with other sun and heat lovers in the flower garden, such as cornflowers, lantana, sedum, marigolds, and zinnias. They also look great contrasting with foliage plants such as sweet potato vine. Mix different pentas varieties in containers to make a colorful pot. They are perfect companions in a butterfly garden with butterfly bushes and butterfly weed.

Try These

Butterfly series produces larger flowers and tolerates stress better than other varieties. New Look series have sturdy stems and don't flop easily. Graffiti series features a more mounding growth habit. The Kaleidoscope series only grows 18 inches tall and has white, pink, or red flowers. The Northern Lights series features tall plants that are more tolerant of cooler temperatures.

Petunia

Petunia × hybrida

Botanical Pronunciation
pe-TOON-e-ah hi-BRI-dah

Other Name
Garden petunia

Bloom Period and Seasonal Color
Summer to fall; white, black, yellow, pink, red, blue, purple, bicolors, and striped

Mature Height × Spread
6 to 24 inches × 2 to 3 feet

Petunias are one of the most recognizable annual flowers. They fill garden centers in spring and end up in garden beds, hanging baskets, containers, and window boxes in many yards. There are varieties in almost any color of the rainbow, including some very attractive black-flowered petunias that I really think are cool. There are many different types of petunias. Grandiflora petunias feature the familiar, large flowers with single- or ruffled-doubled petals that grow in a mound, but also can cascade. Multiflora petunias have more, but smaller-sized, flowers and are compact growing. Milliflora petunias are the smallest type in growth and flower size. Groundcover types, like the popular Wave series, have sprawling vines that can grow 2 to 3 feet wide.

When, Where, and How to Plant

You can start petunia seeds indoors under grow lights 10 to 12 weeks before your last frost date or purchase transplants from garden centers. Because of the wide variety of petunias available and the time involved in starting petunias from seed, it's often easier simply to buy the plants in spring. Set out transplants after all danger of frost has passed, in well-drained soil, spaced 6 to 12 inches apart in a full sun location. Petunias can grow in part sun, but they won't be as floriferous.

Growing Tips

Keep plants well watered and fertilize every 3 weeks with an organic plant food. Keep petunias well weeded until the sprawling types, such as the groundcover petunias, can fill in an area.

Regional Advice and Care

Petunias are a low-maintenance annual that provide lots of color for your effort. Come midsummer they may get leggy, especially if they're not grown in full sun. Simply pinch back the stems to just above a side branch, fertilize, and they will regrow and bloom again. Many new petunia varieties are self-cleaning, meaning they don't need deadheading to look great. Older varieties will need periodic deadheading, though, to keep them tidy. Petunias like cool weather and in warmer parts of New England may stop flowering in midsummer. Be patient. When it cools, they will return to form.

Companion Planting and Design

Petunias can be grouped together mixing different colors in a garden bed or container. Petunias can also be paired in pots with taller-growing annuals such as geraniums, other cascading annuals such as ageratum, and attractive foliage plants such as coleus and dusty miller.

Try These

The Candy series is a multiflora type that has mounded, 6-inch-tall plants. The Picobella series is a milliflora type with small, 1-inch diameter flowers on 8-inch-tall plants. The Ultra series is a grandiflora type with striped or solid colored flowers. The Wave series is a groundcover type with colorful flower that bounce back well after a rain. 'Black Velvet' is a silky textured flower with almost midnight black coloring.

Poppy

Papaver spp.

Botanical Pronunciation
pap-AY-ver

Bloom Period and Seasonal Color
Summer and periodically in fall; red, orange, white, yellow, purple, and pink

Mature Height × Spread
8 inches to 3 feet × 1 foot

Poppies are like splashes of delight across a meadow, garden, or field. There are many different types that can be started from seed, and they self-sow readily. The California poppy is a low-growing form producing a wave of golden, white, or red flowers. Icelandic and Shirley poppies stand up to 2 feet tall and come in a broader array of colors from white to red. Breadseed poppies can grow even taller still; they have single or double flowers in different shades of pink and purple. The seeds can be used in baking. Unlike other annuals, poppies won't flower continuously throughout the summer, but will rebloom several times depending on the variety. (Note that Oriental poppies are featured in the perennials chapter of this book.)

When, Where, and How to Plant
Sprinkle poppy seeds in spring on garden beds as soon as the ground can be worked. Poppies have a taproot and don't transplant well. Plant in full sun in well-drained soil.

Growing Tips
Keep the garden bed well watered to stimulate germination. Once established, poppies are drought tolerant. As long as the soil has moderate fertility, poppies don't need extra fertilization.

Regional Advice and Care
Once the first flush of flowers fade in early summer, remove the seedpods to encourage more blooming. You can leave the seedpods of some poppies, such as the breadseed types, on the plant because they're very attractive. You also can collect the seedpods and seeds of breadseed poppies for baking. To encourage self-sowing, leave all the seedpods on the plants after flowering in late summer or fall. In spring, weed out the self-sown poppy seedlings as they tend to sow too thickly. Thin self-sown plants to 6 to 10 inches apart as crowded poppy plants will be small and won't flower as well. Control slugs on young plants with organic baits, traps, and sprays.

Companion Planting and Design
Poppies look best mixed with other wildflowers, such as daisies and bachelor's buttons, in an informal bed or meadow. Any self-sown flowers will vary in flower color from the original parents, so it will be hard to keep a specific color in your garden unless you reseed fresh each spring. Mix larger poppies, such as the breadseed type, among flowering perennials or tall annuals to provide extra color. Cut the dried seedpods of this type of poppy for use in flower arranging.

Try These
Look for mixes of the different types of poppies to get a broad range of colors. 'Thai Silk' California poppy features semidouble flowers while 'Red Chief' California poppy has bright red- and orange-colored blooms. 'Champagne Bubbles' is a dwarf Icelandic poppy. 'French Flounce' breadseed poppy has giant, fluffy, ruffled double flowers in a mix of colors. 'Hungarian' breadseed poppy is known for its pastel pink flowers and black seeds used in baking.

Salvia

Salvia splendens

Botanical Pronunciation
SAL-vi-a SPLEN-dens

Other Name
Scarlet sage

Bloom Period and Seasonal Color
Midsummer to fall; red, pink, salmon, blue, purple, and white

Mature Height × Spread
1 to 3 feet × 1 to 2 feet

I used to think of annual salvias as those overused flowers with spiky stems and fire engine red blooms. However, with newer varieties featuring blue, purple, salmon, white, burgundy, and pink flowers, I'm giving them a fresh look. Unlike perennial salvias that will bloom off-and-on in summer, these plants are bred to bloom their heads off all summer. Salvias are a mainstay in the annual flower garden providing vivid colors on moderate-sized plants. They are versatile, too. They grow well in containers and can be used as a cut flower. They attract butterflies and hummingbirds to the garden, adding more visual interest.

When, Where, and How to Plant

Start salvia seed indoors under grow lights 6 to 8 weeks before your last frost date or purchase transplants in local garden centers. Plant salvias in a full to part sun location in well-drained, fertile soil after all danger of frost has passed. The more sun they receive, the more flowers they will produce. Space plants about 8 to 12 inches apart in beds and containers. Pinch out the top few inches of the young plant's main stem after planting to encourage more branching and, eventually, even more flowering.

Growing Tips

Keep salvia plants well watered and weeded. Consider mulching around the base of plants to keep the soil moisture constant. Fertilize every three weeks with an organic plant food.

Regional Advice and Care

Newer types are self-cleaning and don't have to be deadheaded to keep blooming. On older varieties, remove the spent flowers to keep the plants blooming and looking tidy. Watch for spider mites, aphids, and whiteflies on plants and spray insecticidal soap to control them. Avoid planting in poorly drained soils as this can lead to root rot.

Companion Planting and Design

Bright-colored salvias look stunning planted *en masse* in all one color or a combination of colors. They also combine nicely with a variety of different flowers in the garden, such as coreopsis, petunias, and dwarf cosmos. Salvias can add some height to containers combined with cascading plants such as calibrachoa. They even can add color to an evergreen shrub border when grown as a bed of colorful salvias in front of the shrubs.

Try These

The Sizzler series features a broad range of bright- and pastel-colored varieties as well as some bicolors. The Firecracker series features dwarf, compact plants. The Lighthouse series features 2- to 3-foot-tall plants that don't need deadheading. The Salsa series features 18-inch-tall plants with flower colors, such as lavender, white, red, pink, rose, and bicolors.

Snapdragon

Antirrhinum majus

Botanical Pronunciation
an-tih-RYE-num MAY-jus

Other Name
Common snapdragon

Bloom Period and Seasonal Color
Spring through fall; pink, red, orange, yellow, and bicolors

Mature Height × Spread
1 to 3 feet × 12 to 18 inches

Snapdragons are fun annuals. Individual flowers look like mouths. It's fun to use snapdragon flowers to play with your kids. Just squeeze the bottom of a flower and watch the "jaws" open and close. Snapdragons feature stalks of brightly colored flowers that bloom best during the cooler parts of spring and fall; they may stop flowering during the heat of summer. The flowers start blooming at the bottom of the stalk and open going up the stem. They make great cut flowers and good companions to other cool-season plants, especially since they can flower in part shade. While the standard snapdragons are tall, bushy plants, newer varieties have a trailing or creeping habit making them perfect for containers, window boxes, and cascading over walls.

When, Where, and How to Plant
Start snapdragon seeds indoors under grow lights 6 to 8 weeks before your last frost date or purchase seedlings from your local garden centers in spring or late summer. Plant in spring as soon as the ground can be worked, around the time you'd plant peas. Find a spot in full sun to part shade in well-drained, compost-amended soil. Space plants 8 to 12 inches apart. Pinch the tips of the plants after transplanting to promote a bushier plant with more flower spikes.

Growing Tips
Keep plants well watered and weeded. Mulch beds to keep the soil evenly moist. Stake taller varieties to keep the flower stalks from curving, especially if they're to be used for cut flowers. Fertilize monthly with an organic plant food.

Regional Advice and Care
Deadhead spent snapdragon flowers to promote a second flush of growth for fall. Snapdragons can withstand frost and, if protected with bark mulch in late fall, may even overwinter in the warmer parts of New England. However, during its second year, plants tend to not be as vigorous as new transplants. Watch for infestations of aphids and spider mites, and control these pests with sprays of insecticidal soap.

Companion Planting and Design
Snapdragons are versatile in the landscape. Plant them near spring bloomers, such as bleeding hearts, as a transition plant to the flowering of warm-season annuals. Plant them in a cutting garden for use as cut flowers indoors. Plant snapdragons in part shade areas to complement foliage perennials, such as brunnera and hostas. You can plant newer cascading varieties in window boxes with other cool-season flowers, such as pansies.

Try These
The Rocket series features 3-foot-tall flower spikes that are perfect for cutting. 'Arrow Formula Mix' has multibranched plants that grow 2 feet tall. The Candy Showers series and the 'Lampion Mix' are trailing snapdragon types with flower colors ranging from deep purple to yellow. 'Montego Mix' is a dwarf snapdragon that only grows 8 to 10 inches tall.

Stock

Matthiola incana

Botanical Pronunciation
math-EYE-oh-luh in-KAY-nuh

Other Name
Gillyflower

Bloom Period and Seasonal Color
Midsummer to fall; red, purple, pink, yellow, and white

Mature Height × Spread
8 inches to 3 feet × 1 foot

A biennial or short-lived perennial in warmer climates, stock flowers are a colorful old-fashioned annual in New England. The plants grow from 8 inches to more than 3 feet tall. Even though the flower spikes and the hairy, grey-green foliage are beautiful, it's the scent that is the calling card of stock. I love the spicy, sweet fragrance of stocks. I think it's similar to vanilla or cloves. To enjoy the fragrance, plant stock flowers in containers on a deck or patio close to where you'll be sitting or in the garden under a window to enjoy the scent. The single- or double-petaled, pastel-colored flowers also attract butterflies and the fragrant flower spikes are good additions to flower arrangements.

When, Where, and How to Plant
Start seeds indoors under grow lights 6 to 8 weeks before your last frost date. Transplant homegrown seedlings or garden center transplants into the garden around the last frost date for your area, spacing plants about 1 foot apart. Plant dwarf varieties closer together for a more dramatic visual and sensual effect. Stock flowers grow best in full sun in well-drained fertile soil. They can tolerate part shade, but the flowering may be decreased.

Growing Tips
Keep plants well watered and fertilized monthly with an organic plant food. Keep plants well weeded and mulched to conserve soil moisture. Deadhead spent flowers to encourage more blooms. Stock flowers have few pests other than the occasional aphid that's controlled with insecticidal soap.

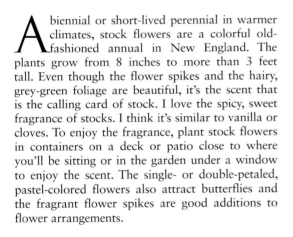

Regional Advice and Care
Stock flowers bloom continuously from summer to fall and grow best during cool weather. They may stop flowering during periods when temperatures are above 80 degrees Fahrenheit in midsummer. You can also grow stock as a fall plant, transplanting seedlings into the garden in late summer. They can take a light frost and continue blooming. Stock flowers self-sow readily, so watch for seedlings next spring and remove them since their quality is less than freshly grown plants.

Companion Planting and Design
Stock flowers grow well in a cottage garden with other pastel-colored flowers, such as salvia, ageratum, and iris, or with other cool-season annuals, such as pansies and snapdragons. Dwarf varieties grow well in containers on a deck, patio, or balcony. Mix and match tall stock flowers in containers with cascading annuals, such as *scaevola* and *calibrachoa*. Grow stock flowers in a cutting garden for indoor flower arrangements. You may have to stake tall varieties to prevent the flower stalks from bending.

Try These
The 'Early Bird Mix' and the 'Formula Mix' feature single- and double-petaled blooms in a variety of colors. These mixes are tall and good for cutting. For dwarf varieties in containers, try the 'Ten Week Mix' and 'Harmony Mix'.

Sunflower

Helianthus annuus

Botanical Pronunciation
hee-lee-AN-thus AN-yew-us

Other Name
Common sunflower

Bloom Period and Seasonal Color
Midsummer to fall; yellow, red, white, and burgundy

Mature Height × Spread
1 to 15 feet × 2 feet

This native North American flower is a dramatic eye-catcher in any garden. The original species features the classic large head with yellow petals. The sunflower head does follow the sun through the sky from east to west, and you'll see fields of these plants nodding all in the same direction in summer. Modern breeding has created a wide range of plant sizes and flower colors. You can now grow dwarf varieties that are 1 foot tall to mammoth varieties that grow more than 15 feet tall. New, multibranching varieties have more flowers per stalk and colors ranging from white to burgundy. Sunflowers attract bees and butterflies, are great cut flowers, and the seeds and immature flower buds are edible for us and for birds.

When, Where, and How to Plant
Plant sunflower seed in compost-amended soil in full sun directly into the garden in spring after all danger of frost has passed, which is about the time to plant tomatoes. Thin the seedlings to 18 inches apart once four leaves have formed. Plant sunflowers in a group to prevent the taller varieties from blowing over in a storm.

Growing Tips
Prevent birds from eating seed or young transplants by covering the sunflower patch with netting or a floating row cover. Once growing, remove the covering. Keep plants well watered and fertilize monthly with an organic plant food. Keep young patches well weeded until the sunflowers can outgrow the weeds.

Regional Advice and Care
To harvest seeds, protect flower heads by covering them in brown paper bags (to keep birds away) once the petals fade but before you can loosen the seeds by rubbing your hands across the head. Cut the head off and let it finish maturing indoors. Harvest immature flower buds using steam and eat like a globe artichoke. It's a surprising treat! Grow plants in an airy location to prevent mildew and other diseases from forming.

Companion Planting and Design
Tall sunflowers look best planted in groups along a fence, wall, or building. This also provides some protection from high winds. Plant medium-sized varieties in a cottage garden or along the back of a perennial flower border. Grow a cutting garden of sunflowers of various colored and shaped heads. Grow dwarf varieties in containers or in front of a flower border.

Try These
'Mammoth Russian' is a tall variety with massive flower heads that are great for collecting seeds for eating or feeding birds. Some nice multiheaded varieties of various colors include 'Soraya' (yellow), 'Italian White' (white), 'Autumn Beauty' (bronze), and 'Chianti' (red). 'Firecracker' (yellow) is a pollen-free variety that's great for flower arranging since it won't drop pollen on the table. However, it won't attract bees. 'Elf' and 'Big Smile' are dwarf varieties that grow well in containers. 'Teddy Bear' features a dwarf plant with chrysanthemum-like yellow flowers.

Sweet Pea

Lathyrus odoratus

Botanical Pronunciation
la-THY-rus od-or-AH-tus

Other Name
Annual sweet pea

Bloom Period and Seasonal Color
Midsummer to fall; white, purple, pink, red, and bicolors

Mature Height × Spread
2 to 8 feet × 1 to 2 feet

This annual vine grows and flowers best during cool weather so it is particularly attractive in the coastal and northern parts of New England. It adds a touch of elegance and, depending on the variety, fragrance to any garden bed or container. Heirloom varieties tend to be the most fragrant, while modern varieties have a wider variety of plant sizes. This vine is a great cut flower for arranging and bringing the scents of summer indoors. There's nothing more enticing than a vase full of fragrant sweet pea blossoms. It needs support to grow, but the tendrils are strong so sweet pea vines will cling to many objects, such as fences, thin poles, netting, and wire.

When, Where, and How to Plant
Sow in a full to part sun location directly in the ground in well-drained, compost-amended soil in spring. Plant climbing sweet peas along a fence, trellis, or wire; plant bush varieties in containers. Nick seeds with a nail file and soak them overnight in warm water to hasten germination. Plant outside once your ground has dried, spacing the seeds 6 inches apart. In cold areas of our region, to get an earlier flowering crop, consider starting sweet pea seeds indoors in pots 4 to 6 weeks before your last frost date.

Growing Tips
Since sweet peas are a legume, they need little additional fertilizer. They do grow best on a neutral pH soil, so add some lime if your soil is acidic. Just keep the soil evenly moist for good germination and growth.

Regional Advice and Care
Sweet peas may dry up and die in midsummer in warmer parts of New England. Enjoy the early summer crop and consider planting a crop in midsummer for fall. Deadhead to encourage more blooms. Avoid planting in the same location each year since diseases can build up in the soil to attack the sweet pea plants. They sometimes get powdery mildew disease. Space vines farther apart to increase air circulation to avoid this fungal disease. Unlike garden peas, sweet peas are poisonous and can't be eaten.

Companion Planting and Design
Grow tall varieties along a fence, lattice, up a lamppost or thin pole, or in a cutting garden. Plant bush varieties in containers or window boxes. Plant fragrant varieties where their aroma can be enjoyed. This traditional English garden plant pairs well with peonies and roses. They also can grow up the stalk of tall flowers, such as sunflowers, adding color before the sunflowers bloom.

Try These
'Old Spice' and 'Mammoth Mix' are fragrant heirloom varieties that come in many pastel colors. They are particularly heat resistant. 'Incense Mix' is a 6-foot-tall mix of colors whose plants have long stems making them great for cutting. 'Villa Roma Mix' is a dwarf variety that only grows 14 inches tall.

Verbena

Verbena hybrids

Botanical Pronunciation
ver-BEE-nah

Other Name
Vervain

Bloom Period and Seasonal Color
Early summer to fall; white, pink, yellow, orange, red, purple, and bicolors

Mature Height × Spread
1 to 5 feet × 6 inches to 3 feet

Verbena is a full sun-loving, colorful annual plant that can fool you since some versions self-sow readily and act like a perennial. They seem to pop up everywhere in my garden. The trailing forms of verbena come in a broad range of colors, adding brightness to window boxes, hanging baskets, containers, and garden beds. Many forms have two or even three colors on the same plant. Taller forms of verbena have less variety of color and a more airy appearance. Butterflies, in particular, love the taller forms. This low-maintenance, drought-tolerant annual just requires light and the occasional deadheading to keep blooming from summer until frost. In fact, too much pampering results in less flowering. It's sometimes best to just leave it alone.

When, Where, and How to Plant
Verbena seed can take up to a month to germinate, so many gardeners simply buy transplants from a local garden center. If you do start seed indoors under grow lights, start them 6 to 8 weeks before your last frost date. Plant in full sun in compost-amended beds after all danger of frost has passed. Space plants about 10 inches apart.

Growing Tips
Verbena needs little additional fertilizer other than spring compost. Keep plants watered once the soil is dry to encourage flowering during hot periods.

Regional Advice and Care
Deadhead spent flowers to encourage more blooms. If the plants get leggy, consider cutting back verbena's trailing vines by one-third to stimulate more side branching and flowering. Verbena is a workhorse in containers and beds in the garden, but *full sun is a must*. If planted in part sun or shade, you can get powdery mildew disease, insect attacks, and little flowering. Basically, it's just more work for you. If plants dry up during the heat of midsummer, simply cut them back, fertilize with an organic plant food, and water; they should bounce back to flower again in a few weeks.

Companion Planting and Design
Verbena are great in hanging baskets, window boxes, and containers paired with other full sun-loving cascading annuals, such as lantana and calibrachoa. Consider mixing and matching them with tall annuals, such as salvia, cleome, and heliotrope, in containers as well. Place containers on a deck or patio or near a window where you can see the butterflies that are inevitably attracted to the flowers. Tall varieties should be planted in the back of annual and perennial flowerbeds to surprise and add color to the midsummer and fall gardens.

Try These
'Homestead Purple' is a popular, purple, trailing variety that now comes in a pink version. 'Tuscany Mix' features colors such as blue, burgundy, and peach. 'Peaches and Cream' is a popular bicolored variety. Butterflies love *Verbena bonariensis*, which is a common tall variety with purple flowers that's good for cutting.

Zinnia

Zinnia elegans

Botanical Pronunciation
ZIN-ee-a-EL-e-ganz

Other Name
Common zinnia

Bloom Period and Seasonal Color
Midsummer until fall; red, pink, orange, yellow, white, and bicolors

Mature Height × Spread
6 inches to 3 feet × 1 to 2 feet

Zinnias are old-fashioned garden favorites that grow in abundance in my garden. The variety of flower shapes, sizes, and colors is amazing. These easy-to-grow annual flowers develop quickly from direct seeding or transplanting to produce single- or double-petaled blooms all summer long until frost. Zinnias add color to the late summer perennial and annual gardens with their showy flowers and nonstop blooming habit. Their needs are simple. Give them plenty of water and grow them in full sun in an airy location to avoid late season diseases. Not only are they beautiful flowers in the garden or containers, zinnias attract butterflies and hummingbirds and can be used as a cut flower indoors in arrangements.

When, Where, and How to Plant
Plant seeds directly in a full sun location into compost-amended garden beds in well-drained soil in spring around the last frost date for your area. For quicker blooms, consider buying transplants from local garden centers in spring or starting seeds indoors under grow lights 4 weeks before your last frost date. Space plants or thin seedlings to 8 to 18 inches apart in beds, depending on the size of the variety. Pinch out the growing tips of young transplants in spring to promote side branching, bushiness, and more flowering.

Growing Tips
Keep plants well watered and fertilize monthly with an organic plant food.

Regional Advice and Care
Deadhead spent flowers all summer long. By late summer in New England, powdery mildew can cause the leaves to die back and the plant to look unsightly. Space plants farther apart to promote air circulation, select disease-resistant varieties, and pull and compost diseased plants to reduce this disease. Japanese beetles *love* zinnias. Trap the beetles, cover prized plants with a row cover, and spray Neem oil to kill adults; spray beneficial nematodes to kill the beetle larvae.

Companion Planting and Design
Zinnias are good additions to a perennial flower border. Grow tall varieties in the middle and back of the border near spring-flowering perennials, such as peonies, iris, and daylilies, to add color in late summer. Plant smaller mounding varieties, such as the Profusion series, in the front of borders or in containers. Zinnias are good additions to the cut flower garden as well. I like growing them in the vegetable garden to attract beneficial insects and add color.

Try These
'Blue Point', 'State Fair', and 'Benary's Giant' are tall, large, double-flowered colorful mixes that are great for cutting and growing in gardens. The Profusion series is a mounding mix of many colors that produces small, single flowers on disease-resistant 1-foot-tall plants. They grow well in containers. The Oklahoma series is a tall, double-flowered, cut flower variety with good powdery mildew resistance. The Ruffles series features double-flowered, frilly petaled flowers with good disease resistance.

BULBS
FOR NEW ENGLAND

There is something magical about bulbs. You plant them in the ground and wait months out of good faith for something to happen. Then in spring (or summer or fall, depending on your bulb), you're rewarded for your patience with a colorful display of flowers. If you're like me, you often forget what you planted in fall, and each spring it's a surprise party of flowers popping up around the yard.

What's a Bulb?

I'm going to use the term "bulb" as a catchall phrase. Depending on the plant, the fleshy underground root may be referred to as a rhizome, corm, tuberous root, or tuber. I like to keep it simple by calling them all bulbs.

Grape hyacinth and tulips in spring

Bulbs can bloom in spring, summer, or fall depending on the type you're growing. In New England we have the perfect climate to grow the spring-flowering bulbs. Daffodils, tulips, scilla, hyacinths, and crocus are some of the bulbs that are planted in fall, need a cold winter for a dormant period, then bloom in spring with the first signs of warm weather. Depending on the weather, we can have bulbs blooming from March (snowdrops) to June (late tulips) with a little planning. Our cool springs allow these bulbs to flower for weeks, extending the color show. These bulbs grow best when grown in full sun in well-drained soil. The key is having full sun on the bulbs in spring, before the deciduous leaves are fully out. Many of these bulbs make great woodland plants that flower and then disappear before the trees leaf out and the heavy shade of summer fills that area.

There are also fall-blooming species of these tough bulbs, such as colchicum, that add color when you least expect it, blooming in September and October. Some of the spring-flowering bulbs, such as snowdrops and hyacinths, have an alluring scent in the garden. It's nice to plant these close to where you can enjoy the fragrance, such as near a deck or patio. These also make great bulbs to force into bloom indoors in pots in winter as a cold-weather treat. Paperwhite narcissus is the most famous indoor bulb for forcing, but people are split about the scent. Some love it, while others can't stand it.

More than Just Spring

We also can grow some tender bulbs in our climate. Dahlias, gladiolus, canna lilies, and caladiums appreciate our warm, long summers. They may take all summer to reach their full glory, but boy is it worth it! Some of these bulbs may need your help to get a jump on the growing season to make it worth the effort. You can grow them in pots so they flower sooner or pot them up indoors to start their growth before it's time to transplant them outside. Plant these heat lovers in a sunny, warm location near your house, garage, or a stone wall, and these bulbs shine. What I particularly like about tropical bulbs is many have interesting foliage. Even if your canna lilies don't get to the flowering stage or your caladiums never bloom, the leaves have a range of colors and patterns that brightens up the landscape. If you want the same plant to come back next year, though, you'll have to dig and store these bulbs. These won't make it through our cold winters.

Dahlia 'Everswinkel'

The one bulb that's a bit of both groups is the lily. It's a hardy bulb in New England, so it comes back year after year. But it also is a summer bloomer with amazing color and, sometimes, fragrance. Asiatic, Oriental, Trumpet, and Orienpet lilies are just some of the types that grow well here. While the colors are outstanding, the scent of the Oriental lilies, in particular, is to die for. One flower bouquet will perfume the whole house.

So consider tucking bulbs in and around the flower garden, between shrubs, in containers, and other places in your yard. You'll *love* the beauty they bring each year.

Allium

Allium spp. and cultivars

Botanical Pronunciation
AL-ee-um

Other Name
Flowering onion

Bloom Period and Seasonal Color
Spring to early summer; white, pink, yellow, and purple

Mature Height × Spread
6 to 36 inches × 10 to 12 inches

Alliums are a broad group of plants in the onion family. While we're all familiar with good common food crops, such as onions, leeks, and garlic, there are many alliums that are grown just for their ornamental characteristics. The ornamental alliums are a diverse group. Some are only 6 inches tall producing dainty flowers, while others can stretch to 3 to 4 feet tall with 8-inch-diameter flowers that are packed in a dense head. Most of these bulbs bloom early in the season providing a dramatic accent to spring-flowering plants. I love seeing tall alliums popping up among my perennial flowers in spring. Combine their tough nature with deer and animal resistance and you get a reliable bulb that will bloom for years.

When, Where, and How to Plant
Alliums are hardy in our region depending on the type. Select varieties hardy to your zone. Plant alliums in fall when you would plant tulips, daffodils, and other spring-flowering bulbs. They prefer a full sun location in well-drained, fertile soil. Alliums will grow in part shade, but may not flower as well. Plant bulbs at a depth 2 to 3 times their diameter. For example, a 2-inch-diameter bulb should be planted 4 to 6 inches deep. Space the bulbs 3 to 8 inches apart, farther apart for larger bulbs.

Growing Tips
Alliums grow best in fertile soil, so amend the soil with compost when planting and spread a light layer over the planting area each spring. Keep the bulbs well weeded and watered. Once established they're drought tolerant.

Regional Advice and Care
Stake tall varieties to prevent the flower stalks from flopping over. Deadhead flowers in summer after the blooms have passed or let them form seeds and self-sow in the garden. Self-sown allium seedlings need a few years of growing to get to the flowering stage, and they can become weedy if you don't thin out the seedlings in summer. Let the foliage naturally yellow and die back in summer before cutting it to the ground. In fall, mulch alliums that are marginally hardy in our area with bark to protect them from winter's cold.

Companion Planting and Design
Alliums grow best tucked in a perennial flower border to "pop up" around other spring-blooming flowers, such as peonies, iris, catmint, and geraniums. You can plant the large-flowering varieties *en masse* for a dramatic effect or short varieties in a rock garden to complement other low-growers, such as columbine and sedums.

Try These
'Purple Sensation' is a large-flowered variety that grows 2 to 3 feet tall producing 4-inch-diameter purple blooms. 'Globemaster' and 'Gladiator' grow even taller (4 feet) with 8-inch-diameter purple flowers. 'Mt. Everest' is a white-flowered version. Drumstick alliums only grow 1 to 2 feet tall and produce 2-inch-diameter reddish-purple blooms. *Allium moly* grows 8 inches tall with yellow flowers in loose clusters.

Caladium

Caladium bicolor

Botanical Pronunciation
kuh-LAY-dee-um BYE-cull-e

Other Name
Elephant's ears

Bloom Period and Seasonal Color
Insignificant flowers; leaves all season;
white, pink, bicolors, and red

Mature Height × Spread
6 to 24 inches × 12 to 18 inches

Caladiums are tropical tubers that grow well as annual bulbs in New England. Although not hardy in our climate, they have strikingly colorful leaves. Many varieties have striking patterns of white, green, pink, and red on the same leaf, and I like how they can light up a shady spot in the garden. Since you aren't waiting for the flowers to bloom, caladiums provide color from spring until fall. Some varieties have arrow-shaped leaves while others have straplike leaves. They love the heat and humidity warmer parts of our region experience, and they really come into their own by midsummer. Dig up and save the tubers for replanting the following spring or allow them to die in fall.

When, Where, and How to Plant
Plant caladiums in late spring or early summer once the soil has warmed to at least 60 degrees Fahrenheit, about the time you'd plant melons. You can also plant tubers indoors 4 to 6 weeks before your last frost date in pots filled with moistened potting soil. Potted tubers grow faster than those planted directly in the ground. Grow them under lights until you move them outdoors, either in the pots or transplanted into the garden. Plant in a partly shaded location in well-drained, humusy soil amended with peat moss. Plant tubers a few inches deep spaced 1 to 2 feet apart.

Growing Tips
Caladiums need well-drained, warm soil that holds moisture well to grow their best. Don't plant too early or the tubers may rot in the cold soils. Keep plants well watered during the growing season. Spread a small handful of bulb fertilizer in the planting hole to stimulate growth.

Regional Advice and Care
Protect caladiums from slugs and snails by placing beer traps around plants, spreading an organic slug bait, such as iron phosphate, and wrapping pots and raised beds with copper tape. To save the tubers, cut back the foliage when it starts to yellow in early fall, lift the tubers without damaging them, remove the soil, and let dry in a warm, well-ventilated location for one week. Once they're dry, place in a perforated plastic bag filled with slightly moistened peat moss and store in a 50 degrees Fahrenheit room. You can also bring pots of caladiums indoors, cut back the foliage, and store them in a basement or heated garage for the winter.

Companion Planting and Design
Caladiums grow well under trees and shrubs where it's shady or paired with other shade-loving perennials, such as hostas, astilbe, and bleeding hearts. Place containers on a deck or patio where the intricately colored leaves can be enjoyed, but where they're shaded from the hot afternoon sun.

Try These
'Carolyn Whorton' features pink leaves with red veins on a 2-foot-tall plant. 'Gingerland' has strappy white leaves with red speckles and green margins. 'Pink Gem' has pink straplike leaves with green edges on 12-inch-tall plants.

Canna Lily

Canna x generalis

Botanical Pronunciation
KAN-uh jen-er-RAY-liss

Other Name
Indian shot

Bloom Period and Seasonal Color
Mid- to late summer; pink, salmon, red, and orange

Mature Height × Spread
3 to 6 feet × 1 to 3 feet

Canna lily is a tropical bulb that grows quickly during our warm summers to produce tall, stately plants with banana-sized and -shaped leaves. From the center of the leaf whorl emerges a flower stalk with brightly colored blooms. Cannas can quickly create a tropical, exotic feel in your garden. They aren't hardy in our region, but grow well in warm ground or containers. I love growing them in containers because they grow faster and flower sooner, allowing me to enjoy them longer. Even if you live in colder areas of our region and you may not have enough warm days for flowering to occur, the colorful leaves are a show in and of themselves.

When, Where, and How to Plant

Plant transplants or rhizomes in early summer once the soil has warmed at least to 60 degrees Fahrenheit, about the same time you'd plant melons. Plant in full sun in well-drained, moist, humusy soil. Amend the soil with an organic plant food when planting. You can also start canna lilies indoors in containers 4 to 6 weeks before your last frost date. Move containers outdoors after all danger of frost has passed or transplant them into the ground. Plant in a bed against a south-facing wall or along a building to maximize its heat. Plant tubers 4 to 6 inches deep. Space them 2 to 3 feet apart; closer together in a container.

Growing Tips

Fertilize monthly with an organic plant food to encourage more growth. Cannas need consistent moisture to grow their best. Keep the plants well weeded and watered.

Regional Advice and Care

Deadhead spent flower stalks and cut back the foliage to the ground in fall after a frost. Tall varieties may need staking to prevent them from flopping. Control Japanese beetles that love to feed on the leaves, with traps, organic sprays, such as pyrethrum, and handpicking. To save plants for next year, cut back the foliage after a frost, dig up the tubers, remove the soil, and let them dry in a warm, airy location out of direct sun. Store in a 50-degrees Fahrenheit basement or garage in a perforated plastic bag filled with slightly moistened peat moss. Discard any rotten or shriveled up tubers in winter.

Companion Planting and Design

Plant tall canna lilies in the back of a perennial flower border next to other tall garden plants, such as Joe-pye weed and plume poppy. Plant shorter varieties in containers to be used as a focal point on your deck, patio, or porch.

Try These

'Tropicanna' is a 5- to 6-foot-tall variety with striking green-, yellow-, pink-, and red-striped leaves and orange flowers. There is a gold-flowered version as well. 'Tropicanna Black' has red flowers and purple-and-burgundy striped leaves. 'Pink Sunburst' is a dwarf canna with pink flowers and yellow-, pink-, and green-striped leaves.

Colchicum

Colchicum autumnale

Botanical Pronunciation
KOLL-chi-kum aw-tum-NAY-lee

Other Name
Naked ladies

Bloom Period and Seasonal Color
Fall; pink, lilac, or white

Mature Height × Spread
4 to 6 inches × 6 to 12 inches

Most gardeners are familiar with spring-flowering bulbs, such as daffodils and tulips, but there is a group of fall-flowering bulbs that grow well in New England, providing color when you least expect it. Autumn crocus or saffron crocus is one type of fall bulb you can grow in our region, but a more dramatically colored fall-flowering bulb is the colchicum. Colchicum is also called naked ladies because in fall, only the flowers emerge from the soil. It's quite a surprise to see up to six bright single- or double-petaled blossoms with yellow anthers popping up around your flowering mums. The flowers die back after blooming. In spring the lance-shaped leaves emerge for a month of growth before dying back.

When, Where, and How to Plant
Colchicum is hardy to zone 4. In colder parts of our region, spread bark mulch over the area where the bulbs are located to protect them from winter. Plant colchicum bulbs purchased from the local garden center in late summer in well-drained soil in full to part sun. The sunnier the location for colchicums, the less likely they will flop over when flowering. Amend the soil well with compost. Plant bulbs 4 to 6 inches deep spaced 6 to 12 inches apart.

Growing Tips
Spread a small handful of a bulb fertilizer in the planting hole. Then, sprinkle fertilizer around plants in spring to encourage more leafy growth that will feed the bulb and produce better flowering in fall. Keep the bulbs well watered their first fall.

Regional Advice and Care
Colchicum will slowly spread over time. To produce more bulbs for your garden, dig and divide bulbs in midsummer when they're dormant. Mark the plant's location so you don't mistakenly weed out the nondescript foliage in spring, thinking it's a weed, when it comes up. Protect the flowers during wet periods from slugs and snails by setting out a beer trap, sprinkling iron phosphate organic bait, or spreading crushed oyster or seashells near the flowers. Colchicum is a good pollen source for bees in fall when little else is available for them.

Companion Planting and Design
Plant colchicum among low-growing evergreens, such as creeping junipers, in front of a perennial flower border or near shrubs for a late season show. Plant them in an area protected from winds so the flowers last longer. Plant bulbs next to other fall bloomers, such as sedum, to provide some complementary color. Plant bulbs close to a walkway or lawn so you can enjoy the brightly colored flowers.

Try These
'Waterlily' is a double-flowered pink variety with 6- to 8-inch-diameter flowers. 'Alba' has single white flowers, while 'Albaplenum' has double white blooms. 'Rosy Dawn' and 'Dick Trotter' both feature single rose-colored flowers with a white center.

Crocus

Crocus spp. and hybrids

Botanical Pronunciation
KROW-kus

Other Name
Dutch crocus

Bloom Period and Seasonal Color
Late winter to spring; blue, white, yellow, purple, and bicolors

Mature Height × Spread
4 to 6 inches × 2 to 4 inches

This low-growing, clumping bulb is an early bloomer in the landscape, offering bright colors that signal the end of winter. The lance-shaped leaves emerge as soon as the ground thaws to produce the cup-shaped flowers. There are two different types of crocus. The most popular is the spring-blooming crocus in a broad array of colors from white to purple to yellow, such as the Dutch hybrids. However, for some fall color, consider planting the autumn crocus that blooms in fall. Saffron is harvested from a fall-flowering crocus species, but saffron crocus are only marginally hardy in many areas of New England. Plus, if you're thinking of starting a new garden business, it takes 4,000 flowers to make one ounce of saffron.

When, Where, and How to Plant

Crocus is hardy throughout our region. Plant spring-flowering crocus bulbs (technically called corms) in fall in a full sun location in well-drained soil. Amend the planting hole with a bulb fertilizer and compost before planting. Plant fall-flowering crocus in late summer and early fall. Plant the small bulbs at a depth 2 to 3 times their diameter. Plant in groups; crocus look best when planted close together, so space them just so they aren't touching.

Growing Tips

Keep the soil well watered after planting. Once they establish, crocus are drought tolerant, especially since they go dormant in summer. Let the leaves naturally fade after the flowers have faded to help the bulb replenish its reserves for next year. Fertilize in fall with a bulb plant food.

Regional Advice and Care

Plant a mix of early- and late-flowering crocus varieties to extend the flowering season. Crocus will slowly spread over time and naturalize. They rarely need dividing. Voles, mice, or chipmunks can eat crocus bulbs. Protect bulbs by spreading crushed oyster shells or seashells in the planting hole or plant them in wire cages buried in the ground. Avoid using bone meal fertilizer since it attracts animals. Protect flowers from deer with netting.

Companion Planting and Design

Plant bulbs in front of a perennial flower border or rock garden. Plant close to spring-flowering perennials, such as bleeding hearts, that will hide the crocus foliage once it starts to yellow. Crocus can be naturalized in lawns, under trees, or in woodlands. Plant in groups and allow them to spread. Plant where they will receive full sun until the leaves come out. If planting in a lawn, don't mow down the foliage until it yellows after the flowers fade.

Try These

For spring-blooming crocus varieties, try 'Blue Pearl' with its pale blue flowers and a yellow throat. 'Jeanne d'Arc' is a pure white-flowering heirloom variety with a purple base. 'Golden Bunch' is a golden-petaled variety with a tangerine-colored throat. 'Ruby Giant' is a large-flowered, ruby-colored variety. 'Cassiope' and 'Conqueror' are blue-flowering, fall-blooming crocus hardy to zone 4.

Daffodil

Narcissus spp. and hybrids

Botanical Pronunciation
nar-SIS-sus

Other Name
Jonquil

Bloom Period and Seasonal Color
Spring; yellow, white, gold, and bicolors

Mature Height × Spread
4 to 24 inches × 3 to 6 inches

If you're looking for an easy-to-grow, spring-flowering bulb that returns faithfully each year, slowly spreading over time that doesn't have problems with animals, choose the daffodil. Daffodils are known for their golden or white, trumpet-shaped flowers on lancelike leaves. There is also a broad range of varieties that feature bicolored flowers in colors of pink, rose, and green as well. The small-flowered versions are often called jonquils. Some jonquils have a strong, sweet fragrance. Daffodils can be planted in small groups in perennial or rock gardens to large swaths in a woodland or bank. I once planted 75 bulbs a year on a bank and in only a few years it was covered with yellow flowers each spring.

When, Where, and How to Plant

Daffodils are hardy throughout our region; select bulbs from your local garden centers. Plant bulbs in fall in a full to part sun location in well-drained, fertile soil. Plant at a depth of 2 to 3 times the bulb's diameter in compost-amended holes. Add a small handful of fertilizer per bulb. Plant in groups, spacing bulbs 3 to 6 inches apart, depending on their size. Plant smaller bulbs closer together.

Growing Tips

Mulch after planting with a 2-inch-thick layer of bark to protect daffodil bulbs through their first winter. Once established they won't need protection. Let the foliage naturally yellow and die after the flowers fade to rejuvenate the bulb for next year's blooming. Sprinkle bulb fertilizer around established plantings in fall.

Regional Advice and Care

Daffodils usually don't need to be divided, but if they stop flowering, dig up bulbs in late spring, separate any small bulblets that have formed around the main bulb, and replant all the bulbs in compost-amended soil. Mice, voles, and chipmunks tend to avoid daffodils.

Companion Planting and Design

Plant daffodils in perennial flower beds next to other spring bloomers, such as bleeding hearts, iris, and peonies. Perennial flowers will cover up the daffodil's dying foliage, which can make a garden look unsightly. Plant in woodlands, on banks, or in lawns. If you're planting in a lawn, don't mow down foliage until it yellows after the flowers fade. Choose varieties based on flower color and bloom time; planting early, mid-, and late season bloomers extends the bloom period.

Try These

'King Alfred' is a classic, large yellow variety. 'Mt. Hood' is a similar white variety. 'Thalia' is small-flowered, white, with a sweet fragrance. 'Tete a Tete' is a similar small, yellow-flowered variety. 'Precocious' is a large white variety with rose pink, frilly centers. 'Tahiti' is a golden color with flecks of orange in the double flowers. 'Cheerfulness' is a double-flowered white variety that offers more than one flower per stalk. Paperwhite is white daffodils that are popular to force or grown indoors in pots in winter.

Dahlia

Dahlia hybrids

Botanical Pronunciation
DAL-yuh

Other Name
Garden dahlia

Bloom Period and Seasonal Color
Late summer into fall; pink, salmon, white, cream, red, and bicolors

Mature Height × Spread
1 to 5 feet × 1 to 3 feet

If you're looking for a big showy flower to cap off the end of the growing season and continue blooming into fall, consider dahlias. Dahlia plants can reach up to 5 feet tall and 3 feet wide, making a statement with their dark green or burgundy- colored foliage. The real show happens in late summer when the flowers appear. There are more than twenty different dahlia flower shapes with the most common ones being the pompon, waterlily, cactus, and decorative. Some are literally the size of dinner plates; that's one big flower! There are single and double flowers available in a wide range of colors. The flowers attract butterflies and hummingbirds, are great for cutting and flower arranging, and are not favored by deer.

When, Where, and How to Plant

Dahlias are not hardy in our region and should be treated as an annual or the tubers should be dug and stored indoors in winter. Plant dahlia tubers in spring once the soil temperature rises above 60 degrees Fahrenheit, about the time you'd plant corn. Plant bulbs in well-drained, compost-amended soil. Place a handful of an organic fertilizer in the hole. You can also plant in containers indoors, 4 weeks before your last frost date. Space plants 2 to 3 feet apart.

Growing Tips

Apply additional organic fertilizer monthly as a sidedressing. Mulch with bark mulch to control weeds and keep the soil evenly moist.

Regional Advice and Care

Support tall varieties and large-flowered varieties with a cage or stake to keep the blossoms from flopping over. Control slugs and snails on young plants by setting out beer traps, sprinkling organic iron phosphate baits, and wrapping copper flashing around the containers. To store, dig tubers in fall after frost has blackened the foliage. Cut the foliage to the ground, lift the tubers, and knock off excess soil. Let the tubers dry in a warm, airy location out of direct sun for one week and then store in a cool basement in perforated plastic bags filled with slightly moistened peat moss.

Companion Planting and Design

Plant tall dahlia varieties in the back of a perennial flower border among other fall bloomers, such as anemones, hardy hibiscus, and ornamental grasses. Plant shorter varieties in containers or in the front of the garden. Consider planting them *en masse* for an amazing wow! effect in late summer.

Try These

'Bishop of York' stands 4 feet tall with single, golden blossoms on dark-colored foliage. 'All That Jazz' has rose-red, zinnia-like, 5-inch-diameter flowers on 4-foot-tall plants. 'Envy' has amazing 11-inch-diameter red blooms on 3-foot-tall plants. 'Frank Holmes' has small pompon-shaped, lavender flowers on 3-foot-tall plants. 'Inflammation' has single apricot-colored flowers on 18-inch-tall plants. 'White Lightning' is a white, cactus-shaped variety on 4-foot-tall plants; it's good for cutting.

Gladiolus

Gladiolus hybrids

Botanical Pronunciation
GLAD-ee-ol-us

Other Name
Sword lily

Bloom Period and Seasonal Color
Summer; white, yellow, pink, red, purple,
and bicolors

Mature Height × Spread
3 to 4 feet × 12 inches

There is no flower more stunning in an arrangement than gladiolus. They are popular cut flowers for all occasions, from weddings to funerals. Even though they are mostly known as a cut flower, gladiolus look beautiful in the flower garden as well, especially when grouped together and planted next to flowers in a complementary color. If you want color, gladiolus is your flower. Varieties are available in almost any color of the rainbow, with many having frilly flowers and bicolored blooms. The swordlike leaves yield a spiky flower stalk with individual flowers that bloom from the bottom up. To keep flowers coming all summer and fall, continue to plant bulbs (known as corms) into early summer.

When, Where, and How to Plant

Gladiolus is not hardy in New England, so bulbs need to be dug up in fall and stored or simply grow them as an annual. Purchase bulbs (corms) from your local garden centers. The largest corms will yield the best flowers. Plant bulbs in spring after all danger of frost has passed, about the time you'd plant corn, in well-drained soil. Gladiolus grows best in sandy loam soil. If you have clay soil, consider raising the beds for better water drainage. Plant the bulbs at a depth of 4 times the diameter of the bulb. Amend the soil with compost and some bulb fertilizer in each hole. Space bulbs 6 to 10 inches apart.

Growing Tips

Keep the soil evenly moist by watering and mulching with bark mulch. For use in flower arrangements, harvest the flower stalks after the first few flowers open. In the garden, let the whole flower stalk bloom and cut it to the ground after the flowers fade.

Regional Advice and Care

As gladiolus grows, tie the flower stalks to a stake or use wire cages to keep the stalks growing straight and not flopping. Thrips can attack gladioli flowers. These small, white insects feed on flowers and leaves causing them to be streaky and discolored. Spray insecticidal soap on the plants to kill thrips. If storing the corms, dip them in hot water for 2 minutes and allow them to dry to kill the thrips.

Companion Planting and Design

Glads are usually planted in rows to be harvested as a cut flower, but they also can be used in the perennial flower border planted with dahlias and tall zinnias to give the garden a late season flower boost. Plant gladiolus near plants that will hide their foliage once their blooms have passed. Shorter varieties grow well in containers.

Try These

'Candyman' has deep pink flowers. 'Dream's End' has a bright orange flower stalk that stands 3 feet tall. 'Frizzled Coral Lace' has ruffled coral- and salmon-colored flowers. The Flevo series comes in many colors, such as red, yellow, and blue flowers, and only grows 2 feet tall, reducing the need for staking.

Glory-of-the-Snow

Chionodoxa luciliae

Botanical Pronunciation
kye-on-uh-DOCKS-uh loo-SILL-ee-ee

Other Name
Boissier's glory-of-the-snow

Bloom Period and Seasonal Color
Spring; blue, pink, white, and bicolors

Mature Height × Spread
4 to 6 inches × 4 to 6 inches

Glory-of-the-snow is so-named because it often is one of the first bulbs to bloom in early spring. This low-growing, spring-flowering bulb also will self-sow and spread to fill in a perennial flower garden, rock garden, woodland, or lawn area with beautiful blue, white, or pink flowers each spring. The upward-facing, starlike flowers are produced on 6-inch-tall flower stalks. They provide a shot of color to the early spring landscape before many other perennials or bulbs are blooming. Glory-of-the-snow is hardy in our region. Glory-of-the-snow will disappear in late spring after its foliage yellows and dies. The bulb will survive for years in the ground slowly expanding and producing more flowers each year.

When, Where, and How to Plant
Purchase bulbs from garden centers, selecting firm bulbs without any signs of damage. Plant in fall when planting other spring-flowering bulbs, such as daffodils. Plant bulbs so they aren't touching, in groups about 3 inches deep or a depth of 2 to 3 times their diameter, in well-drained soil. They look best planted *en masse*. They also can be planted in lawns. Randomly throw the bulbs on the lawn and plant them where they drop for a more naturalistic effect. Mix a small amount of a bulb fertilize in each hole.

Growing Tips
Glory-of-the-snow is actually native to warmer areas of the world and will grow best if the soil doesn't dry out in spring and summer. Keep newly planted bulbs well watered the first year. Let the flowers go to seed after blooming and allow the seed to spread and populate the area. Don't mow down the foliage until after it yellows. In a few years the glory-of-the-snow plants will spread throughout your garden. To prevent self-sowing, mow down the spent flowers after they fade, but allow the foliage to naturally yellow to rejuvenate the bulb.

Regional Advice and Care
Glory-of-the-snow need little care other than occasional fertilization with a bulb plant food in fall to promote better growth. The bulbs can be divided to produce more plants. Mark the bulb's location in spring before the foliage dies back, dig up and lift the bulbs in late summer, separate off the bulblets and replant the mother bulb and bulblets. To prevent their spread, weed out seedlings in the spring from rock or flower gardens. Otherwise, glory-of-the-snow is a carefree bulb.

Companion Planting and Design
Plant glory-of-the-snow bulbs with other spring bloomers, such as small-flowered daffodils, crocus, and tulips. Plant bulbs in groups in lawns, under deciduous trees, and in woodlands to naturalize.

Try These
'Gigantea' has large, 2-inch-diameter blue flowers. 'Alba' is a common white variety. 'Pink Giant' has pink flowers with white centers.

Grape Hyacinth

Muscari spp.

Botanical Pronunciation
mus-KAR-ee

Other Name
Common grape hyacinth

Bloom Period and Seasonal Color
Spring; blue, yellow, and white

Mature Height × Spread
6 to 10 inches × 4 to 6 inches

The name "grape hyacinth" is truly a misnomer. They aren't related to hyacinths and even though their small flowers are shaped like tiny grapes, they aren't edible. But this spring-flowering bulb is a hardy mainstay in any flower garden. It's a tough little plant that only grows 6 to 10 inches tall with beautiful blue, white, or yellow fragrant flowers in spring. The flower stalks stand above the grasslike leaves. The whole show is over in spring and the foliage dies back in summer. They are equally at home in a formal garden as a woodland setting. Bees particularly enjoy the early blooming flowers, and they make good plantings under fruit trees to help with pollination.

When, Where, and How to Plant
Grape hyacinths are hardy throughout our region. Purchase bags of these small bulbs from garden centers in fall. Plant when you would plant other spring-flowering bulbs, such as daffodils. Plant grape hyacinths in groups of about 25 bulbs or more, spread throughout a wide hole. Space the bulbs 3 inches apart and plant about 4 inches deep. Mix a bulb fertilizer into the hole and cover with native soil.

Growing Tips
Grape hyacinths need little care other than watering the first year and leaving the grasslike leaves uncut until after they start to yellow. To prevent their spread, remove the green seedpods. If you want them to self-sow, let the seedpod mature and drop its seeds. The foliage reappears in fall. Mark where the bulbs are planted so you don't mistakenly weed them out in autumn.

Regional Advice and Care
Squirrels and chipmunks sometimes will dig up grape hyacinth bulbs after planting. To prevent their theft, sprinkle cayenne pepper, crushed oyster shells, or crushed seashells in the planting holes. You can also cover the area with a fine mesh netting to thwart them. After the first year, the little critters should forget about the bulbs. Deer tend to leave grape hyacinths alone.

Companion Planting and Design
Plant grape hyacinths with other spring-flowering bulbs, such as glory-of-the-snow, crocus, species tulips, and small daffodils. They also look great in the front of the perennial flower border, in rock gardens, and naturalized in lawns and woodlands. Consider planting swaths of grape hyacinths throughout a deciduous woodland in curving patterns and specialty designs.

Try These
'Dark Eyes' has a light blue flower with an attractive white edging around the flower rim. 'Sky Blue' has a soft, azure blue color. 'Album' is, of course, white. 'Snow Queen', also known as 'Venus', has white flowers, but they turn blue with age. 'Yellow Fragrance' has distinct golden flowers that have a fragrant aroma.

Hyacinth

Hyacinthus orientalis

Botanical Pronunciation
hi-a-SIN-thus or-ee-en-TAL-is

Other Name
Garden hyacinth

Bloom Period and Seasonal Color
Spring; white, yellow, blue, pink, and purple

Mature Height × Spread
8 to 12 inches × 4 to 8 inches

Hyacinths are known for their cone-shaped clusters of small, tubular-shaped flowers. Depending on the varieties, the clusters can be loose or densely packed. Multiflora hyacinths have loosely arranged flowers. The flowers may be single or double on the flower stalk. This colorful bulb blooms around the same time as many tulips and is a nice complement to those bulbs with its blue, white, or pink blossoms. The biggest draw for growing hyacinths, though, is their fragrance. The heady, sweet fragrance will perfume a garden and almost overwhelm you indoors if brought in as a cut flower. I like to force hyacinths into bloom indoors in winter to capture that heady perfume and remind me of more colorful days to come.

When, Where, and How to Plant

Hyacinths are hardy throughout our region. Purchase bulbs from garden centers in fall and plant when you would plant other spring-flowering bulbs in a sunny, fertile soil location. Be careful handling the bulbs since they contain a chemical that may irritate the skin and give some people a rash. Wear gloves as a precaution. Plant bulbs in groups spaced 6 inches apart and planted as deep as 3 times their diameter. Place a small handful of bulb fertilizer in the planting hole.

Growing Tips

Keep the bulbs watered the first year and well weeded. Mulch first year plantings in fall with bark mulch if they are growing in colder areas of our region for added winter protection. Sprinkle bulb fertilizer each fall over the bulb planting bed to encourage better growth.

Regional Advice and Care

Cut back spent blossoms once they have faded, but let foliage naturally yellow before cutting it back to rejuvenate the bulbs. Prevent the heavy flowers from flopping by grouping them together and reducing added fertilizer. Hyacinth bulbs are a favorite food of chipmunks, mice, and voles. Protect bulbs by placing a small handful of cayenne pepper, crushed oyster shells, or crushed seashells in the planting hole or grow the bulbs in wire cages.

Companion Planting and Design

Plant hyacinths in groups among other spring-flowering bulbs, such as tulips, daffodils, and crocus. You can force bulbs to bloom in pots, indoors in winter. Plant in fall in a container filled with moistened potting soil. Chill the bulbs in a cool basement (below 50 degrees Fahrenheit) for 16 weeks. Bring them into a warm, sunny room to sprout. You can leave them in the basement until spring and then bring the pots outdoors to bloom in their containers.

Try These

For classic single-flowered varieties, try 'City of Haarlem' with yellow flowers; 'Blue Jacket' featuring bluish-purple flowers; and 'Carnegie' with white blossoms. 'Fondant' is a popular pink single-flowered selection. 'Anastasia' is a low-growing multiflora variety with fragrant blue blossoms. 'Hollyhock' is a popular double-flowered bright pink variety, and 'General Kohler' is a light blue double-flowered variety.

Lily

Lilium spp. and hybrids

Botanical Pronunciation
LIL-ee-um

Bloom Period and Seasonal Color
Summer; white, yellow, pink, red, orange, and bicolors

Mature Height × Spread
1 to 6 feet × 1 to 2 feet

True lilies shouldn't be confused with the similar-looking daylily. True lilies are bulbs that die back in fall but return each year. Daylilies aren't even in the lily family and are herbaceous perennials. (I cover daylilies in the perennials chapter.) The range of lily varieties and colors is staggering. From the tall trumpet lilies to the fragrant Oriental lilies to the classic Easter lily, these spectacular flowers put on a show in the summer garden and are great for cutting as well. I often pick a bouquet of fragrant Oriental lilies to perfume my house in summer. Lilies produce tall flower stalks with multiple flower buds per stalk. By selecting different varieties you can have blooms in your garden most of the summer.

When, Where, and How to Plant
Most lilies are hardy throughout our region, but they may have difficulty returning each year if grown in heavy, wet clay soil. Buy bulbs in spring or fall and plant in full sun in well-drained soil. Plant as deep as 3 times a bulb's diameter, spaced at least 1 foot apart. Sprinkle a small handful of bulb fertilizer in the hole.

Growing Tips
Fertilize in spring with an all-purpose bulb food. Keep the bed free of weeds and mulched to preserve soil moisture. Lilies will tolerate dry periods once established.

Regional Advice and Care
Stake tall varieties to keep them from flopping. Cut back spent flower stalks after blooming, but let the leaves naturally yellow and die to rejuvenate the bulb. Mice, voles, and chipmunks feed on lily bulbs. Sprinkle a handful of crushed oyster shells or seashells in the planting hole or grow the bulbs in a cage. The red lily leaf beetle is a devastating insect especially on Asiatic and Oriental lilies. Handpick the bright red adults in spring as the lilies emerge. Spray an appropriate insecticide to control the black, sluglike larvae that hatch on the leaf undersides.

Companion Planting and Design
Plant lilies in a perennial flower border near lower growing annuals and perennials, such as lady's mantle, geraniums, and mounding zinnias. These low growers will hide the unsightly bottom of the lily plants. You can also grow lilies in a cutting garden.

Try These
Asiatic lilies bloom in early summer on 3- to 4-foot-tall flower stalks and feature colorful flowers, but no fragrance. 'Gran Paradiso' (red), 'Chianti' (pink), and 'Gironde' (yellow) are popular. Oriental lilies bloom in midsummer on 2- to 5-foot-tall flower stalks and are fragrant. Varieties include 'Stargazer' (white with pink) and 'Pink Pearl' (pink). Trumpet lilies grow up to 6 feet tall with trumpet-shaped, colorful flowers. Easter lilies are in this group, but they are marginally hardy in colder parts of our region. Orienpets are a cross between Oriental and trumpet lilies. They grow tall and colorful, but still have fragrance. 'Caravan' is a popular yellow and red.

Siberian Squill

Scilla siberica

Botanical Pronunciation
SILL-uh sye-BIR-i-kuh

Other Name
Scilla

Bloom Period and Seasonal Color
Early spring; blue, white, and pink

Mature Height × Spread
4 to 6 inches × 4 to 6 inches

Siberian squill is a hardy bulb that is most noted for naturalizing in lawns and gardens turning the ground a carpet of blue, pink, or white in early spring. I often see this bulb naturalized around old farmhouses in Vermont where it has taken over the landscape in spring. This low-growing small bulb isn't fussy about growing conditions and is tough enough to bloom through snow and cold. It easily spreads by seed and can turn into a spring groundcover in your garden. The swordlike leaves emerge in early spring and a flower stalk bearing 3 to 5 umbrella-shaped blooms soon follows. The flowers fade in a few weeks. Bees love the early blooming flowers, but deer seem to leave them alone.

When, Where, and How to Plant

Siberian squill hails from Russia so naturally it's hardy throughout our region. Purchase bulbs in fall from a local garden center and plant with other spring-flowering bulbs in a full to part sun location on well-drained soil. Plant groups 3 to 5 inches below the soil spaced a few inches apart for the best effect. Mix a small amount of bulb fertilizer in each hole.

Growing Tips

Siberian squill needs little fertilization once it's planted. Keep the bulbs consistently moist after planting but once established, squill needs little supplemental water. To allow them to naturalize, let the flowers fade and seedpods form to disperse the seed. Let the leaves naturally yellow before mowing them down, about 6 weeks after they bloom. If you don't want them to spread, remove the spent flowers, but don't cut the leaves until they yellow.

Regional Advice and Care

Siberian squill look best naturalized in a broad area around your yard. Throw bulbs around an area randomly and plant them where they fall to give the planting a natural look. You can transplant clumps of Siberian squill to naturalize areas of your yard; do this in late spring after the blooms fade and the leaves start to yellow. Keep the clumps well watered the first year. Protect newly planted bulbs from maurading squirrels by adding a small amount of crushed oyster shells or seashells to the planting hole.

Companion Planting and Design

Plant Siberian squill in lawns, woodlands, rock gardens, and in front of shrub and flower borders. Plant many bulbs at once to have a truly dramatic effect. Plant them where other spring flowers, such as glory-of-the-snow, crocus, and snowdrops grow, or under spring-flowering shrubs, such as flowering quince, daphne, and forsythia and with perennials, such as bleeding heart and iris.

Try These

'Spring Beauty' has large, bell-shaped blossoms with a true blue flower. 'Alba' features bright white blooms. 'Rosy' has pale pink blossoms.

Snowdrops

Galanthus nivalis

Botanical Pronunciation
guh-LAN-thus nih-VAY-liss

Other Name
Common snowdrop

Bloom Period and Seasonal Color
Early spring; white or white-and-green

Mature Height × Spread
4 to 6 inches × 6 to 8 inches

Snowdrops are so named because they are one of the earliest bulbs to grow and flower in the landscape. They often are growing and flowering beneath or even through banks of snow in late winter. I've been known to shovel snow off areas where I planted snowdrops to reveal the flowering bulbs. These small dainty flowers are great harbingers of spring. The nodding white or pink single- or double-petaled flowers can have a magnificent scent and can be cut and brought indoors for the first fragrance of the season. The swordlike foliage will last for a few weeks after blooming, but by mid-spring, snowdrops are pretty much finished. They are reliably hardy and clumps will slowly expand and spread over time.

When, Where, and How to Plant
Snowdrops are hardy throughout New England. Purchase bulbs from a local garden center in fall and plant when you would plant other spring-flowering bulbs, such as daffodils. Snowdrops are small bulbs, so consider buying a larger quantity to have a stronger visual effect. Plant snowdrops in groups in wide, shallow holes in a part sun location in well-drained soil. Too much spring sunshine will cause the flowers to wither faster. They're best planted under a shrub or tree for this reason. Space individual bulbs 3 inches apart in the holes planted 2 to 4 inches deep. Plant bulbs on the shallower side on clay soils.

Growing Tips
Water newly planted bulbs well. After flowering, let the foliage naturally die back. It will disappear quickly in spring. Just mark where the bulbs are and fertilize in fall with a bulb plant food.

Regional Advice and Care
Few animals seem to like snowdrops. Squirrels may dig up newly planted bulbs in fall out of curiosity. Add some hot pepper flakes to the planting hole to discourage them. Not only will snowdrop clumps slowly expand over time, they will self-sow and start popping up in other locations in your landscape. However, unlike Siberian squill, they will not spread quickly. If the clumps get large and have few flowers, divide snowdrops after flowering, separating out the bulbs and replanting.

Companion Planting and Design
To appreciate these small flowers, plant them close to walkways, on garden edges, or under a favorite tree or shrub. Try to plant in areas that lose their snow quickly in spring so you can see the flowers when they are blooming. Snowdrops look great paired with other spring-blooming bulbs, such as Siberian squill, crocus, and glory-of-the-snow. They also look good planted under early-blooming shrubs, such as forsythia and flowering quince.

Try These
'Giant Snowdrop' has white fragrant flowers on large, for snowdrops, plants. 'Sam Arnott' has white flowers and a strong, almost honeylike fragrance. 'Flore Pleno' has ruffled, double-petaled, green- and white-flowers.

Tuberous Begonia

Begonia tuberhybrida

Botanical Pronunciation
bay-GO-nee-a tu-ber-HY-brid-a

Other Name
Tuberous rooted begonia

Bloom Period and Seasonal Color
Summer to fall; red, pink, yellow, orange, white, and bicolors

Mature Height × Spread
8 to 18 inches × 8 to 18 inches

Tuberous begonias are colorful flowers grown from underground bulbs or tubers that produce beautiful single- or double-petaled blooms all summer until frost. Unlike the traditional wax begonias commonly found in garden centers as bedding plants in spring, tuberous begonias have large, showy flowers and put on quite a show. I remember seeing an exhibition of these flowers, and they were so perfect it was hard to believe they were real. The plants can be upright or cascading depending on the variety. They are sensitive to wind, rain, and adverse weather, but in a protected location, and especially when grown in a container, they're a striking flower in the garden. Like other begonias, tuberous begonias foliage can have attractive coloring and markings.

When, Where, and How to Plant
Tuberous begonias are not hardy in New England, so tubers must be stored in winter or grown as an annual. They can be grown from seed, but it is easier to purchase bulbs or plants in spring from garden centers. Plant in the garden or a pot after all danger of frost has passed. They grow best in a partly shaded location protected from the afternoon sun. To get a jumpstart on the season, plant bulbs indoors 8 weeks before your last frost date in containers. Grow in a sunny window until you can plant them outdoors.

Growing Tips
Tuberous begonia flowers and leaves are sensitive to wind and rain. Plant in a protected area and try not to get the leaves or blooms wet when watering. Many gardeners grow tuberous begonias in hanging baskets under a porch or eave. Fertilize every 3 weeks with an organic plant food and keep well watered. Don't overwater or the stems will rot.

Regional Advice and Care
Keep plants deadheaded to stimulate more blooming. To save the bulbs, before a frost in fall, cut back all foliage to the soil line, dig the bulbs, let them dry in a warm, airy location for a few weeks, and then store in perforated plastic bags filled with moistened peat moss in a cool, dark basement. To control powdery mildew, clean up diseased foliage, grow in a well-ventilated location, and spray an organic fungicide.

Companion Planting and Design
Tuberous begonias look great planted in small groups or singly in a container. They also look good planted with cascading annuals, such as alyssum and lobelia. In a shade garden, pair them with hostas and bergenia.

Try These
'Non-Stop' is a new line of tuberous begonias that is more heat tolerant and doesn't require deadheading. They come in a wide range of colors, such as apricot, red, pink, orange, yellow, and white, and have heart-shaped leaves. The Illumination series features cascading double flowers in a variety of colors and bicolors. Ornament series features large double flowers in a variety of colors on burgundy-colored leaves.

Tulip

Tulipa spp. and hybrids

Botanical Pronunciation
TEW-li-pa

Bloom Period and Seasonal Color
Spring to early summer; almost every color of
the rainbow

Mature Height × Spread
4 to 24 inches × 6 to 8 inches

Tulips are the standard bearer for spring-flowering bulbs. They are a vast group with a variety of plant sizes, flower shapes, and colors. Sizes range from the diminutive species to the tall Darwin varieties. Colors can be a deep purple, almost black, to the most pristine white, in single or double petals. The petals can also be curved, frilly, and striped with different colors. By growing early-, mid-, and late-season varieties you can extend the tulip flowering season for weeks. Most may need more care than daffodils to keep blooming, but the show they put on is worth the effort. I've particularly become fond of the species tulips for their more wildflower-like appearance and low maintenance.

When, Where, and How to Plant
Purchase bulbs in fall from your local garden centers and plant when you would other spring-flowering bulbs. Plant tulips in groups at a depth 3 times the diameter of the bulb and spaced 3 to 4 inches apart. Plant bulbs in a full to part sun location on well-drained soil with a small handful of a bulb fertilizer in each hole.

Growing Tips
Fertilize in fall or early spring when tulips first start growing. Keep the soil evenly moist, but not overwatered to prevent bulbs from rotting. Deadhead spent flowers, but allow foliage to naturally yellow and die to rejuvenate the bulbs.

Regional Advice and Care
Most tulip types, except species tulips, stop flowering after a few years. If your tulips are sending up just leaves or the flowers are getting fewer and smaller each spring, divide the bulbs. After the leaves have yellowed, dig up the bulbs and separate the small bulblets from the mother bulb. Replant, adding a small handful of fertilizer. Keep mice, voles, and chipmunks from eating the bulbs by placing crushed oyster shells or seashells in the planting hole or planting the bulbs in a wire cage underground. Spray deer repellent to thwart deer from eating the flowers.

Companion Planting and Design
Grow tulips in large groups of all one color or multiple colors for an overwhelming, botanic gardenlike display. They look good mixed with other perennials and shrubs, such as catmint, peonies, iris, forsythia, and daphne. Plant them near perennials with lots of foliage, such as peonies and daylilies, to hide the yellowing tulip foliage in late spring. Tulips make excellent cut flowers.

Try These
Species tulips 'Lilac Wonder' and 'Lady Jane' are low-growing tulips that not only come back every year and flower, but will slowly spread. For traditional varieties, try 'Darwin' and 'Triumph' with their tall stems and colorful flowers that are great for cutting. Lily-flowered tulips have curved, lilylike leaves and petals. 'Angelique' is a popular peony-flowered tulip with frilly, pink, double blossoms. 'Parrot' tulips have serrated-edged petals in a broad range of colors.

LAWNS
FOR NEW ENGLAND

Americans love their lawns. We grow more than 46 million acres of lawn in this country. To put that number into perspective, that's the area of Rhode Island, Pennsylvania, and Delaware combined. We also love to have beautiful lawns. We apply 3 million pounds of fertilizer, 70 million pounds of pesticides, and 17 trillion gallons of water a year to keep our lawns green and beautiful. That's quite a bit of resources.

Lawn and island plantings

But the fact remains that New Englanders love their lawns as much as anyone in the country. We also are blessed with a climate that makes lawn grass growing fairly easy. It just takes following some basic guidelines to grow a naturally healthy lawn without lots of energy or effort. I don't want to sound anti-lawn, because I'm not. I have a lawn, and it grows great for my use. But we need to be more thoughtful and careful with our lawns. Lawns have become placeholders in the landscape. On the plus side, lawns absorb rainfall, preventing soil erosion and runoff going into our streams and lakes. Lawns cool the air on a hot summer day. Lawns are easy to maintain; simply mow them regularly. But, lawns can also be an ecological desert, with little plant diversity for pollinators and wildlife to thrive. And all those chemicals we add can pollute our waterways. It's time to think about why we have a lawn and what the purpose of that lawn is in our yards.

Why Have a Lawn?

How much lawn you have and how you care for it will partly depend on what you do with it. If you have kids or grandkids who love to play outdoors, consider having a big swatch of lawn. Place that lawn in an area where they can kick soccer balls, run, and play without harming gardens, the house, or outdoor furniture.

If you have a smaller yard and love gardens (and I hope you do; after all, you're reading this book), then your lawn can be a gathering place for guests. Plant a lawn area where you can entertain, pitch a tent, or generally have folks gather in the middle of your yard. Use the lawn grass as a pathway to channel visitors from one area of your yard to another. Lawns make great paths between island beds. Plant your lawn with some forethought, so it's a functioning part of the landscape and not just an afterthought.

While many of us probably would like to reduce the size of our lawn, the fact remains that lawns are here to stay. Short of replacing the whole lawn to grow trees, shrubs, flowers, edibles, and vines, you'll have to care for that lawn. Most people would like a green, lush lawn without having to resort to harmful chemical fertilizers and pesticides. Luckily, you *can* have such a lawn. The keys to growing a healthy lawn with fewer or no chemical inputs are using the right grass variety for your site; watering, fertilizing, and mowing properly; and staying on top of regular lawn upkeep.

Pick the Right Grass for Your Location

The first step to a healthy lawn in our climate is picking the right grass type to sow. Lawn grasses are grouped as warm- and cool-season types. Warm-season grasses grow south of a line running roughly from Washington D.C. to San Francisco, California. These grasses include Bermuda and St. Augustine grass. North of that line is where the cool-season grasses thrive. These include Kentucky bluegrass, fescue grass, and perennial ryegrass. Let's take a look at each of these cool-season grass types.

- **Kentucky Bluegrass** - This is the soft lawn grass everyone *loves*. The blue-green grass blades form a thick mat on the soil, making walking barefoot across it a pure joy. Kentucky bluegrass needs full sun, lots of water, and fertile soil to grow its best. Because it grows so lushly, it's prone to thatch (dead grass) buildup, and it generally needs more water, fertilizer, and maintenance than other grass types.

- **Fescue Grass** - Fescue grass is categorized as fine or tall fescue. Fine fescue is a low-maintenance, scruffy grass with thin grass blades. It grows in part shade and can grow well on poor, even acidic, soils. Tall fescue is a more attractive, larger-bladed grass. A new type, called turf-type tall fescue, is a versatile grass and is the one most New Englanders can appreciate. It has an attractive look like Kentucky bluegrass, but it tolerates low fertility soils, compacted areas, drought, and foot traffic. It fills in quickly and grows well in full sun or part shade.

Lawns not only provide recreational space, they also control erosion, reduce noise, absorb air pollution, and trap dust particles.

- **Perennial Ryegrass** - This grass is better looking than a fine fescue, but not the same as a bluegrass. It's cold and heat tolerant, doesn't require highly fertile soils, and is quick to establish, often crowding out weeds. It's often mixed with Kentucky bluegrass seed, getting quickly established before the bluegrass can take over.
- **No-Mow Grass** - These grasses are meant for meadows, fruit tree orchards, or any spot where you won't be mowing regularly, and when you do, you will mow high. They mostly are types of fine fescue grasses that tolerate shade and poor soil. They don't like heavy foot traffic and aren't very thick. Simply mow these grasses 3½ inches high periodically in summer to maintain them, and they'll give you a rough-looking, but green carpet.

When you buy grass seed, you'll often find mixes. Conservation mix is a popular one many contractors use. Based on your site, select the mix that will grow the best. If you have a full sun lawn on fertile soil and you really want a manicured look, find a mix that's high in Kentucky bluegrass seed. If you have a part sun lawn with average fertility and have kids and multiple functions happening on the lawn, select one that is mostly turf-type tall fescue. If you have a part shade area on poor soil with low foot traffic, consider a no-mow mix or one high in fine fescue.

For truly shady areas, such as under large trees or evergreens, *don't* try to grow grass. Consider growing shade-loving groundcovers, such as vinca, or in heavy shade, simply mulch with bark mulch.

Whatever lawn grass you decide to sow, consider mixing in 10 percent white clover. Clover is often identified as a weed, but in fact, it is an essential part to a healthy lawn. Clover has strong roots that fix atmospheric nitrogen, in turn feeding the lawn. It also stays green during droughts and, if allowed to flower, provides nectar to bees and butterflies.

Another option would be to purchase lawn grass sod. Sod has the advantage of creating an instant lawn with no weeds. It is more expensive than sowing seeds, heavy to work with, and you'll have limited choices of the mix of lawn grasses in the sod. However, you'll simply roll out the sod, water it well, and you'll have a lawn that you can dance on in a few weeks.

Planting Your Lawn Grass

If you're starting a new lawn or replacing part of an old one, here are some simple steps to ensure that your grass seeds grow quickly into a lush lawn.

1. Select the right grass seed for your sun and soil conditions. If patching a lawn area, try to match a similar grass mix as the one growing on your lawn.
2. Sow seeds in spring or early fall for the best success. Summer-sown grass seeds will need extra water to germinate during the dry, hot conditions.

Use a hand spreader to spread grass seed thickly and evenly over the entire area, slightly overlapping the edges of the grass that isn't covered with soil. When you're done seeding, the ground should look like it snowed lightly.

Sprinkle wheat straw, which you can get at garden centers and home improvement stores, over the newly seeded area. This will help the seeds stay moist until they sprout. It's easy to grow new grass seed as long as you keep it moist. The biggest problem that people have when overseeding or replanting lawns is that they don't keep the grass seed moist while it's sprouting. The straw mulch helps eliminate that problem.

3. Till up or rake off all the old grass and weeds, removing stones and other debris.

4. Amend the soil, based on a soil test, with lime or sulfur to bring the pH to between 6.5 and 7.2. Add other nutrients as needed and a thick layer of compost to increase soil fertility and water retention.

5. Spread the lawn grass seed on the area with a seed spreader at the rate suggested on the seed package. Generally, Kentucky bluegrass seed is sown thicker than fescue and perennial ryegrass seed. Place one-half of the amount of seed in the spreader and cover the whole area. Then take the second half of seed and spread it over the area again, going perpendicular to the first pass.

6. Roll the soil with a lawn roller to pack the seeds into the soil. Water well.

7. Spread straw over the sown area and keep watering for the first few weeks until the lawn grass germinates and starts filling in.

Mowing

Once your lawn is up and growing, you'll need to maintain it so weeds don't take over. The key with keeping out weeds is to grow a thick, lush, healthy lawn. Mowing is one of the key ways to keep your lawn healthy. Mow your lawn 2 ½ to 3 inches high. This is generally higher than most people like to mow, but it has some noteworthy advantages. A healthy lawn has a deep, well-developed root system. By mowing the lawn high, you allow more nutrients to feed those roots, allowing them to prosper. Lawns cut low may look more manicured, but they reduce the size of the root system, and the lawn doesn't fill in as well. This opens the opportunity for weeds to invade. By mowing high, it's also easier to leave the grass clippings on your lawn. Ideally, you should use a mulching mower or mulching mower blade to chop up the grass clippings into small pieces that decompose quickly. It's estimated that you can achieve one-third

While mowing each new row, place your mower so that it overlaps the previous row by 25 percent. By doing this, you cut the entire lawn evenly.

of the nitrogen needs of your lawn simply by mulching the grass blades when mowing. By keeping your mower blades sharp, you can also reduce gasoline use by 22 percent and reduce tearing of the grass blades, which opens them up to disease infection.

Never mow your lawn more than one-third of its height at any time. This will harm the growth point of the grass blade. If it's been rainy and you can't mow, consider mowing high and then a few days later mow again at the proper height.

Each spring check the thatch layer (dead grass) in your lawn. If it's thicker than one-half inch, rake out the thatch or consider renting a dethatching machine. Thatch prevents water and nutrients from entering the soil and smothers the grass blades, creating dead areas.

Fertilizing and Watering

It's important to keep your lawn well watered, especially the first year. It's always best to water in the morning so the lawn can dry before evening. Wet grass in the evening is more prone to disease infection. Some lawn grass types, such as Kentucky bluegrass, need lots of water to stay green all summer, especially during droughts. In general, apply 1 inch of water each week. Underwatered lawns will go dormant and dry up in summer. Overwatered lawns are more prone to disease problems.

To determine how much water you're using on your lawn, simply place 8 to 10 cat food or similarly sized empty cans around a lawn sprinkler. Run the sprinkler until 1 inch of water has been collected in most of the cans. Time how long that look and set your timer to water.

Even lawns on fertile soils will need supplemental fertilization. Generally, lawns in New England use a 3-1-2 NPK ratio of fertilizer. That's the ratio of nitrogen to phosphorous to potassium. Look for these three numbers on bags of fertilizer. Some soils in New England already have too much phosphorous and any additional phosphorous fertilizer will just runoff and pollute our waterways. Look for no phosphorous fertilizers in these areas. I usually recommend organic fertilizers

Rent a core aerator and aerate the lawn once yearly in the fall to keep the soil from becoming compacted.

because they're slow release and feed the soil microorganisms slowly over time, building a healthier soil and lawn.

If you only are fertilizing your lawn once a year, do so in early fall. Fall fertilization helps feed the grass roots, creating a healthy root system and grass. Also, because the days are shorter, you won't get the quick flush of new growth requiring extra mowing. Lawns fertilized in fall also green up earlier in spring.

More Cool Organic Techniques

To really grow a healthy lawn that eventually won't need many "extras" at all, follow these organic lawn care techniques.

- **Aeration** - Aerate lawns in spring to allow water, air, and nutrients to reach the grass roots. In a small lawn, simply take an iron rake and make holes every 6 inches across the lawn. In larger lawns, rent an aeration machine that extracts soil plugs out of the lawn and deposits them on the grass. These plugs of soil will eventually decompose. Aerating your lawn is particularly important for grass grown on clay soil or lawns with lots of foot traffic and soil compaction.
- **Topdressing** - Lawns need a thick, healthy soil to grow best. Topdressing the soil each fall with a ¼-inch-thick layer of compost will help create this thick root system. Simply dump the compost in piles on the lawn and gently rake it to a thickness so the grass blades are showing.
- **Overseeding** - Each fall spread a layer of grass seed over your lawn as a way to make it thicker and more lush. Overseeding helps fill in thin areas, that prevent weeds from invading.
- **Pests** - You can get a sense that if you care for your lawn properly you shouldn't have problems with pests and weeds. A thick, healthy lawn is your solution to weeds. Don't add too much nitrogen fertilizer to prevent diseases. Some problems are due to environmental conditions. Moss occurs on acidic lawns grown in shade with shallow soils. Mushrooms may be due to some buried building debris or stumps that are decomposing. Some pests, such as skunks, are searching for food, such as grubs. Kill the grubs with beneficial nematodes and the skunks shouldn't bother your lawn. Scare off moles and voles with sprays of castor oil.

With just these few simple steps, you can "have your cake and eat it too" to satisfy both your desire to have a lawn and do so responsibly.

PERENNIALS

FOR NEW ENGLAND

Perennials give us a vast array of bloom colors and foliage shapes and textures to create a beautiful garden palette in our yards. While annuals put on quite a flower show for one season, perennials come back for years, consistently flowering at their given time. Some perennials even spread and multiply. They can be divided to create new plants that can be shared or used to start new beds.

Pink roses with salvia, catmint, and lady's mantel

Mix + Match + Patience = Nonstop Show

One of the keys of designing and growing perennial flower gardens is also one of its challenges. Since individual perennials often only flower at certain times, to get that continual flower show and interest many of us crave, we'll have to mix and match different perennial flowers in the bed. Some gardeners will agonize over making the right choices for complementary colors and matching foliage. Certainly understanding the ultimate height, flower color, and bloom time will help you decide what perennial flower to plant where. But also pay attention to foliage colors and textures; sun, soil, and fertility needs of the plant; and potential animal, insect, and disease pests. All of these conditions may be more important dictating where you plant which flower than matching the right colored blossoms.

Be patient. More so than any other ornamental, perennial flowers require experimentation to get the look and feel you desire. Start by making a list of the flowers you love. Decide where they will grow best in your yard. Then plant other perennials, with similar growing requirements, that bloom before and after them. If you need a place to start, plant tried-and-true perennials, such as peonies and daylilies, that will be the anchors in your garden, and then work from there. Consider not only the complementary flower colors and bloom times, but also foliage. Many perennial flowers, such as hosta and coral bells, have attractive textures and colorful foliage that will keep the garden interesting long after the flowers have passed. It's not just about flowers and leaves. Some perennials have attractive seedheads, such as coneflowers and ornamental grasses, which will provide an interesting landscape even into winter.

Surprises Await

Perennial flower gardening makes you open to change. Many times, even in the most precisely designed perennial garden, surprises may erupt. A self-sown black-eyed Susan may end up near a phlox and provide the perfect flower color combination. Bee balm may creep into the coneflowers making a perfect haven for hummingbirds and butterflies. Clematis can grow into peony foliage offering color in summer long after the peony blossoms have faded. One year I grew rose campion in my garden and I thought it died. The next year I noticed it growing among the burgundy-colored ninebark leaves. It was a combination I would never have thought of, but it was magnificent. The magenta flowers provided a vivid contrast to the dark ninebark leaves. While planning is important, it's also good to be open to the inspirations that nature provides. Ultimately, a flower gardener realizes the garden is never a static thing and is always changing year after year.

Many perennial gardeners mistakenly believe that perennials require no maintenance. *Every* garden needs to be maintained. Certainly perennials don't have to be planted each year, but they still require watering, weeding, mulching, fertilizing, and periodic moving and dividing to make the garden look its best. Plus, part of the fun of the perennial flower garden is to change its look based on your whimsy and inspiration.

While a garden made up of just perennials can be a work of art, don't forget accent plants of flowering bulbs, annuals, and small shrubs. Spring-flowering bulbs can give your perennial flower garden a jumpstart early in the season. Annuals keep the color coming in between the bursts of perennial flower color. And small shrubs provide structure to the garden, giving it interest when little else is happening in our New England landscapes.

Garden cement paver brick path with grass lawn and hosta plants

Artemisia

Artemisia spp.

Botanical Pronunciation
are-ti-MEEZ-ee-a

Other Name
Wormwood

Bloom Period and Seasonal Color
Spring to fall; silvery green foliage

Mature Height × Spread
1 to 3 feet × 1 to 3 feet

Artemisia is a perennial flower mostly grown for its stunning silvery green foliage. There is also an annual version called dusty miller, often grown as a bedding plant. Although artemisia's yellow flowers bloom in late summer, they're of little interest. The real show is the foliage. It provides a dramatic contrast to many, more colorful, perennial flowers. Since its color is evident from spring to fall, it's a perfect companion to many other perennial flower garden plants and shrubs. Because of artemisia's ability to survive and thrive in hot, dry conditions once established, it makes a good addition to south-facing flower gardens located in full sun. Artemisia can be an aggressive spreader, so divide plants regularly or plant where its growth isn't an issue.

When, Where, and How to Plant

Artemisia is hardy throughout New England. Plant transplants in spring to early fall in a full sun location in well-drained soil. Space plants 18 inches apart to account for its spreading nature. Avoid planting in heavy clay, wet soils where root rot can become a problem.

Growing Tips

Keep newly transplanted plants well watered and weeded. Once established, artemisia is drought tolerant. Fertilize each spring with a thin layer of compost spread around the roots.

Regional Advice and Care

Remove flowers that form so the plant puts more energy into leaf growth. Divide the plants every 3 to 4 years in spring or fall to promote new, healthier growth and to create new plants to spread elsewhere in your garden or to share. Cut back spreading plants to keep them from invading into unwanted areas. In warm areas of our region, the foliage may start looking tattered by midsummer. Simply cut back the foliage, water, and the new, more attractive growth should regrow. For tall varieties, consider staking or planting in groups to reduce flopping. Artemisia stems also look good in flower arrangements.

Companion Planting and Design

Artemisia is an all-purpose companion in the flower garden. Its silver foliage covers up yellowing bulb foliage in spring. I like how the white leaves shine in moonlight, and they also provide great contrast to blue flowers, such as veronica and salvia, in summer. Artemisia is a good complement to chrysanthemums in fall. Grow taller varieties in the middle or back of a perennial flower border and shorter, mounding varieties in the front. Shorter artemisia varieties also grow well in containers and rock gardens complementing other perennial and annual flowers.

Try These

'Silver King' and 'Silver Queen' are compact, 3-foot-tall varieties with fuzzy silver-green leaves. 'Powis Castle' is a 2-foot-tall variety with lacy, silver foliage. 'Silver Mound' is a popular, mounding, 1-foot-tall variety with finely cut silver leaves. It's a good addition to rock gardens and containers. 'Brocade' artemisia grows only 6 to 8 inches tall and 1 foot across with woolly, white, lobed leaves.

Aster

Aster spp. and hybrids

Botanical Pronunciation
ASS-ter

Other Name
Michaelmas daisy

Bloom Period and Seasonal Color
Late summer to fall; blue, purple, red, pink, and white

Mature Height × Spread
1 to 6 feet × 2 to 4 feet

This native wildflower is a sure sign of late summer and early fall in New England. You can see it blooming in the wild next to goldenrod along roadways, in abandoned fields, and in meadows. Cultivated varieties of the wild aster are easy to grow, have better plant form, larger and more varied flowers, and a better growth habit. The two main types are New York (*A. novi-belgii*) and New England asters (*A. novae-angliae*). New England asters tend to have denser and frillier flowers than New York asters. The attractive, daisylike single or double flowers are a favorite of bees, butterflies, and other pollinators. While many varieties can stand up to 6 feet tall, newer hybrids are shorter and bushier, offering options for small spaces, and even container gardeners.

When, Where, and How to Plant

Asters are hardy throughout our region. Purchase plants from your local garden centers and plant from spring to early fall. You can plant divisions from a friend or neighbor's garden. Plant asters in full sun in compost-amended, well-drained soil. Asters don't grow well in poorly drained, clay soils.

Growing Tips

Keep new transplants well watered. Once established, asters are very carefree. Add compost around the base of plants each spring. Mulch to preserve soil moisture and prevent weed growth.

Regional Advice and Care

Divide plants in spring as needed. Pinch the tops of young shoots in spring to promote branching, more flowering, and a shorter plant. Stake tall aster varieties to keep them from flopping over. Powdery mildew disease thrives during our humid summers, and asters are susceptible. Look for white, then yellowing leaves in late summer. To avoid this disease, plant resistant varieties, water from the bottom to avoid wetting the leaves, and plant in an airy location where leaves will dry quickly once wet. Cut back and clean up foliage in fall to prevent disease from overwintering near the plants.

Companion Planting and Design

Plant tall varieties in the back of flower gardens near earlier-blooming perennials, such as daylilies and Shasta daisy, to provide a continuum of color into fall. Mix and match shorter varieties near earlier-blooming, lower-growing perennials, such as coreopsis and geraniums. Plant next to other late-summer bloomers, such as Russian sage and ornamental grasses, for a colorful fall flower show.

Try These

'Purple Dome' is a dwarf, New England variety that grows less than 2 feet tall. 'Alma Pötschke' is a New England aster that grows 4 feet tall with red flowers. 'Professor Anton Kippenberg' is a New York aster that grows 1 to 2 feet tall with light blue flowers. 'White Lady' is a New York type that grows 5 to 6 feet tall. 'Patricia Ballard' is a New York aster that grows 2 to 3 feet tall with pale blue, double flowers.

Astilbe

Astilbe spp. and hybrids

Botanical Pronunciation
a-STIL-bee

Other Name
False spirea

Bloom Period and Seasonal Color
Late spring into summer; cream, white, pink, lilac, and red

Mature Height × Spread
1 to 5 feet × 2 to 3 feet

Astilbe is a part-shade-loving perennial with airy white, pink, red, or lilac flowers. I grow it to provide color to darker areas of the garden and soften the look of sunnier spots. The deeply lobed, fernlike green leaves add to the whimsical look of this plant. Some varieties even have copper-colored leaves. This easy-to-grow perennial flower grows best in the cool periods of late spring and early summer. In warmer parts of our region the foliage may brown and die back during hot, dry periods in midsummer. However, the plants are virtually trouble-free as far as insects and diseases are concerned. After the main flowering has past, the flowers will often dry on the plants and remain attractive for weeks.

When, Where, and How to Plant

Astilbe varieties are hardy throughout our region. Plant in spring to early fall in a part sun or part shade location, spacing plants 1 to 3 feet apart depending on the variety. Astilbe plants can take more sun when grown in cooler parts of New England, but they need more shade in warmer locations. Astilbe will grow in a full shade location, but may not flower well. An east-facing location with morning sun is usually best. Astilbe grows well in moist, fertile soil with a slightly acidic pH.

Growing Tips

Keep plants well watered and mulched with a layer of bark mulch. Replenish the mulch each spring and fertilize in spring with compost spread around the plant roots.

Regional Advice and Care

Astilbe needs little care once established. They can be divided every four to five years to create more plants and to keep the existing plants healthy. Deadhead spent flowers if they don't look attractive. Astilbe flowers also make nice additions to floral arrangements when used as a cut flower. Cut back and clean up foliage in fall to prevent disease from overwintering near the plants.

Companion Planting and Design

Astilbes are great plants to grow in brightly lit woodland areas, such as under tall maples or oaks. They're a perfect companion to other perennials, such as heucheras, hostas, and yellow rocket, in a shade garden. They also look great grown *en masse* in a shade garden, along a stream, or near a pond, creating a beautiful tapestry of color and foliage in the landscape.

Try These

'Bridal Veil' has white plumes that grow on 3-foot-tall plants. 'Rheinland' is an early blooming, 2- to 3-foot-tall plant with pink plumes. 'Purple Candles' has deep purple blooms on 3- to 4-foot-tall plants. 'Fanal' is a red-flowering variety that grows 2 feet tall. 'Color Flash' grows 1 foot tall and has unique bronze- and copper-colored leaves with pink flowers. 'Bressingham Beauty' grows 3 to 4 feet tall with rich, pink flowers.

Baby's Breath

Gypsophila paniculata

Botanical Pronunciation
jip-SOF-i-la pan-I-cu-LAH-ta

Other Name
Perennial baby's breath

Bloom Period and Seasonal Color
Early summer to fall; white and pink

Mature Height × Spread
2 to 3 feet × 3 to 4 feet

This airy perennial flower is a common sight in floral bouquets as a filler plant. In the garden it produces wispy clouds of single or double, white or pink flowers with lacy green leaves. Baby's breath fills the same role in a flower border as it does in a cut flower arrangement. It fills in well around other perennial and annual flowers providing a nice contrast to bolder-colored and bigger-leaved flowers. Baby's breath can withstand dry periods and attracts butterflies to the garden. And, of course, you can use them as cut flowers in your own flower arrangements, especially since it dries easily. There is also an annual baby's breath (*Gypsophila repens*) that's low-growing and can be started from seeds.

When, Where, and How to Plant
Baby's breath is hardy throughout New England. Plant transplants of perennial baby's breath in spring, after all danger of frost has passed, to early fall in well-drained, compost-amended soil. Baby's breath grows best in full sun, but will tolerate some afternoon shade in the warmer parts of New England. Baby's breath grows best in neutral to slightly alkaline soil, so consider adding lime to raise the pH to between 7.0 to 7.5 for best growth. Space plants 2 feet apart in beds if growing them *en masse*.

Growing Tips
Keep young plants well watered, but once it's established, baby's breath is drought tolerant. Fertilize in spring with compost and mulch to preserve the soil moisture.

Regional Advice and Care
Baby's breath will flower in early summer and, if it's cut back, will rebloom in late summer and early fall. Avoid growing in poorly drained soils or the plants may not survive the winter. If grown individually, the plants may need staking or support. Cut back and clean up foliage in fall to prevent disease from overwintering near the plants.

Companion Planting and Design
I like growing baby's breath as a "see through" plant in the landscape. I plant it in the front of a flower border with bolder colored flowers behind it, such as roses, zinnias, and coreopsis, that show through the foliage. Planted next to tulips and daffodils, it also can cover up spent bulb foliage in late spring. It is a nice addition to the back of a rock garden where it often grows smaller due to the lower soil fertility. The pink-colored varieties of baby's breath pair well with other silver-leaved perennials, such as artemisia and lamb's ears. Consider adding it to a cut flower garden for bouquets in summer and fall.

Try These
'Bristol Fairy' and 'Perfecta' are popular double-flowered white varieties with strong sturdy stems that are good for cutting. 'Snowflake' is a large, free-branching, double-flowered white variety with sharply pointed leaves. 'Pink Fairy' produces double, pink-colored flowers on 2-foot-tall plants.

Bee Balm

Monarda didyma

Botanical Pronunciation
muh-NAR-duh DID-ih-muh

Other Name
Bergamot

Bloom Period and Seasonal Color
Midsummer to late summer; red, pink, and white

Mature Height × Spread
2 to 4 feet × 2 to 4 feet

Bee balm is a native, spreading perennial that is a delight not only for us, but also for butterflies, beneficial insects, and hummingbirds. The colorful tubular flowers come in red, white, purple, or pink, and form in whorls around the bloom creating an almost hairy appearance. Bee balm provides mid- to late summer color in the flower garden. The leaves and flowers can be used to make tea, hence one if its common names, Oswego tea. It's an aggressive plant and can quickly take over an area if it's grown on fertile soil and you aren't cutting it back each year. But its spreading nature also makes it a great choice to fill in perennial flower borders, wildflower areas, and meadows.

When, Where, and How to Plant
Bee balm is hardy throughout our region. It is easy to transplant from divisions so select a favorite variety from a friend or purchase a transplant from your local garden center. Plant from spring to early fall in a full or part sun location in well-drained, moist, slightly acidic soil. Space plants 2 to 3 feet apart.

Growing Tips
Keep plants well watered and mulched with bark mulch. Plants may wilt during midsummer hot spells if they're not properly watered so be vigilant. To fertilize, add a layer of compost around the roots in spring.

Regional Advice and Care
Deadhead spent flowers to increase the flowering duration. Divide bee balm every two to three years once the plant's center dies out and it begins to spread into unwanted territory. Dig up plants in spring when growth first emerges and move them to another location or share them with others. Bee balm is susceptible to powdery mildew disease. It will cause the leaves to first look white, then yellow and die. Plant in areas with good air circulation, grow powdery mildew resistant varieties, and spray plants with an organic fungicide in early summer to thwart this disease. Cut back and clean up foliage in fall to prevent diseases from overwintering near the plants.

Companion Planting and Design
Bee balm is a perfect cottage garden plant. I like to let it ramble through a perennial flower border next to tall garden phlox, rudbeckia, roses, and peonies. It looks best when allowed to grow in groups to create a vivid color statement. Grow shorter varieties of the flower in flower borders. These tend not to spread as aggressively as taller varieties.

Try These
Look for powdery mildew disease-resistant varieties to avoid having to spray for this common disease in New England. Tall varieties, such as 'Jacob Cline' (red) and 'Marshall's Delight' (purple), don't get this disease. For shorter, mildew resistant varieties that grow less than 2 feet tall, try 'Petite Wonder' (pink) and 'Petite Delight' (rose). 'Snow White' is a 3-foot-tall variety with cream-colored flowers.

Bellflower

Campanula spp.

Botanical Pronunciation
kam-PAN-u-la

Other Name
Garden bluebell

Bloom Period and Seasonal Color
Late spring to early fall; blue, white, red, and pink

Mature Height × Spread
6 inches to 6 feet × 6 inches to 3 feet

This diverse group of perennial flowers range from creepers to tall garden flowers. The one thing they all have in common is their bell- or saucer-shaped flowers. Bellflowers are a classic cottage garden plant filling in among other colorful perennials providing a fairylike appearance with their nodding blooms. The blooms last for weeks in the garden providing color throughout the middle of the summer. Creeping varieties can be grown in front of flower borders or in rock gardens. Some varieties have more tube-shaped flowers, offering another variation. Butterflies and bees love the flowers and the plants. The flower sprays make nice additions to arrangements as a cut flower as well.

When, Where, and How to Plant

Bellflowers are hardy throughout our region. The tiny seeds can be sown directly in the garden in spring after all danger of frost has passed. You can also purchase transplants and plant in spring to early fall in well-drained, fertile soil. Most bellflowers grow best sited in full sun, but they also will flower in part sun, especially in warmer parts of our region. Plant transplants or thin seedlings to be spaced 1 to 2 feet apart.

Growing Tips

Although established plants are drought tolerant, keep young plants well watered. Add a topdressing of compost in spring for fertilizer and mulch with bark mulch to keep the soil cool and moist.

Regional Advice and Care

Bellflowers are low-maintenance plants in our region. They will spread and some varieties will need to be divided in spring every two to three years to keep them blooming strong and prevent their spread. Deadhead spent flowers of tall varieties to extend the bloom time. Cutting back tall flower stems by one-third after blooming will sometimes stimulate new growth and reblooming later in summer and early fall. Watch out for aphids on leaves and slugs or snails eating the foliage. Spray insecticidal soap to control aphids and use iron phosphate bait, beer traps, or erect a copper barrier on raised beds to control slugs and snails. Cut back and clean up foliage in fall to prevent disease from overwintering near the plants.

Companion Planting and Design

Bellflowers look great in a cottage garden planted with Siberian iris, columbine, roses, and lady's mantle. Creeping varieties can grow over rock walls or in rock gardens with iberis and sedums.

Try These

The peach-leafed bellflowers come in colors such as white, pink, or blue, cup-shaped flowers in 2- to 3-foot-tall plants. The chimney bellflowers grow up to 6 feet tall in colors of blue or white. They make excellent cut flowers. The Serbian bellflower grows less than 6 inches tall and spreads with unusual, star-shaped flowers. Canterberry bells are an old-fashioned selection with white or blue flowers on 3-foot-tall flower stalks.

Black-Eyed Susan

Rudbeckia spp.

Botanical Pronunciation
rud-BECK-ee-ah

Other Name
Brown-eyed Susan

Bloom Period and Seasonal Color
Midsummer to fall; yellow, red, green, and bronze

Mature Height × Spread
1 to 5 feet × 2 to 3 feet

A standard late summer flower in gardens and wildflower meadows, black-eyed Susans brighten up the landscape with their daisy-like blossoms. The wild species have black centers and yellow petals and are often seen growing in abandoned fields and meadows. Recent breeding has created a whole range of flower colors on black-eyed Susans from mahogany to green on single or even double flowers. These new varieties are great as cut flowers and add a new dimension to this tried-and-true perennial. However, I have found these new hybrids don't tend to be as hardy as the original yellow-petaled species. Some can reach 5 to 6 feet but most varieties grow only a few feet tall. They're great pollinator plants, attracting bees, butterflies, and hummingbirds.

When, Where, and How to Plant

Black-eyed Susans are hardy throughout our area, but some newer hybrids only last a few years. They can be started from seed indoors under grow lights 6 to 8 weeks before your last frost date and transplanted or sown directly in the garden in spring. You can also purchase transplants from the local garden center and plant from spring to early fall. Directly sown seeds tend to flower the second year, while transplants will flower the first year. Plant black-eyed Susans in full or part sun in well-drained soil. Space plants 1 to 2 feet apart or let them naturalize in groups.

Growing Tips

Keep plants well watered the first year. Once established, they are drought tolerant.

Black-eyed Susans don't require additional fertilizing during the growing season. In fact, too much fertilizer can create weak stems that tend to flop.

Regional Advice and Care

If you're growing them in a meadow or naturalized setting, let black-eyed Susans spread. They self-sow readily. In the garden divide plants every two to three years to prevent them from taking over. Instead of deadheading spent blooms, consider leaving the cones on the flowers for birds to eat the seeds in late summer and fall.

Companion Planting and Design

Grow the yellow-flowered black-eyed Susans as wildflowers in a meadow. If growing these in a flower garden, weed out self-sown seedlings in spring or they can take over. Grow black-eyed Susans next to ornamental grasses, tall garden phlox, and asters. Grow the newer varieties that don't spread as readily in perennial flower gardens next to Russian sage, coneflowers, and sedum or in a cut flower garden.

Try These

'Goldstrum' is a popular, yellow-petaled variety that's similar to the wild species, flowers for along period, and is *tough*. 'Cherokee Sunset' is a newer variety that's short-lived but self-sows and has flowers in colors with shades of yellow, orange, and bronze. 'Toto' is a dwarf variety that only grows 1 foot tall. 'Irish Eyes' features a green center or cone with yellow petals.

Blazing Star

Liatris spicata

Botanical Pronunciation
lye-AY-triss spy-KAY-tuh

Other Name
Gayfeather

Bloom Period and Seasonal Color
Mid- to late summer; white, rose, and lavender-purple

Mature Height × Spread
1 to 4 feet × 2 feet

This North American prairie native grows pretty well in our neck of the woods too. Blazing star thrives on neglect, producing multiple, tall spikes of white, rose, or magenta-purple flowers in mid- to late summer. The hairy flowers on the cone-shaped stalks are unusual because they open from the top down on the flower stalk. They're stunning in themselves as they rise above their grasslike foliage, through the air up to 4 feet tall. They are also favorites of bees, butterflies, and hummingbirds. Once established, the plant is drought tolerant and tame in the garden, slowly expanding over time. Blazing star actually grows from underground corms or bulbs. You can help spread them around by digging and dividing the bulbs in fall.

When, Where, and How to Plant
Blazing star is hardy throughout our area. Start blazing star from corms or purchase transplants from your local garden centers. The largest corms (3 inches in diameter) and transplants will be most likely to form flowers the first year. Plant in full or part sun in well-drained soil. Poor water drainage can lead to root rot. Space plants about 1 to 2 feet apart in the garden.

Growing Tips
Blazing star doesn't need additional fertilizer other than compost at the time of planting. In fact, too much fertility will cause the flower stalks to flop. Although blazing star can take dry conditions, during the heat of summer, be sure to apply about 1 inch of water a week or the flower stalks may be stunted.

Regional Advice and Care
Deadhead flower stalks that have bloomed and they may rebloom in early fall. After a frost, cut back foliage in fall and compost. To help blazing star spread, dig corms in late fall, remove the smaller bulblets, store indoors in a cool, dark location in winter, and replant about 1 to 2 inches deep in spring. These bulblets will eventually form new plants that will flower in the same color as the mother plant.

Companion Planting and Design
Blazing star is a versatile plant. It can grow in a wildflower meadow next to black-eyed Susans and coreopsis or a cottage garden with baby's breath, Shasta daisies, and dianthus. Plant blazing star in the garden where you can surprise visitors with its tall flower spikes and where you can easily see the butterflies that will frequent the flowers. Blazing star also makes a nice cut flower, so consider adding it to your cut flower garden.

Try These
'Kobold' and 'Floristan' come in purple or white flowers. It stands 2 to 3 feet tall and has a long bloom period. These two types are good cutting varieties. 'Snow Queen' grows 3 to 4 feet with creamy white flowers.

Bleeding Heart

Dicentra spectabilis

Botanical Pronunciation
dye-SEN-truh speck-TAB-ih-liss

Other Name
Old fashioned bleeding heart

Bloom Period and Seasonal Color
Spring; red, pink, and white

Mature Height × Spread
2 to 3 feet × 1 to 3 feet

This eastern United States native plant is a beauty in spring with its characteristic heart-shaped flowers that come in red, pink, or white. At the bottom of each flower is a colored "drop" that refers to the common name. The plant has fernlike or lobed leaves, depending on the variety. The flowers form on stalks in spring about the time late-flowering hellebores bloom. They grow best in part sun or shade, adding brightness to a woodland planting or shade garden. The plant can actually get quite large when it's mature. After flowering, they slowly die back and go dormant so that by midsummer there's no sign of your bleeding hearts. It's good to plant bleeding hearts where other perennials will fill in after it dies.

When, Where, and How to Plant
Although you can start bleeding hearts from seed, it's easiest to take divisions from a friend's plant, transplant self-sown seedlings in the garden, or purchase transplants from a local garden center. Plant in spring to early summer in part sun or part shade in well-drained, moist soil. Space plants 1 to 2 feet apart.

Growing Tips
Bleeding hearts need little maintenance. They grow best in a consistently moist, humus-rich soil. Pay attention to watering and add a layer of compost in spring for fertilizer.

Regional Advice and Care
After flowering is finished, deadhead flower stalks to tidy up the plant. Once the foliage starts yellowing, I like to cut the whole plant back to the ground. Mark the spot where your bleeding heart is growing so you don't accidentally dig it up in summer or fall when planting annuals or bulbs. Bleeding hearts can grow too large for a space, so every two to three years divide the plants after flowering to keep them inbounds and to share with others. Dig up the whole plant, separate into 1-foot-wide sections with a sharp spade, and replant in compost-amended soil in a similar location.

Companion Planting and Design
Consider planting bleeding hearts in a woodland setting with other wildflowers, such as trout lilies and trilliums. In a shade garden, plant near ferns, coral bells, hostas, and astilbe. Plant bleeding hearts near spreading perennials, such as lungwort, that will fill in the area once it dies back or plant shade-loving annuals, such as begonias, in that spot. Bleeding heart flower stalks also make nice additions to a spring cut flower arrangement with forget-me-nots and dwarf iris.

Try These
'King of Hearts' is an old-fashioned type with long sprays of pink flowers and blue-green foliage. 'Alba' has pure white flowers. 'Golden Heart' has pink flowers with unusual yellow-green, lobed foliage. "Fringed" bleeding heart is a different species (*D. eximia*) that is also attractive. It has unique cut leaves and pink flowers on 1-foot-tall plants.

Butterfly Bush

Buddleia davidii

Botanical Pronunciation
BUD-lee-a da-VID-i

Other Name
Summer lilac

Bloom Period and Seasonal Color
Late summer to fall; purple, white, pink, red, yellow, and lavender

Mature Height × Spread
5 to 8 feet × 4 to 6 feet

The butterfly bush is aptly named. It is a magnet for butterflies, hummingbirds, and all sorts of beneficial insects that absolutely flock to this plant in late summer and fall when it's in full bloom. This sun-lover provides great color and stature in the garden, often growing from ground level to up to 8 feet tall in one growing season! The showy, cone-shaped flowers bloom on new wood each year. In warmer climates, butterfly bush is grown more as a shrub, but in New England it can be marginally hardy in cold areas. It's best grown as an herbaceous perennial. Even if the plant dies back to the ground in winter, the new growth that emerges from the roots in spring will eventually flower.

When, Where, and How to Plant
Butterfly bushes are hardy to zone 5. In colder areas they can be coaxed to overwinter if the plant roots are protected with mulch. Plant locally purchased plants from spring to summer in full sun in compost-amended, well-drained soil. Full-sized butterfly bushes should be spaced 3 to 4 feet apart. Dwarf varieties can be grown in containers or spaced only a couple of feet apart.

Growing Tips
Keep plants well watered. Fertilize in spring with a layer of compost and an organic plant food. Plants are less likely to survive cold winters if they're planted in poorly drained soils.

Regional Advice and Care
Since the butterfly bush is marginally hardy in many parts of New England, plant it in a protected spot, cover the roots with bark mulch in late fall, and cut it back to the ground each spring. The new growth will grow quickly to flower. Deadheading also encourages more flowers to form. Butterfly bushes can self-sow readily and some consider it invasive. Weed out any new seedlings each spring and deadhead spent blossoms to prevent self-sowing.

Companion Planting and Design
Plant butterfly bushes in groups in the back of perennial flower borders. It has a somewhat randy, unkempt appearance so is best planted around other perennials that can hide some of its growth. Plant them where the butterflies can be easily viewed and with other fall-blooming butterfly attractors, such as asters, goldenrod, and tall garden phlox. Plant dwarf varieties in front of flower borders or in containers on a deck or patio. Container varieties can be treated as an annual by placing them in a protected garage or basement in winter or planted in the ground in fall to overwinter.

Try These
'Black Knight' has a dark purple flower and better hardiness than most butterfly bush varieties. 'White Profusion' has short, white flowers. 'Honeycomb' is one of the best yellow-flowered varieties. 'Blue Chip' is a dwarf that only grows 2 to 3 feet tall with small blue flowers. There are also 'Lilac Chip' and 'Ice Chip' in this dwarf series.

Butterfly Weed

Asclepias tuberosa

Botanical Pronunciation
uh-SKLEE-pee-us too-bur-OH-zuh

Other Name
Orange milkweed

Bloom Period and Seasonal Color
Late summer to fall; orange, red, yellow, and pink

Mature Height × Spread
2 to 4 feet × 2 to 4 feet

This native has less stature, compared to the butterfly bush, but is just as effective at drawing in winged friends, such as butterflies, ladybugs, and beneficial insects, into the garden. It's particularly a favorite of the Monarch butterfly. Butterfly weed is also hardier and more adapted to a wider range of soils, making it a good choice if you're having a hard time growing butterfly bush successfully. The plant is slow to emerge in spring, so don't give up hope. My butterfly weed often will just start growing when other plants are fully leafed out around it. But it makes up for lost time quickly growing to 4 feet tall and wide with brightly colored flowers. Once it's growing, it has few problems.

When, Where, and How to Plant

Butterfly weed is hardy throughout New England. Sow seeds indoors in peat pots 6 to 8 weeks before your last frost date, thinning to one plant per pot. Plant the entire peat pot when it's time or plant locally purchased plants. Add to the garden in spring after the danger of frost has passed, or in summer in full sun in compost-amended, well-drained soil. Poor soil drainage is the one thing butterfly weed won't stand. Space plants 2 to 3 feet apart. Butterfly weed has a taproot, so once planted it's difficult to move.

Growing Tips

Keep the plants well watered the first year and fertilize once in spring with compost. Butterfly weed is slow growing at first in our cool soils, so mark where you planted it so you don't accidentally dig it up when planting annuals and other perennials in spring.

Regional Advice and Care

Deadhead spent flowers to encourage more flowering and reduce self-sowing. Weed out self-sown seedlings each spring. Be careful when pruning the plant as the stems have a milky sap that might irritate your skin. Cut back the plant to the ground in fall after a frost and compost it. It needs little care once established in the garden and can be drought tolerant. Aphids can sometimes be a problem and are easily controlled with sprays of insecticidal soap. Butterfly weed plants can withstand damage from the Monarch butterfly caterpillars. Don't spray to kill them or you'll not have any beautiful butterflies.

Companion Planting and Design

Plant butterfly weed close to where you can view the butterflies from a window or deck. Since butterfly weed can have loud, hot flower colors, pair it in the garden with complementary-colored perennials, such as Russian sage, coneflowers, and ornamental grasses. It can also be grown in the cut flower garden for arrangements.

Try These

Orange is the color of the hardy native species and it's often sold just as *Ascelpias tuberosa*. 'Hollow Yellow' is yellow. 'Cinderella' has pinkish red flowers. 'Gay Butterflies Mix' has plants in colors of red, orange, and yellow.

Candytuft

Iberis sempervirens

Botanical Pronunciation
i-BE-ris sem-per-VI-renz

Other Name
Evergreen candytuft

Bloom Period and Seasonal Color
Late spring; white and pink

Mature Height × Spread
6 to 12 inches × 1 to 2 feet

This low-growing, evergreen groundcover is a delight in the perennial flower garden in spring. The bright white flowers light up the border when in bloom, sometimes covering the foliage with so many flowers you can't see the leaves. The blooms may take on a pinkish tinge when exposed to cool nights. It slowly spreads making it perfect for growing on top of walls, in rock gardens, and along walkways. The evergreen foliage makes candytuft a nice complement to other low-growing perennial flowers in the garden when it's not in bloom. It's a low-maintenance plant too. All it needs to keep looking attractive is an annual pruning and some winter protection in cold winter areas of our region.

When, Where, and How to Plant

Candytuft is hardy throughout our region, although the leaves may look ratty in winter if not protected in cold areas. Plant transplants purchased from local garden centers in spring to early fall in compost-amended soils. It flowers best in full sun but can take part sun. It's important to plant in a permanent location in well-drained soils because candytuft doesn't like being transplanted, and it grows poorly in wet soils. Space plants 6 to 12 inches apart.

Growing Tips

Keep new transplants well watered. Fertilize in spring with compost and mulch with bark mulch to help keep weeds away.

Regional Advice and Care

Cut back plants by one-third every few years to promote less woody stems and more flowering.

Deadhead spent flowers after blooming in late spring to promote a second flush of blooms in summer. Candytuft does best with some protection in winter in most areas of New England. Cover the plants in late fall with pine boughs or bark mulch. Gardens with consistent snow cover all winter often can grow candytuft more easily than in gardens where snow comes and goes. Stems may root where they contact the ground, making it easy to dig and divide new plants from established plantings. Prevent powdery mildew on the leaves by spacing the plants farther apart and growing candytuft in a breezy location where the leaves can dry out quickly.

Companion Planting and Design

Plant candytuft in front of flower borders or in rock gardens. It pairs well with spring-flowering bulbs, such as daffodils and hyacinths. Other good companions would be similar low-growing flowers, such as creeping phlox and alyssum. It also can be grown in containers, but they would need to be brought into a garage or basement in winter for protection.

Try These

'Snowflake' produces low mounds of pure white flowers. It is known to rebloom well in fall. 'Snow Mantle' is a compact version of 'Snowflake'. 'Little Gem' and 'Purity' only grow 6 inches tall and stay more compact. 'Pink Ice' is a newer pink-colored variety.

Catmint

Nepeta × faassenii

Botanical Pronunciation
NEP-eh-tah fah-SEEN-ee-eye

Other Name
Dwarf catnip

Bloom Period and Seasonal Color
Late spring to midsummer (can rebloom in fall);
blue, white, and violet

Mature Height × Spread
12 to 16 inches × 1 to 3 feet

This cool-weather-loving perennial flower most commonly has blue, trumpet-shaped clusters of flowers and grey-green foliage with a characteristic mint aroma. Although often called catnip, it's not as attractive to cats as the real catnip. I have noticed our cat will indulge herself though, if given the chance. The plant can grow up to 3 feet tall, but often will sprawl forming a grey-green groundcover. It blooms profusely in late spring and early summer. It often will stop flowering for a time in midsummer with hot weather, only to resume again in early fall, especially if it's cut back vigorously. Butterflies, hummingbirds, and beneficial insects *love* catmint flowers.

When, Where, and How to Plant
Catmint is hardy throughout our region, although some varieties may need winter protection in cold areas. Although it can be grown from seed, it's much easier to purchase plants from a local nursery or obtain divisions from a friend's garden in spring when it first starts growing; catmint is easy to divide. Plant in spring to early fall. Plant catmint in full or part sun in well-drained, humus-rich, compost-amended soil. If growing in warmer parts of our region, plant where it will have afternoon shade. Space plants 1 to 2 feet apart in the garden.

Growing Tips
Keep first year plants well watered. Once established, they can be drought tolerant. Spread compost around the base of plants in spring and mulch with bark to help keep weeds away and the soil consistently moist.

Regional Advice and Care
Catmint can be kept in almost continual bloom from late spring to fall if you aggressively deadhead flowers and cut the plant back by two-thirds after each flush of blooms. After a few years, dividing the plant in spring will help rejuvenate its growth and produce more plants for friends and other plantings. Catmint has few pests, and the seeds are sterile so it doesn't spread by self-sowing.

Companion Planting and Design
Catmint is a classic cottage garden plant that often accompanies peonies, roses, coreopsis, and delphiniums. Because of its spreading nature, it's a great filler plant to provide color and green foliage between later-blooming flowers. It grows well as a rock garden plant and planted near a wall where it can cascade over. It can have a bit of a rangy appearance, so isn't a good choice for very formal settings.

Try These
'Walker's Low' is a newer variety with blue-violet flowers and a neater appearance than other varieties since it doesn't sprawl as much. 'White Wonder' and 'Snowflake' have unusual white blooms and only grow 1 foot tall. 'Six Hills Giant' is known for its vivid blue flowers and is a large plant. 'Blue Wonder' has 1- to 2-foot-tall stems with dark blue flowers.

Columbine

Aquilegia spp. and hybrids

Botanical Pronunciation
ack-wih-LEE-jee-uh

Other Name
Granny's bonnet

Bloom Period and Seasonal Color
Spring; white, yellow, blue, purple, red, orange, and bicolors

Mature Height × Spread
1 to 3 feet × 6 to 24 inches

Often one of the first spring wildflowers to appear in our woodlands, columbine is a versatile plant. There are species and hybrid varieties that look equally at home in a wildflower meadow as well as the flower border. These perennial bloomers come in a wide range of colors. Their flowers float above the oval, fan-shaped foliage. The plants may only be short-lived perennials, but they do self-sow readily providing years of flower color. The flowers also cross (hybridize) easily so new plants may have different colors than the mother plants. I have wild plants naturally growing in rock ledges behind our house in part shade giving a good indication that columbine can thrive in dry, well-drained soil conditions.

When, Where, and How to Plant

Columbines are hardy throughout New England. They're easy to grow from seed directly sown in the garden or started indoors under grow lights 8 to 10 weeks before your last frost date. Columbine transplants are often available in garden centers as well. Plant in spring, after all danger of frost has passed, or summer in well-drained soil in part sun or part shade. The species types are more adapted to growing in the shade. Thin seedlings or space transplants one foot apart. Seed-grown columbine may not bloom the first year in the garden.

Growing Tips

Keep the soil moist, especially when growing hybrid columbines during the hot summer, to keep plants healthy. Mulch around the base of plants to maintain soil moisture and prevent weed growth. Apply a layer of compost in spring for fertilizer.

Regional Advice and Care

Species versions of columbine naturalize readily in part-shaded woodlands or rocky ledges but well-drained soil is a *must*. Deadhead spent flower stalks in late spring to tidy up the plants and prevent self-sowing, if you don't want more seedlings. Mother plants will tend to die off after three to four years. Tunneling leaf miner insects can attack columbine foliage. Shear the plants after blooming and remove the foliage to eliminate this pest. The plant will regrow the same summer, but will not flower again.

Companion Planting and Design

Grow the species in woodlands, wildflower patches, and rock gardens. In the garden, hybrid versions, with their larger, sometimes double and more colorful flowers, offer a nice transition from spring bulbs to spring-flowering perennials. Columbine also makes good cut flowers in arrangements.

Try These

The Canadian columbine is a wild species with red and yellow flowers. 'Black Currant Ice' is a newer variety with nodding purple and yellow flowers that grows 1 foot tall. The McKana series feature 2- to 3-foot-tall plants with a mix of flower colors. The Origami series has 1- to 2-foot-tall plants that bloom longer than other hybrids. The Barlow series has unique blue, red, or black shaggy double flowers.

Coneflower

Echinacea purpurea

Botanical Pronunciation
eck-ih-NAY-see-uh pur-PUR-ee-uh

Other Name
Purple coneflower

Bloom Period and Seasonal Color
Early to late summer; purple, white, yellow, pink, and orange

Mature Height × Spread
1 to 4 feet × 1 to 2 feet

Known for its medicinal benefits, coneflowers are a beautiful native, low-maintenance perennial. Coneflowers have gone through a revolution in the past years as breeders have taken the purple- or white-flowered native species and produced different-sized plants with an array of flower colors and shapes. New varieties offer flower colors such as yellow, white, red, pink, and orange. Some have double flowers that don't even look like coneflowers any longer. Some plants are small enough to fit in containers and small space gardens. Unfortunately, I find these newer varieties aren't as tough or hardy as the original species. However, they still are worth growing as an attractive addition to your flower garden. The flowers and cones also make excellent cut flowers.

When, Where, and How to Plant
Coneflowers are hardy throughout New England, but some newer varieties may be short-lived perennials. You can start coneflowers from seed, but the plants may take a few years to bloom in the garden. It's better to purchase transplants from a local garden center or obtain self-sown seedlings from a friend's garden. Coneflowers grow best in full or part sun in well-drained soil. Plant in spring to early fall in compost-amended soil. Space plants 1 to 2 feet apart depending on the selection.

Growing Tips
Coneflowers don't require special fertilizer or watering. They're drought tolerant once established and an annual application of compost in spring is plenty for fertility. Hybrid varieties

may need more pampering and fertilizing to look their best.

Regional Advice and Care
Coneflowers self-sow readily, but a seedling's flowers may not come true to the color of the parent plant. If you're growing them in a meadow or large border and you want a mass of coneflowers, leave the flower heads on the plant after petals fall to sow seeds. In smaller gardens, deadhead spent flowers in summer to prevent self-sowing and weed out any seedlings the following spring. If powdery mildew is a problem on your coneflowers, plant in an open area with good breezes that will dry out the foliage and plant resistant varieties.

Companion Planting and Design
Coneflowers look great planted *en masse* in a wildflower setting or mixed with other perennials, such as rudbeckia, Shasta daisies, and tall garden phlox, in a perennial border. Plant dwarf varieties in front of flower borders or in containers. Container-grown coneflowers will have to be protected in winter by moving the plants into a garage or basement.

Try These
The purple coneflower species is the toughest type of coneflower to grow and often found in wildflower mixes. For flowers of a different color, 'Fragrant Angel' is a white variety with scented petals. 'Orange Meadowbrite' has thin orange petals. 'Pixie Meadowbrite' only grows 18 inches tall. 'Harvest Moon' features golden petals. 'Hot Papaya' has unusual double, fuzzy red flowers.

Coral Bells

Heuchera spp. and hybrids

Botanical Pronunciation
HEW-ker-a

Other Name
Alum root

Bloom Period and Seasonal Color
Late spring to midsummer; white, red, pink, and coral

Mature Height × Spread
1 to 2 feet × 1 to 2 feet

Coral bells are a great option for plants that grow well in shade. I particularly like their colorful leaves and small, airy, bell-shaped ornamental flowers that brighten up a dark area. Coral bells have been going through quite a breeding frenzy. The focus has been on creating varieties with more colorful leaves. While the tall, delicate flowers add a touch of whimsy to a perennial flower border and are loved by butterflies and hummingbirds, it's the leaves that provide color all season. The multicolored leaf varieties give this plant versatility when it's grown in rock gardens, shade gardens, woodlands, or even in containers. The leaves can be rounded, lobed, or hairy in shape and texture. The flower stalks add a nice touch to flower arrangements.

When, Where, and How to Plant
Coral bells are hardy throughout New England, but may need winter protection in the coldest areas. Seed-grown coral bells take a long time to grow and flower so it's best to purchase plants in spring from local garden centers or take divisions from established plants from a friend's garden. Plant from spring to early fall in a location with some afternoon shade. They don't flower well in full shade. Plant in well-drained, slightly acidic, humus-rich soil, which stays moist but not too wet. Space plants 1 foot apart and in groups for the best effect.

Growing Tips
Keep plants well watered and fertilize in spring and early fall with an organic plant food. Keep plants well weeded, and spread mulch to keep the soil cool and moist and prevent weed growth.

Regional Advice and Care
In cool summer areas coral bells can take full sun and grow well. Otherwise the colorful foliage will have a washed out appearance. Deadhead flower stalks to prolong the flowering period. Control slugs and snails with iron phosphate baits, beer traps, and copper flashing on containers and raised beds. Protect plants in cold winter areas by topping the bed with pine boughs or bark mulch in winter.

Companion Planting and Design
Plant coral bells with other shade lovers, such as hostas, small astilbe, lungwort, and forget-me-nots. Plant in groups and mix and match leaf colors for a more dramatic effect. Plant in rock gardens and in part-shade woodlands as a wildflower plant.

Try These
'Electric Lime' has bright lime green leaves and white flowers. 'Dolce Creme Brulee' has copper- and bronze-colored leaves with pink flowers. 'Plum Pudding' has purple leaves with silver veins and beautiful pink flower stalks. 'Blondie' has red leaves with a tinge of orange and unique yellow flowers that blooms well into summer. 'Ring of Fire' has leaves that start out lime green, then darken with age. They have bright red veins and soft pink flowers.

Daylily

Hemerocallis spp. and hybrids

Botanical Pronunciation
hem-er-o-KAL-is

Other Name
Tawny daylily

Bloom Period and Seasonal Color
Early to late summer; orange, yellow, pink, red, purple, cream, and bicolors

Mature Height × Spread
1 to 4 feet × 1 to 4 feet

If you're looking for a carefree, low-maintenance perennial flower to grow, consider the daylily. This plant is hardy and tough and almost always flowers as long as you give it at least one-half day of sun. There are hundreds of varieties available in a rainbow of colors. The best way to buy daylilies is to select the shades you want when they're blooming since there is such a wide variation in colors. You can also select varieties that bloom from summer to fall to extend the bloom season or select repeat bloomers. They grow in about any condition as evidenced by the clumps of tawny orange daylilies growing along roadsides throughout New England. The flower buds, flowers, and root tubers are also edible.

When, Where, and How to Plant

Daylilies are hardy throughout our area. Plant them anytime from spring to early fall. Select divisions of favorite varieties from friends or purchase them in bloom at garden centers. Choose a full or part sun location; too much shade will prevent blooming. Daylilies are not fussy about soil conditions and are drought tolerant once established. I've even seen forgotten, unplanted daylily divisions sitting on the garden's edge blooming in summer. Space plants 1 to 2 feet apart.

Growing Tips

Daylilies require little care. Water newly planted varieties well the first year, add some compost each spring for fertilizing, and mulch with bark mulch to maintain soil moisture. Once established, they need little extra watering.

Regional Advice and Care

Daylily flowers only open for one day, but the scapes (flower stalks) produce many flowers. Deadhead spent flower scapes after all the buds have opened. Cut back the foliage in fall and compost. Daylilies can grow in all the climates of New England from the mountains to the seashore. They have no serious diseases or insect problems. They may need to be divided every three to four years if they're overcrowded and stop flowering. Divide clumps in spring and replant soon afterward.

Companion Planting and Design

Daylilies look great massed together in a bed or paired with other summer- and fall-blooming perennials such as rudbeckia, heliopsis, asters, and chrysanthemums. They're a good plant to grow on a bank or in an abandoned area since they require little care.

Try These

Daylily varieties come in many colors, and the flowers come in many shapes, such as single, double spider, recurved, and flat. Select varieties that bloom early, mid-, and late season and repeat bloomers to extend the flowering season. Some repeat-blooming varieties to try include 'Stella de Oro' (yellow), 'Happy Returns' (red), and 'Joan Senior' (white). 'Hyperion' is an older variety with bright yellow flowers that blooms in midsummer and has a strong fragrance. 'Siloam Double Classic' is an early bloomer with puffy, pink double flowers. 'Eenie Joy' has yellow flowers on only 1-foot-tall stalks.

Delphinium

Delphinium spp. and hybrids

Botanical Pronunciation
del-FIN-ee-um

Other Name
Larkspur

Bloom Period and Seasonal Color
Early to midsummer; blue, pink, white, rose, and purple

Mature Height × Spread
2 to 6 feet × 1 to 2 feet

There is no more stately a flower than the delphinium. This English garden standard has spiky flower stalks that can reach 6 feet tall depending on the variety. They are breathtaking when grown in clumps. The flowers are single or double with contrasting colored centers or "bees." The flowers surround the stalk so the delphiniums look like majestic, colorful pillars in the back of the flower border. They're not without their nuances though. The spikes need support and the plants can be finicky about lasting more than three to four years in the garden. The blooms can be used in cut flower arranging, and bees, butterflies, and beneficial insects appreciate the tall blooms.

When, Where, and How to Plant

Delphiniums are hardy throughout New England. They're difficult to grow from seed so it's best to buy plants locally from garden centers in spring to plant from spring to summer. Delphiniums like a slightly alkaline soil, so add lime to raise the pH above 6.5 (if needed). They need well-drained, moist, compost-amended soil to grow their best. Plant delphiniums in full sun on the south side of a house or garage protected from strong winds. Space plants 2 to 3 feet apart.

Growing Tips

Keep plants well watered. Mulch around the base of plants to keep weeds away and the soil consistently moist. Fertilize monthly with an organic plant food.

Regional Advice and Care

Tall varieties of delphiniums need support. Place stakes or plant rings around developing flower stalks when they are 1 foot tall to protect them breaking due to summer thunderstorms. There's nothing worse than having your fully opened delphinium stalk snap in half due to a windstorm. Delphiniums are magnificent when they're blooming, but shabby when they've finished flowering. Remove the spent flower stalks soon after blooming and secondary stalks often form, giving you more flowers in late summer. Plant away from eaves of the house where rain dripping off the roof can damage the blossoms.

Companion Planting and Design

While tall delphiniums grow well in the back of a border or against a house, shorter varieties look good in the front of your garden. Pair tall delphiniums with iris and phlox and lower-growing varieties with alyssum and ageratum. Plant them in a cutting garden. Cut flower stalks when they're three quarters open for best blooms.

Try These

'Pacific Giants Mix' is a standard group of varieties with blue, violet, and rose double flowers. 'Blue Springs' only grow 2 feet tall with blue flowers. The Magic Fountain series has a mix of white and blue flowers that grow 3 feet tall and are good for cutting. 'Magic Fountain Sky Blue' is a particularly beautiful selection. The New Millennium series from New Zealand has large flowers on strong stems, and the plants are longer lived.

False Indigo

Baptisia australis

Botanical Pronunciation
bap-TIZZ-ee-uh aw-STRAY-liss

Other Name
Blue wild indigo

Bloom Period and Seasonal Color
Late spring to summer; blue, white, red, and yellow

Mature Height × Spread
3 to 4 feet × 3 to 4 feet

This native perennial has a shrublike appearance even though it dies back to the ground each winter. It's in the legume family, and the pealike leaves give away its heritage. It was once used as a substitute for making the blue dye called "indigo." False indigo is a long-lived perennial flower in the garden with beautiful blue flowers in late spring. There are other species of false indigo with white, red, and yellow flowers as well. The dark green leaves make a good backdrop to other flowers throughout the summer. The flowers give way to pealike seedpods that turn black when mature. They're ornamental in their own right and are often used in flower arranging. The dried seeds rattle in their pods, making them fun toys for kids.

When, Where, and How to Plant
False indigo is hardy throughout our region. Seeds are hard to germinate and plants started from seed take up to three years to flower. It's best to purchase plants from a local garden center and plant from spring to early fall. False indigo grows best in full or part sun in well-drained, compost-amended soil. The plants have taproots so they're difficult to move once planted. Space plants 3 to 4 feet apart.

Growing Tips
False indigo likes moisture, but once established the plants are drought tolerant. Mulch to keep the soil wet and weeds away. Since it's a legume, it needs little additional fertilizer (it "makes" its own).

Regional Advice and Care
If growing false indigo in part shade, place stakes or a cage around the plant as the flower stalks may get floppy. If you're not using the seedpods for arrangements, deadhead spent flowers. Once it gets cooler in fall and the leaves start turning black, cut back the whole plant to the ground. If leaves are prone to powdery mildew disease, remove weeds and other perennials close to the plant to open up the area around the plant to promote more air movement. Control aphids on the new foliage with sprays of insecticidal soap.

Companion Planting and Design
Plant false indigo in a perennial flower border near peonies, iris, and salvias to complement those flowers. Place later-blooming perennials, such as daylilies and coneflowers, in front of false indigo to take advantage of its dark green foliage backdrop. False indigo can also be planted as a meadow plant or in the wildflower patch.

Try These
'Purple Smoke' is a newer hybrid variety with dark purple flower stalks. 'White Wild Indigo' is a *Baptisia alba* species with white flowers. The 'Decadence' series features red, yellow, and blue flowers on more compact plants. 'Carolina Moonlight' is a cross of two species that produce blue-green leaves and buttery yellow flower stalks.

Ferns

Various genera

Botanical Pronunciation
Varies

Bloom Period and Seasonal Color
Grown mostly for their green ferns; some turn golden in fall

Mature Height × Spread
1 to 4 feet × 1 to 3 feet

New England woodlands and shady areas are loaded with native ferns. They are so ubiquitous in our region that we often overlook them as garden plants. Ferns create a green understory in the forest and fill in shade gardens providing color and texture, often where little else can grow. From the small maidenhair fern to the tall cinnamon fern, the diversity of this group of plants is impressive. Some are clump forming, while others spread by fibrous roots. Given shade and moist soil conditions, ferns can spread to fill in a garden or understory in a woodland, sometimes becoming too aggressive for a small space garden. Some ferns even have edible shoots in spring and others have attractive fronds that can be used in arrangements.

When, Where, and How to Plant
Ferns are hardy throughout New England. Ferns grow best in a part or full shade area with consistently moist soil. Some ferns will grow well in part sun given enough water. Divide ferns in spring from a friend's garden or purchase them from a garden center. Plant ferns from spring to early summer. Ferns can tolerate low fertility soil and most grow best in slightly acidic soil. Plant ferns on well-drained, humus-rich soil amended with peat moss and compost. Space plants anywhere from 1 to 3 feet apart.

Growing Tips
Once established in the right location, ferns need little care. Keep the soil moist and heavily amended with organic matter, such as peat moss, to encourage the fern roots to spread.

Regional Advice and Care
In the shade, ferns will out compete other weeds and flowers so they're a good groundcover plant. They will outcompete your perennial flowers so don't let them overrun an area. Divide ferns in early spring to create more plants to share and to keep them inbounds. Cut back the fern foliage in fall after a frost. Mulch ferns with pine needles to keep the soil consistently moist and acidic.

Companion Planting and Design
Ferns pair well with many other shade-loving perennials, such as hosta, astilbes, bleeding hearts, lungwort, and violas. They can be allowed to naturally spread under the canopy of deciduous trees, such as maples.

Try These
Japanese painted fern varieties, such as 'Ursula Red', are popular, 1-foot-tall ferns with red and silver leaf coloring. They can grow in part sun. Cinnamon ferns grow 3 to 5 feet tall with dark green fronds turning to a golden color in fall. They produce cinnamon-colored fronds that appear like flower stalks. Ostrich ferns grow 4 to 5 feet tall, and their edible, unfurled fronds in spring can be eaten as fiddleheads. Maidenhair ferns only grow 1 foot tall and have elegant, bright green, fingerlike fronds with shiny black stems. Christmas ferns have 2-foot-tall upright, evergreen fronds often used in holiday decorations.

Foxglove

Digitalis spp. and hybrids

Botanical Pronunciation
didge-ih-TAY-liss

Other Name
Common foxglove

Bloom Period and Seasonal Color
Spring to early summer; blue, pink, peach, red, yellow, purple, and speckled

Mature Height × Spread
2 to 4 feet × 1 to 3 feet

This common cottage garden plant can be a biennial or perennial depending on the species. Biennials just grow leaves the first year and flower the second year. Since they self-sow readily, you'll often get colonies of foxgloves blooming each year making it look as if they're perennials. There are also some short-lived perennials in this group that grow well in New England. The small foxglove blooms are born on flower stalks. The tube-shaped flowers are perfect for attracting butterflies and hummingbirds to the garden. The leaves and flowers, however, contain digitalis and can be harmful if eaten. Foxglove flower stalks make excellent cut flowers and can be very showy in a perennial flower border.

When, Where, and How to Plant

Foxgloves are hardy throughout New England. Plant seed in summer or early fall in the perennial garden in moist, slightly acidic soil. Some newer varieties can be sown in early spring and will flower the first year. Keep well watered. Thin plants to 12 to 18 inches apart. You can also plant transplants purchased from the local garden center in spring. In hot areas, plant in part shade. In cool areas, plant in full or part sun.

Growing Tips

Keep plants well watered and weeded. Mulch to maintain soil moisture conditions and prevent weed growth. Add compost each spring to fertilize the plants.

Regional Advice and Care

Taller varieties, or varieties grown for cutting, may need staking to keep from falling over. After blooming, let the foxglove plants drop their seed, then remove that plant since it will look unkempt and die soon anyway. Keep the area properly thinned of new seedlings each spring or you will have an overcrowded planting with small flower stalks and unhealthy looking plants. Foxgloves also can be left to naturalize in a wildflower area since they self-sow so readily.

Companion Planting and Design

Tall foxgloves look great in the back of a perennial flower border, especially against a dark wall or dark-foliaged plants, such as peonies and Shasta daisies. Plant shorter foxglove varieties among flowers, such as columbines, roses, sweet William, snapdragons, and poppies. They provide some vertical color. Grow varieties along partly shaded woodland walks and in wildflower patches.

Try These

Some common hybrid foxgloves to grow include 'Excelsior'. It has colorful flowers that grow on all sides of the flower stalk, not just one side, and they face outward rather than downward. The Dalmatian series features 2- to 3-foot-tall flower stalks in peach, pink, and white that flowers in just 4 months from seeding. The Camelot series produce huge, speckled flowers on 4-foot-tall stalks. 'Carillon' is a 12-inch-tall, long-blooming yellow variety.

Hardy Geranium

Geranium spp.

Botanical Pronunciation
jer-AE-nee-um

Other Name
Cranesbill geranium

Bloom Period and Seasonal Color
Late spring to early summer (some rebloom through the summer); white, blue, and pink

Mature Height × Spread
6 to 24 inches × 1 to 2 feet

Geraniums aren't really geraniums. The geranium most gardeners refer to is actually *Pelargonium*, an annual flower. I cover those in the chapter on annuals. True geraniums are hardy perennials in New England that are low-growing and free-flowering in colors such as blue, white, and pink. They are also called cranesbill geraniums because the seedpod resembles this bird's bill. The flowers form above the lobed foliage and will bloom off and on all summer, especially if the plant is religiously deadheaded. This sprawling plant can spread to a few feet wide, but is kept inbounds with periodic pruning and dividing. The small, cup-shaped flowers are appealing to bees and butterflies.

When, Where, and How to Plant
Hardy geraniums grow throughout New England. Plant locally purchased transplants or divisions from a friend's garden in spring after all danger of frost has passed until early fall. They grow and flower best in compost-amended soil, but will still flower in part sun and even in clay soils. Space plants 1 foot apart in beds.

Growing Tips
Keep hardy geranium plants well watered and fertilized each spring with a layer of compost. Mulch around the base of plants to inhibit weed growth and keep the soil moist.

Regional Advice and Care
Hardy geraniums will repeat flowering if they're deadheaded and cut back after the initial blooming period. Plants have a tidier look and flower better if divided every three to four years. To divide, in spring dig up the clump and separate into 1-foot-diameter divisions for replanting elsewhere or to give away. Hardy geraniums are one of the lowest maintenance perennials you can grow in your garden. However, in part shade or during wet summers they can get powdery mildew. Keep plants pruned and well spaced, and clean up the dead leaves in fall to reduce the incidence of this disease.

Companion Planting and Design
Hardy geraniums are great filler plants in the perennial garden. Because they sprawl and flower in summer, they can fill in next to other plants that have finished blooming, such as peonies and iris, or complement other summer bloomers, such as roses, daylilies, and coreopsis. If they're growing in the front of your flower border, keep them trimmed so they don't look so messy. Plant more trailing varieties along a wall to cascade over the edge.

Try These
One of my favorite hardy geranium varieties is 'Rozanne'. This variety has violet-blue flowers on a plant that grows to 2 feet tall. 'Johnson's Blue' is another similarly sized blue variety. 'Ann Folkard' is a magenta-colored flower variety that only grows 8 inches tall and is great in a rock garden or along a wall. 'Album' has white flowers on 12-inch-tall plants.

Hardy Hibiscus

Hibiscus moscheutos

Botanical Pronunciation
hi-BIS-kus mos-KEW-tos

Other Name
Swamp rose mallow

Bloom Period and Seasonal Color
Late summer to fall; white, pink, red, and bicolors

Mature Height × Spread
2 to 5 feet × 2 to 5 feet

Yes! you can grow hibiscus in New England. Often people think of the tropical houseplant when I mention this plant, but there is a hardy version that looks just as beautiful. The hardy hibiscus is a slow grower, but it builds size and energy through the summer to finally start flowering in late summer and continues until frost. It puts on quite a show. The flowers are colorful and can be 10 to 12 inches in diameter. They are sometimes called the dinner plate hibiscus for that reason. The plant can grow 5 feet tall and wide, filling in an area in the perennial garden. The flowers only last one or two days, but they come in succession to keep the flower show going.

When, Where, and How to Plant

Hardy hibiscus is grown throughout our region. You can start seeds indoors 2 months before your last frost date and transplant seedlings into the garden. For just a few plants it may be easier to purchase plants in spring from your local garden center. Plant after all danger of frost has passed and throughout the summer in well-drained, fertile soil. Hardy hibiscus like the heat and full sun, so consider planting them near a south-facing wall or building. Space plants 2 to 3 feet apart in the garden.

Growing Tips

Hardy hibiscus like moist soils, so keep plants well watered and mulched with bark mulch to prevent weeds from crowding them and maintain the soil moisture. Fertilize in spring with a layer of compost.

Regional Advice and Care

Hardy hibiscus is slow to emerge in spring in cold areas so be patient. They may not pop out of the ground until June. Pinch the shoots of young plants in early summer to encourage branching and more flower stalks to form. Hardy hibiscus can also self-sow and become weedy. The self-sown seedlings will not necessarily be the same color as the parents, but they can be transplanted and moved throughout the garden if you wish. Keep plants deadheaded so they look tidy and prevent the seeds from sowing if you don't want seedlings. After a frost cut back plants to the ground and compost the flower stalks.

Companion Planting and Design

Plant hardy hibiscus in the back of a perennial flower border or among other perennials that have finished flowering, such as peonies, iris, and coneflowers. They can tolerate wet soils so they are a good choice where Joe-pye weed and other moisture-lovers thrive.

Try These

'Lord Baltimore' is an old-fashioned variety with red flowers. 'Lady Baltimore' is similar with white flowers and a red throat. 'Kopper King' grows 4 feet tall with attractive burgundy foliage and pink flowers with a red throat. 'Plum Crazy' has frilly pink flowers. 'Blue River II' has stunning white flowers.

Hollyhock

Alcea rosea and hybrids

Botanical Pronunciation
al-SEE-uh ROSE-ee-ah

Other Name
Mallow

Bloom Period and Seasonal Color
Early to midsummer; white, pink, red, yellow, black, purple, and bicolors

Mature Height × Spread
2 to 8 feet × 1 to 3 feet

An old-fashioned cottage garden isn't complete without a clump of hollyhocks blooming in the background. These tall, stately plants have flowers that form all along their stalk that can reach 8 feet tall. Newer varieties can grow only to 2 feet tall, making them good choices for small space gardens. When in full bloom the flower stalk looks like a pole of color standing in back of your garden. Hollyhocks are actually biennial plants, dying after they bloom in their second season; however, they self-sow readily. If you let a few plants drop their seeds each year, you'll be rewarded with a continual hollyhock display with little work. The colors of the offspring may not match the parents, but the variety of colors is appealing.

When, Where, and How to Plant
Hollyhocks are hardy throughout New England. Sow seeds directly into the soil in spring one week before the last frost date for your area. You can also start seedlings indoors 4 to 6 weeks earlier before setting them out in the garden or purchase transplants from the local garden center. Transplants can be planted from spring to early fall. Hollyhocks grow best in full or part sun in well-drained, moist soil. Keep the seedbed and young seedlings well watered. Thin hollyhock seedlings 2 feet apart.

Growing Tips
Hollyhock seed sown in spring won't bloom until their second year. Transplants should bloom the first year. Amend the soil with compost each spring and keep the soil moist with regular waterings.

Regional Advice and Care
Grow hollyhocks in groups to support one another, and stake tall varieties so they don't blow over during summer storms. Hollyhocks can get rust disease on their leaves. It usually starts on lower leaves as yellow spots and works its way up the flower stalk making the whole plant look unsightly. To slow its progression, mulch the plants and plant away from the overhang of house eaves to keep the foliage dry. Japanese beetles love hollyhock flowers. Trap, handpick, and spray pyrethrum on plants to control this pest.

Companion Planting and Design
Plant hollyhocks in back of your perennial flower border, or against a garage, wall, or house. Plant them near a window so you can enjoy the flowers and watch the butterflies and hummingbirds that frequently visit. Mix and match flower colors with the color of the structure they stand in front of and with plants around them. Hollyhocks pair well with plants that can hide their sometimes bare lower branches, such as daylilies, daisies, and rudbeckia.

Try These
Some old-fashioned varieties to try include 'Chatter's Double' with its mix of pink, scarlet, white, and yellow blooms. 'Peaches N Dreams' has frilly, double peach-colored blooms. 'The Watchman' has striking, almost black, single flowers. 'Queeny Purple' is a modern dwarf variety that grows 2 feet tall with frilly purple flowers.

Hosta

Hosta spp. and hybrids

Botanical Pronunciation
HOS-tuh

Other Name
Plantain lily

Bloom Period and Seasonal Color
Summer to fall; white and violet flowers; grown for foliage

Mature Height × Spread
6 inches to 3 feet × 1 to 4 feet

Hosta is the queen of the shade garden. They spread and fill in dark areas, providing beauty and interest. Hostas are more often grown for their colorful and textured leaves than their flower stalks. The plant and leaves can be tiny, fitting neatly into a small container, or monstrous, taking up an entire bed. The colorful leaves range from dark green to golden with some striped types. Although the foliage is the big show, the flowers shouldn't be totally discounted. The flower stalks arise later in the season with tube-shaped white- or violet-colored flowers that hummingbirds and butterflies love. Some varieties even have fragrant flowers. I like arranging them indoors as cut flowers.

When, Where, and How to Plant

Hosta is hardy throughout New England. Plant hostas in spring, summer, or fall. Purchase transplants from a local garden center or take divisions from a friend's garden. Plant hostas in a full or part shade location in well-drained, compost-amended soil. The yellow-leafed varieties tolerate part sun better than other leaf colors. Other varieties will get sunburned or the leaf colors will fade in the bright light. Space plants 6 inches to 3 feet apart, depending on the variety.

Growing Tips

Hostas like a humus-rich, moist soil. Amend the soil annually in spring with compost and keep the bed well weeded until the hostas get established. Mulch plants with bark mulch to keep the soil evenly moist and help with weed prevention.

Regional Advice and Care

Divide hostas in spring to create new plants every few years. Hostas can have problems with slugs and snails. These creatures love the shady, moist conditions hostas thrive. Control slugs and snails by cultivating regularly to dry out the area between plants, setting up beer traps, spreading iron phosphate organic bait around plants, and mulching around plants with raw sheep's wool, crushed seashells, or sharp (builder's) sand. (Gardeners in England have found the sheep's wool repels slugs.)

Companion Planting and Design

Hostas grow best with other shade lovers, such as ferns, astilbe, lungwort, and ornamental grasses. You can also plant hostas in a naturalized setting, such as a shaded woodland near a stream, to create a soft, soothing landscape.

Try These

There are so many varieties it's hard to pick only a few to highlight. Your first criteria should be leaf color and texture and plant size. 'Autumn Frost' has green-edged-in-gold leaves. 'Elegans' has striking, heart-shaped, grey-blue leaves. 'Sum and Substance' has huge, frilly green leaves that spread 3 feet tall and 5 feet wide. 'Key West' has lime green leaves. 'Bitsy' is a dwarf variety that only grows 12 inches tall with green or yellow leaves depending on the variety. 'Royal Standard' has green leaves that are more sun tolerant than other varieties and fragrant white flowers.

Iris

Iris spp. and hybrids

Botanical Pronunciation
EYE-riss

Bloom Period and Seasonal Color
Spring to early summer; black, white, blue, peach, pink, yellow, red, and purple

Mature Height × Spread
8 to 36 inches × 1 to 2 feet

The *Iris* genus is a diverse group of plants that adds color and splendor to spring and early summer gardens. This is an easy-to-grow group of plants, and there are many different species of iris that grow well throughout New England. The most common are the bearded iris (*Iris germanica*), Siberian iris (*Iris siberica*), and Japanese iris (*Iris ensata*). There are also fall-planted iris bulbs (*Iris reticulata*) that bloom in spring and are grown similar to daffodils and tulips. The perennial flower iris produces strong flower stalks with beautifully colored flowers that are standards in cottage gardens and are a good cut flower. The leaves are swordlike and flat. They remain an attraction even after the flowers fade. Some varieties even rebloom again in late summer.

When, Where, and How to Plant
Siberian and Japanese iris grow in clumps from root systems similar to other perennials. Bearded iris grows from underground rhizomes. Plant bearded iris rhizomes or Siberian and Japanese iris plants obtained from a local garden center or divisions from a gardening friend, from spring to late summer. Iris grow best in full or part sun, in well-drained, compost-amended soil. Siberian and Japanese iris grow better in wetter soil conditions than does bearded iris. Plant bearded iris rhizomes so they're barely covered with soil. Space 1 to 2 feet apart.

Growing Tips
Keep young plants well watered and mulched to keep the soil moist all summer. Fertilize each spring with compost.

Regional Advice and Care
All three of these iris types will need dividing every three to four years. Divide iris when they start flowering less and the centers of clumps start to die. Cut back the foliage to 6 inches tall in late summer. To divide Siberian and Japanese iris, dig up the entire plant, divide the clumps, and reset them in compost-amended soil. For bearded iris, dig up the rhizomes and inspect them for damage and holes. The iris borer insect causes the holes. Discard any soft, rotting rhizomes due to these holes to reduce the borer infestation. Replant in compost-amended soil, spacing the rhizomes about 1 foot apart.

Companion Planting and Design
Iris grow well in a flower border with other spring-blooming perennials such as peonies and catmint. Grow Japanese or Siberia iris in a perennial flower garden or near a pond or wet area. They grow well in moist conditions. Grow bulb iris in a rock garden or a low perennial border with other spring-flowering bulbs and perennials.

Try These
For bearded iris hybrids, try 'Beverly Sills' (peach), 'Batik' (blue and white freckled), 'Apollo' (yellow and white), and 'Edith Wolford' (blue and white). 'Immortality' is a white, reblooming bearded iris. Some nice Siberian iris varieties include 'Caesar's Brother' (blue), 'Butter and Sugar' (white and yellow), and 'Gull's Wings' (white). Some good Japanese varieties are 'Great White Heron' and 'Blue Pompom'.

Japanese Anemone

Anemone spp.

Botanical Pronunciation
an-eh-MOE-nee

Other Name
Windflower

Bloom Period and Seasonal Color
Late summer to fall; white, lavender, and pink

Mature Height × Spread
2 to 4 feet × 2 feet

Japanese anemones are the crowning glory of a late summer garden. The buttercup-like, pink, lavender, or white single or double flowers with yellow centers are held up on wiry stems. The dainty flowers dance in the breeze, hence its other common name, windflower. They're different from the bulbing anemones that bloom in spring. The perennial Japanese anemone is an autumn bloomer and a larger plant that adds color to the late summer perennial flower border and cottage garden. Japanese anemone grows well in moist soil conditions and can take part sun or part shade. I find the flower color is actually best with some afternoon shade. They will spread if they're grown under the right conditions.

When, Where, and How to Plant

Japanese anemones grow throughout our region. In colder areas consider planting them close to buildings for added winter protection. It's easiest to purchase Japanese anemones from the local garden center or get divisions from a garden friend. Plant in spring after all danger of frost has passed and until early fall in well-drained, compost-amended, humus-rich soil. Japanese anemone roots do not like to dry out, so keep the plants moist and well mulched. Space plants 1 to 2 feet apart.

Growing Tips

Japanese anemones are very forgiving of any soil type as long as it's well drained yet still stays moist. Fertilize in spring with compost and an organic plant food. Keep the plants mulched with bark mulch each season to maintain soil moisture and keep weeds away.

Regional Advice and Care

Japanese anemones can grow 4 feet tall; some double-flowered varieties may need staking to keep them from falling over. Japanese anemones spread by underground runners so they can be divided every few years to keep them inbounds and produce more plants. Dig entire clumps in early spring, divide them into fist-sized new plants, and replant in a similar soil and sun condition or give them away to friends or family. After frost has killed the plants, cut them back to the ground and compost the tops.

Companion Planting and Design

Japanese anemones are great additions to part sun gardens paired with monkshood, hosta, ornamental grasses, and bergenia. They look best when allowed to form into groups and have room to spread. Plant them where you can also enjoy butterflies landing on the blossoms. You can also grow them in open woodlands and along wet areas to naturally spread.

Try These

'Honorine Jobert' is an heirloom white variety that blooms for weeks in fall. 'Bressingham Glow' is a double, rose-pink variety. 'Whirlwind' is a white variety that only grows 2 feet tall. For a touch of lavender, try 'Kriemhilde'. 'Max Vogel' has semidouble pink flowers.

Lamb's Ears

Stachys byzantina

Botanical Pronunciation
STAY-kiss biz-un-TYE-nuh

Other Name
Woolly betony

Bloom Period and Seasonal Color
Summer; white or violet flower spikes; grown
for silvery green foliage

Mature Height × Spread
6 to 18 inches × 12 to 36 inches

There is no better way to entice a child into your flower garden than to grow lamb's ears. This low-growing perennial has soft, silvery green leaves that, when touched, remind you of a lamb's ear. Kids love to pat the plant and pick leaves to share. Lamb's ears are also favorites of adult gardeners too. This low-maintenance perennial can slowly spread to fill in the front of flower borders or creep along in rock gardens. It produces spiky white- or violet-colored flowers in midsummer that bees love. If you want just leaves, there are some new varieties that rarely bloom. Because of the leaves, lamb's ears are an attractive plant spring, summer, and fall in the garden.

When, Where, and How to Plant
Lamb's ears are hardy throughout New England. Purchase plants from your local garden center or get divisions from a friend's garden. Plant in spring, after all danger of frost has passed, to early fall in full or part sun, in well-drained, compost-amended soil. Space plants about 1 foot apart.

Growing Tips
Lamb's ears need little care once established. Amend the soil with a light layer of compost in spring and keep young plants watered. Older plants are drought tolerant. Mulch plants with a light organic mulch, such as cocoa bean hulls, to highlight the foliage.

Regional Advice and Care
Lamb's ears produce summer flowers that can be left on the plant for bees to enjoy or removed as soon as they form so the plant puts more energy into producing leaves. After three to four years, lamb's ears plants may die out in the center and need dividing. Divide in spring, removing the whole plant and separating out fist-sized divisions to replant or give away. Lamb's ears spread faster in warmer areas and may need to be divided more frequently to keep them from spreading too far. Because the leaves are close to the ground, they may brown and rot during humid, wet weather. Periodically pinch off discolored and ratty leaves to keep the plant looking tidy.

Companion Planting and Design
Lamb's ears are a nice addition to the perennial flower garden. The leaves brighten up a garden and complement blue-colored flowers, such as salvia, veronica, and catmint, particularly well. They can also be grown in an herb garden or rock garden too. Certainly if you are planting a children's garden, a clump of lamb's ears is a must.

Try These
'Silver Carpet' and 'Helen Von Stein' are two newer varieties that feature large, whitish green leaves, and they do not bloom. Nonblooming varieties don't spread as quickly. 'Striped Phantom' has variegated foliage and few flowers. 'Cotton Boll' has flower stalks with cottony flowers.

Lenten Rose

Helleborus orientalis

Botanical Pronunciation
hel-LEB-or-us or-ee-en-TAL-iss

Other Name
Christmas rose

Bloom Period and Seasonal Color
Early spring; white, rose, pink, yellow, violet, and maroon

Mature Height × Spread
12 to 24 inches × 1 to 3 feet

Lenten rose, also called just hellebore, are some of the first perennial flowers to bloom in spring, often sending up flowers in the snow. In warm climates it may bloom as early as Christmas, but in New England, it's more likely to be blooming in March or April. Its evergreen foliage looks best when it's grown in part shade. The nodding flowers form in colors, such as white, pink, and maroon, and they continue blooming into summer. Some flowers are double petaled and newer varieties have flowers that hang above the green foliage, making them easier to appreciate. This long-lived perennial doesn't spread quickly, but it does provide color to shade gardens and the evergreen foliage adds winter interest in an otherwise barren landscape.

When, Where, and How to Plant

Lenten rose are hardy throughout our region. Purchase plants from your local garden centers and plant in spring after all danger of frost has passed. Plant in a part sun or part shade location in well-drained, humus-rich soil. Lenten rose can take morning sun and still grow well but the leaves stay more vibrant-looking when they're grown in some shade. Lenten roses grow best in moist soils with a neutral pH soil. Add lime if the pH is low.

Growing Tips

Keep the soil consistently moist by watering during dry periods and adding bark mulch around plants. In spring, fertilize with a layer of compost.

Regional Advice and Care

The evergreen foliage is often ratty looking in spring after the snow melts. Snip off unsightly leaves, being careful not to remove the flower buds as the new ones start to emerge. Lenten rose rarely needs dividing, but can be moved if necessary by digging it up after flowering. Slugs and snails can enjoy the evergreen foliage. Sprinkle iron phosphate organic bait, set up beer traps, or surround the plants with sharp sand or crushed oyster shells to ward off these mollusks. Removing some of the bark mulch will also reduce their hiding places.

Companion Planting and Design

Lenten rose plants are good companions with many shade garden plants. Hostas, astilbe, lungwort, campanula, and ferns are some of the perennials that look great next to Lenten roses. Consider planting spring-flowering bulbs, such as scilla and crocus, near Lenten roses to complement their flowers.

Try These

Christmas rose (*H. niger*) is a white-flowered variety that will bloom at Christmastime in southern climates, but much later in New England. Newer varieties are noted for their tall flowers that are easier to view. 'Amethyst Gem' is a newer, double violet-red with pink edges variety; it has outstanding flowers. 'Golden Lotus' features double yellow flowers tinged in pink. 'Pink Frost' starts out pink and fades to rose.

Oriental Poppy

Papaver orientale

Botanical Pronunciation
puh-PAY-vur ore-ee-un-TAY-lee

Other Name
Compact Oriental poppy

Bloom Period and Seasonal Color
Spring to early summer; red, orange, salmon, white, and bicolors

Mature Height × Spread
2 to 4 feet × 2 feet

Oriental poppies produce large, colorful flowers early in the growing season that stand 2 to 4 feet tall perched on sturdy stems. They like our cool New England summers. The silky textured flowers can be up to 6 inches wide, making a dramatic statement when in bloom. Unlike the seed grown, smaller poppy types, such as California poppies, breadseed poppy, and Flanders poppy, the Oriental poppy is a true perennial. The mother plant returns each year and slowly expands over time to produce a larger plant and more flowers. The only downside of Oriental poppies is they die back in summer, so they are best planted in a garden with lots of other summer bloomers to fill in the gaps left by the Oriental poppy.

When, Where, and How to Plant

Oriental poppies are hardy throughout New England. You can grow Oriental poppies from seed started indoors under grow lights. These poppies resent being transplanted, so grow them in biodegradable pots that can be planted directly into the garden. An easier way to get started is to purchase plants from a local garden center and plant from early spring into early summer. Oriental poppies flower best in full or part sun in well-drained, fertile soil. Dig a good-sized hole for your transplant since it has a taproot. Amend the planting hole with compost, and space plants 1 to 2 feet apart.

Growing Tips

Oriental poppies will flower early and then the plant will die back. The plant will reemerge in late summer, but it will not flower again. Amend the soil annually in spring with compost. Even though Oriental poppies can be drought tolerant once established, keep young plants well watered.

Regional Advice and Care

Protect plants in spring from slugs and snails with beer traps, iron phosphate organic bait, and sharp (builder's) sand or crushed seashells. Cut back the foliage of the poppy plant to the ground once it starts to yellow in early summer. You can deadhead spent flowers, or leave the flowers to form seedpods that are attractive in their own right. Oriental poppies don't divide well because of their taproot. If you must move your plant, so do in fall and try to dig a deep hole to remove as much of the taproot as possible. Protect the new poppy foliage in fall with bark mulch or pine boughs.

Companion Planting and Design

Plant Oriental poppies in the middle or back of the flower border to let other flowers fill in once they die off. You can hide their withering foliage with summer-blooming perennials, such as Siberian iris, baby's breath, Russian sage, daylilies, and rudbeckia.

Try These

'Watermelon' is a dwarf, 2-foot-tall variety with salmon-pink flowers. 'Patty's Plum' has reddish purple flowers. 'Doubloon' has bright orange flowers and 'Forncett' has frilly pink petals. 'Royal Wedding' features white flowers with a dark purple center.

Ornamental Grasses

Various genera

Botanical Pronunciation
Varies

Bloom Period and Seasonal Color
Late summer and fall; brown, purple, red, and silver

Mature Height × Spread
1 to 6 feet × 1 to 3 feet

Ornamental grasses have become all the rage in landscaping circles, and there is a wide variety of these grasses that grow well in our region. The key is to select the right ones that are hardy for your area. Ornamental grasses fill many rolls in the garden. They provide a solid backdrop for more colorful perennials. They can complement other flowers and shrubs with their interesting leaf textures, colors, and flower heads. Ornamental grasses' nodding flower heads also provide beauty and movement in fall and winter to provide interest in an otherwise bleak winter landscape. Ornamental grasses provide habitat for birds and insects, making them key players in an ecologically oriented yard.

When, Where, and How to Plant
Ornamental grasses are best purchased as transplants from local garden centers in spring or obtained from a friend's garden as divisions. Plant grasses from spring to early fall in full or part sun to form the best flower heads in well-drained, compost-amended soil. Space the plants according to their growth habit, from 1 to 3 feet apart.

Growing Tips
Keep newly planted grasses well watered after planting. Once established, ornamental grasses are drought tolerant. Apply a layer of compost each spring to encourage their growth.

Regional Advice and Care
Not all types of ornamental grasses are hardy throughout New England. Also, ornamental grasses vary widely in their mature sizes and ability to spread. Ornamental grasses need little care once established. They can be divided in spring to create more plants or keep their growth inbounds. Leave the flower heads to enjoy in fall and winter and cut back ornamental grasses in early spring before new growth emerges. Some grasses will self-sow readily and volunteers should be thinned out in spring.

Companion Planting and Design
Plant ornamental grasses with other late summer- and fall-blooming perennials, such as Russian sage, rudbeckia, asters, and sedum or with evergreens and shrubs. Tall ornamental grasses, such as feather reed grass, can be grown into an informal hedge to screen an unsightly view. Mounding types, such as hakone grass, make great additions as a groundcover or edging plant.

Try These
'Karl Foerster' feather reed grass grows 5 to 6 feet tall producing purple flower heads that fade to tan. Hakone grass is only hardy in southern New England. It grows into a 2-foot-tall mound with green and yellow grass blades. Northern sea oat grass is a native grass that grows 3 to 4 feet tall with beautiful oat seedheads that turn brown in fall and are good for flower arrangements. Oat grass self-sows readily. Switch grass is another native that offers airy plumes with good fall color. Blue fescue grass, with blue foliage and tan flower heads, only grows in 1-foot-tall mounds.

Peony

Paeonia spp.

Botanical Pronunciation pay-OHN-ee-uh

Other Name Garden peony

Bloom Period and Seasonal Color
Late spring to early summer; white, coral, pink, red, yellow, and bicolors

Mature Height × Spread
3 to 4 feet × 3 feet

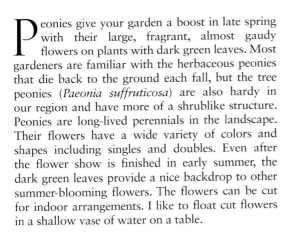

Peonies give your garden a boost in late spring with their large, fragrant, almost gaudy flowers on plants with dark green leaves. Most gardeners are familiar with the herbaceous peonies that die back to the ground each fall, but the tree peonies (*Paeonia suffruticosa*) are also hardy in our region and have more of a shrublike structure. Peonies are long-lived perennials in the landscape. Their flowers have a wide variety of colors and shapes including singles and doubles. Even after the flower show is finished in early summer, the dark green leaves provide a nice backdrop to other summer-blooming flowers. The flowers can be cut for indoor arrangements. I like to float cut flowers in a shallow vase of water on a table.

When, Where, and How to Plant
Purchase varieties in spring or fall from your local garden center or receive divisions from a friend's garden in fall. Peonies flower best in full sun in well-drained fertile soil, amended with compost. Plant so the crown is no more than a few inches below the soil line, or the peony plant may be slow to start flowering. Space plants 3 feet apart.

Growing Tips
Keep the plants well watered and mulched to prevent weed growth and keep the soil moist. Fertilize annually in spring with compost and an organic plant food.

Regional Advice and Care
Because the herbaceous peonies grow from the ground each spring, the flower stalks may need help supporting their large, heavy flowers. Use wire peony cages, chicken wire fencing, or twine tied to garden stakes to support peonies and prevent the flowers from flopping. Tree peonies don't need additional support. Peonies can be divided and moved in fall. Herbaceous peonies may not flower for a year or two after dividing and transplanting. During periods of rainy spring weather, peony flowers may be attacked by botrytis fungal blight disease, which causes the flower buds to dry and die before opening. To prevent this disease, space plants farther apart so the leaves and buds dry out faster. Spray with an organic fungicide.

Companion Planting and Design
Peonies look great planted together in their own bed. Consider mixing and matching early, mid, and late season varieties to extend the flowering. Also, pair peonies with other spring flowering perennials, such as iris, catmint, and clematis.

Try These
'Blaze' has single, bright red flowers. 'Festiva Maxima' is a fragrant white variety with just some splashes of red coloring on the petals. Fern-leaf peony (*P. tenufolia*) has double red flowers, but its calling card is its unusual, serrated, fernlike foliage on 2-foot-tall plants. 'Coral Supreme' has beautiful coral-colored double flowers. 'Sarah Bernhardt' has fluffy, double pink flowers. 'Bartzella' is one of the newer herbaceous and tree peony crosses that features rare yellow flowers.

Phlox

Phlox paniculata

Botanical Pronunciation
FLOKS pa-nik-ew-LAH-ta

Other Name
Tall garden phlox

Bloom Period and Seasonal Color
Midsummer to fall; white, red, violet, purple, and bicolors

Mature Height × Spread
3 to 4 feet × 1 to 2 feet

This tall native perennial puts on quite a summer flower show when it's planted in groups. This perennial phlox is different from the creeping phlox (*Phlox subulata*) that hugs the ground and flowers in spring. Tall garden phlox grow up to 4 feet, creating a great backdrop to other perennials. They provide color in summer and fall when many other perennial flowers are fading. The clumps will slowly spread over time filling in an area and providing an even greater color punch. The flowers are good for cutting and are fragrant. Not only are the colors enticing to us, hummingbirds and butterflies can't resist them. With their tall stature, phlox make good additions to the back of a perennial flower border.

When, Where, and How to Plant

Phlox are hardy throughout our region. Plants are readily available; purchase phlox from a local garden center or obtain divisions from a friend's garden. Plant in spring to early fall in full or part sun in well-drained, fertile soil. Amend the soil well with compost before planting because phlox grow best with high fertility. Space plants 2 feet apart.

Growing Tips

Keep plants well watered and mulch with bark mulch in spring. To prevent root rot, keep the mulch from touching the crown. Fertilize each spring with a layer of compost.

Regional Advice and Care

Phlox will spread, so divide the clumps in spring every three to four years to create more plants to replant or share, to reinvigorate the mother plant, and to keep the plant inbounds. Powdery mildew is a big disease issue on phlox in our humid New England summers. Select disease-resistant varieties, space plants farther apart to increase air circulation allowing the leaves to dry out faster, and spray with an organic fungicide as soon as any signs of the white powder or yellowing leaves is seen on the plants. Deadhead spent flowers to prolong the bloom season. Cut plants back to the ground in fall, and remove them after the flowering is finished and the leaves have yellowed.

Companion Planting and Design

Plant phlox in a perennial flower border with other fall bloomers, such as Japanese anemone, goldenrod, asters, and chrysanthemums. To produce a stronger visual effect, plant them *en masse* and just let them spread to fill in the back of a flower border or even a meadow.

Try These

'David' was one of the first mildew-resistant varieties on the market and this white-flowered variety is still one of the best. 'Laura' is a purple-flowered, mildew-resistant variety that has a white flower center. 'Volcano Purple' is a disease-resistant, compact 2-foot-tall selection. 'Bright Eyes' is a pink variety with red centers. 'Franz Schubert' is an old-fashioned lilac variety. 'Starfire' is cherry red.

Pinks

Dianthus spp. and hybrids

Botanical Pronunciation
dye-AN-thus

Other Name
Cottage pinks

Bloom Period and Seasonal Color
Spring to early fall; red, pink, white, and rose

Mature Height × Spread
6 to 24 inches × 8 to 12 inches

While there are annual and biennial versions of pinks, such as sweet William and carnations, the perennial species of pinks is hardy in New England and makes an excellent low-growing, blooming flower for gardens and containers. Pinks will start blooming during the cool days of spring and continue off and on into early fall. The spiky, blue-green leaves are topped with delicate, spicy, clove-scented single or double flowers, usually in the pink, red, or white color range. Some of the flowers have contrasting colored eyes, increasing its visual appeal. Old-fashioned varieties are more fragrant than modern hybrids. I like growing them as edging plants in front of a garden and in a cut flower garden since they make good additions to flower arrangements.

When, Where, and How to Plant
Pinks are hardy throughout New England. Start pinks from seed sown indoors under grow lights 6 to 8 weeks before your last frost date. Seeds can also be sown directly in the garden in spring, but they probably won't bloom the first year. It's easiest to purchase transplants from a local garden center or plant divisions from a friend's garden. The best time to plant is from spring to early fall in a full or part sun location in well-drained soil. Consider planting in raised beds if you have clay soil to help with water drainage. In warmer parts of our region, plant pinks where they will get afternoon shade to keep them in bloom throughout the summer. Space plants 6 to 12 inches apart.

Growing Tips
Pinks grow best in cool, moist conditions, but once established, they're tolerant of drought. They like a slightly alkaline soil so keep the pH close to 7 by adding lime, based on a soil test. Fertilize in spring with a layer of compost and add mulch to reduce weed competition.

Regional Advice and Care
Create more pinks by dividing the clumps in spring. This also will rejuvenate older plants that may not be flowering as well. Dig up the whole clump, separate it into wedge-sized divisions, add compost, replant in a new location, and water well. Deadhead spent flowers to encourage more blooms. Pinks will self-sow, so weed out unwanted seedlings in spring so they don't get overcrowded.

Companion Planting and Design
Grow pinks in a cottage garden with other plants of similar stature, such as low-growing roses, lavender, lamb's ears, and geraniums. They also grow well in containers, but the container must be moved to a protected spot in winter, such as a basement or garage. Grow pinks in a rock garden or along the edge of a low-growing shrub or flower border too.

Try These
'Birmingham' is a long-stemmed, double-flowered white variety. 'Pomegranate Kiss' and 'Fire Star' are frilly petaled, bright red varieties. 'Purpleton' has double flowered, pinkish purple blooms.

Russian Sage

Perovskia atriplicifolia

Botanical Pronunciation
pe-ROF-ski-a a-tri-pli-si-FO-li-a

Other Name
Azure sage

Bloom Period and Seasonal Color
Midsummer to fall; light blue and lavender blue

Mature Height × Spread
1 to 4 feet × 1 to 3 feet

Russian sage has become one of the new darlings for low-maintenance perennial gardens. The tall airy plant has fragrant, grey-green foliage reminiscent of Western sagebrush, with spiky lavender-blue flowers. The most outstanding feature of this perennial is its carefree nature. You really can plant it and forget about it. It tolerates dry conditions and below average soil fertility, attracts butterflies, and isn't bothered by insects or animals. Since it blooms from summer to fall it adds great foliage and flower color to the garden when few other flowers are blooming. It's equally valuable grown *en masse*, looking like a purple haze in the garden when in bloom, to being grown near other brightly colored annual and perennial flowers.

When, Where, and How to Plant

Russian sage grows throughout our region. You can start plants from seed, but it's easier, and more likely to flower the first year, if you purchase transplants from a local garden center or plant divisions from a friend's garden. Plant Russian sage from spring to early fall, spacing plants 2 to 3 feet apart. Russian sage likes full sun and tolerates almost any soil conditions as long as the soil is well drained.

Growing Tips

Keep first-year plants well watered. Once established, Russian sage is drought tolerant. A light layer of compost in spring is all that's required for fertilization.

Regional Advice and Care

Russian sage tolerates alkaline soil and salty, windy conditions. It's a good choice to grow near the ocean. Russian sage can tend to flop as the stems get long. To prevent flopping, grow shorter varieties, stake or cage your plants, or pinch back the growing tips when the plant is 1 foot tall. Divide plants every three to four years to encourage better flowering. Dig up the whole clump of Russian sage in spring, divide it into wedge-sized pieces, and replant in a location with similar growing conditions. Deadhead spent flowers to encourage more blooming into fall. The flower heads also look attractive when left to dry on the plant to provide winter interest in the garden.

Companion Planting and Design

Russian sage grows well in a sunny flower border next to other grey-green foliage plants, such as lamb's ears and artemisia. The plant can grow a bit rangy so don't plant it in a formal border. The soft foliage and blue flowers contrast well with bolder-colored yellow and orange flowers, such as coreopsis and daylilies. Plant Russian sage near rock walls or as a backdrop in rock gardens since it enjoys well-drained soils.

Try These

'Blue Mist' has pale blue-colored flowers. 'Longin' grows more upright and is less likely to flop over. 'Little Spire' only grows 2 feet tall. 'Filigran' has more dissected leaves with an even airier appearance than the species form.

Salvia

Salvia spp.

Botanical Pronunciation
SAL-via

Other Name
Garden sage

Bloom Period and Seasonal Color
Summer; blue, purple, rose, and white

Mature Height × Spread
1 to 3 feet × 1 to 2 feet

Plants in the *Salvia* genus include a broad group of annual and perennial plants that are mainstays in the flower garden. While most gardeners are familiar with annual salvias (I cover those in the annuals chapter of this book), there are perennial salvias as well. Some of these perennials are hardy throughout our region, and some are even native to North America. Perennial salvias are upright plants that produce colorful flower spikes from summer into fall. Although not as floriferous as the annual versions, varieties of perennial salvia make a statement in the garden, especially when grown in groups. The culinary herb of sage is also in this family. Some of these have attractive flowers and foliage to make nice additions as edible landscape plants in the garden.

When, Where, and How to Plant

Select salvias hardy for your area. You can start salvia from seed sown indoors under grow lights about 6 to 8 weeks before your last frost date. You can also purchase salvia transplants from local garden centers or obtain divisions from a friend's garden. Plant from spring to early fall in full or part sun, in well-drained, fertile, compost-amended soil. Spacing is 1 to 2 feet apart.

Growing Tips

Salvia roots don't like to dry out, so water salvia deeply to promote deep root growth. Mulch salvias annually to maintain the soil moisture conditions to prevent weed growth. Fertilize in spring with compost and a small handful of an organic plant food.

Regional Advice and Care

Keep plants deadheaded to encourage more flowering throughout the summer. Once the plants get large, divide salvia in spring, digging up the whole clump and separating some wedge-sized sections to replant or give away. For marginally hardy salvias, mulch the plants in late fall with bark mulch to protect them in winter. Cut back all salvias to the ground in fall after a frost.

Companion Planting and Design

Combine perennial salvias with a variety of low-growing, summer-flowering perennials, such as yarrow, catmint, sedum, rudbeckia, coreopsis, and daisies. For the best visual display, plant salvia in groups of at least three plants. You can also plant salvias in containers, but they will need to be protected in a warm location, such as a basement or garage, in winter.

Try These

Look for varieties that are hardy in your area. A popular USDA zone 4 hardy species is *Salvia nemorosa*. It has many hardy varieties to choose from, such as 'May Night', with its deep blue-violet flowers. 'East Friesland' has deep purple flowers on compact 1-foot-tall plants. 'Rose Queen' has rose-colored flowers and "Snow Hill" features white flowers. 'Tricolor' is a variety of *Salvia officinalis* or culinary sage. It features yellow, green, and red leaves. *Salvia verticillata* features 'Purple Rain' and 'White Rain' with 2- to 3-foot-tall plants with vivid flowers.

Scabiosa

Scabiosa columbaria

Botanical Pronunciation
scab-ee-OH-suh coh-lum-BARE-ee-yah

Other Name
Pincushion flower

Bloom Period and Seasonal Color
Late spring to fall; white, blue, and pink

Mature Height × Spread
12 to 18 inches × 12 to 16 inches

This low-growing perennial is called the pincushion flower for good reason. The round, colorful flowers are shaped like small cushions with pins sticking out. The flowers start opening in late spring and continue blooming, off and on, until fall. They really like the cooler weather, so in the hot parts of our region they may stop blooming in midsummer. But don't give up on them because they will start flowering again in early fall. In cooler regions, they may flower all summer. The plants have ferny foliage and wiry stems that produce the flowers. The flowers are a magnet for butterflies and bees and can be cut and used in flower arrangements as well. The scabiosa seedpods are also attractive when used in arrangements.

When, Where, and How to Plant

Scabiosa is hardy throughout New England. Plant seeds indoors under grow lights 4 to 6 weeks before your last frost date. You can also direct sow seed in the garden after all danger of frost has passed, but they may not flower until late in the summer. For growing just a few plants, purchase transplants from a local garden center. Plant scabiosa from spring to summer in full or part sun in well-drained soil. Wet clay soil may stop scabiosa from overwintering well. Space transplants or thin seedlings 12 to 18 inches apart.

Growing Tips

Keep scabiosa well watered the first year. Older plants are more drought tolerant. Fertilize in spring with a small handful of an organic plant food.

Regional Advice and Care

Scabiosa will self-sow and create groups of seedlings in spring. Thin these seedlings to the proper spacing if you want to save them. Scabiosa has few insect and disease problems. Spray insecticidal soap on aphids feeding on new growth in spring. Plants can be divided every three to four years to produce new transplants to grow and share. Deadhead plants to encourage more flowering. In cold parts of our region, cover plants with bark mulch or pine boughs to protect them from the winter's cold.

Companion Planting and Design

Scabiosa can grow in a perennial flower border, cottage garden, rock garden, or wildflower meadow. This diverse plant looks great grouped together to form a mass of pincushion flowers or paired with other low-growing, cottage garden plants, such as alyssum, salvias, sedum, and low-growing roses. Let them naturalize in a wildflower meadow or grow scabiosa in a rock garden with columbine and pinks. Their interesting wiry flowers and foliage makes for a conversation piece.

Try These

'Butterfly Blue' has lavender-blue, 2-inch-diameter flowers on 12-inch-long stems. 'Pink Mist' is a pink version of 'Butterfly Blue'. 'Black Knight' produces dark-burgundy-colored flowers. 'Fama White' and 'Fama Blue' produce good cut flower blooms on plants that bloom quickly from direct sowing.

Sedum

Sedum spp. and hybrids

Botanical Pronunciation
SEE-dum

Other Name
Stonecrop

Bloom Period and Seasonal Color
Midsummer into fall; pink, red, white, and yellow

Mature Height × Spread
4 to 24 inches × 1 to 2 feet

Sedums are a versatile group of plants. Some are low-growing groundcovers while other sedums grow taller, making them good companions in the flower border. All sedums have fleshy leaves and colorful flowers that look good even after they're past their prime. The fleshy leaves hold moisture, which makes this an excellent plant for dry areas, and some varieties have attractive foliage as well. While the creeping forms will spread and form a low-growing mat of foliage over time, tall garden sedums are more clump forming and stand up well next to tall garden perennials for a late summer flower show. I often leave my tall sedums in the garden well after they have finished flowering because the dried flowers still look attractive.

When, Where, and How to Plant
Sedums are hardy throughout New England. Plant locally purchased transplants or divisions from a friend's garden from spring to early fall in full or part sun in well-drained soil. Sedum plants grow best with a neutral to slightly alkaline pH. Space creeping varieties 6 inches to 1 foot apart and tall varieties 1 to 2 feet apart.

Growing Tips
Keep young plants well watered. Older plants are drought tolerant. Sedums don't need highly fertile soils to grow well but you can add a light layer of compost each spring.

Regional Advice and Care
Tall sedums may get leggy and flop over, especially if they're grown in a part sun location. Cage plants to keep them upright, or pinch new growth in spring to promote more branching and shorter plants. Divide tall sedums every few years once the center of the clump starts to die out. Dig clumps in spring, divide into wedge-shaped sections, and replant in a similar location or give plants away. Since the dried flower heads are equally as attractive as the flower head in full bloom, don't deadhead sedums. After a freeze, cut the whole plant back to the ground and compost the tops.

Companion Planting and Design
Creeping sedum varieties grow best in rock gardens or along a flower border. Pair them with other low-growing flowers, such as alyssum. Tall garden sedum varieties grow well with other summer bloomers, such as coneflowers, rudbeckia, and Russian sage.

Try These
'Autumn Joy' is the best-known tall sedum. It has pink flower buds opening to a copper color on a hardy 2-foot-tall plant. 'Elsie Gold' is similar to 'Autumn Joy', but has cream-colored leaf edges. 'Maestro' has beautiful mauve-colored flowers and burgundy-colored leaves that make this an attractive perennial even when it's not in bloom. 'Cloud Nine' has variegated leaves. For low-growing varieties, 'Vera Jamison' grows less than 1 foot tall; it has pink flowers and dark foliage. *Sedum kamtschaticum* is a creeping species whose pink flower buds open to yellow flowers. There is a variegated leaf version as well.

Shasta Daisy

Leucanthemum superbum

Botanical Pronunciation
lew-KAN-thee-mum sue-PER-bum

Bloom Period and Seasonal Color
Early to late summer; white

Mature Height × Spread
1 to 3 feet × 2 feet

Daisies are one of the easiest flowers to grow in the landscape. The wild or oxeye daisy is a common flower in New England wildflower mixes and is often seen in meadows and abandoned fields in our region. An improved version of the wild daisy, the Shasta daisy features larger flowers and is a more stately plant. Shasta daisies have become popular perennial flower border plants because of the long bloom time of the white flowers with a yellow eye and their tolerance to dry soils. I often have my Shasta daisies blooming twice during a growing season, especially if I deadhead them regularly. Shasta daisies make great cut flowers, and bees and butterflies love to visit the flowers.

When, Where, and How to Plant
Most varieties of Shasta daisies are hardy to zone 5. With some protection in winter they can survive colder zones in our region. If you have problems getting your Shasta daisy plant to survive the winter, look for hardy varieties, such as 'Alaska', or consider growing the more cold-tolerant oxeye daisy. While you can sow seeds indoors under grow lights to transplant into the garden, it's easier to plant locally purchased transplants or divide some in spring from a friend's garden. Plant Shasta daisies in spring to early fall. Space plants 1 to 2 feet apart in a full sun location in well-drained, fertile soil.

Growing Tips
Apply a layer of compost in spring around the plants for fertilizer. Keep young plants well watered. Once established, Shasta daisies are drought tolerant, so they require little additional water.

Regional Advice and Care
Every three to four years when the center of the clump starts to die out, divide Shasta daisy plants in spring. Dig up the whole clump and separate wedge-shaped divisions to be replanted elsewhere in the garden or given away. Most modern varieties have strong stems and don't need staking to keep the plants from flopping over. However, if plants are grown in part sun, the stems may be weaker and will need some support. Deadhead spent flowers, cutting back the stems to the first set of leaves, once the flowers start to fade to encourage more blooms throughout the summer.

Companion Planting and Design
Shasta daisies grow well with other tall, summer-blooming perennials, such as coneflowers, rudbeckia, bee balm, and Joe-pye weed. Shasta daisies are a more formal addition to the wildflower meadow. Consider planting Shasta daisies in a cutting garden for use in flower arrangements.

Try These
'Becky' is a widely popular, 3-foot-tall Shasta daisy variety with strong, straight stems. 'Alaska' also grows 3 feet tall with large, 6-inch-wide flowers. 'Snow Lady' is a long-blooming dwarf variety. 'Crazy Daisy' has frilly, white flower petals. 'Cobham Gold' is a double-flowered variety that grows to 2 feet tall.

Tickseed

Coreopsis spp.

Botanical Pronunciation
cor-ee-OP-sis

Other Name
Coreopsis

Bloom Period and Seasonal Color
Early to late summer; yellow, pink, and red

Mature Height × Spread
1 to 2 feet × 1 to 2 feet

Tickseed is a common native perennial flower that tolerates a wide range of sun and soil conditions. There are many newer varieties of tickseed with a wide range of flower colors, such as pink, red, and bicolors, but these tend not to be as consistently hardy in all parts of our region. Tickseed leaves vary in shape from lobed to thin and threadlike, depending on the variety. The plant produces small, single or semidouble, daisylike flowers in summer. The flowers of some varieties are good for cutting. Since they grow in less than fertile soil conditions as long as the soil is well drained, tickseed ranks with daylilies as one of the easiest perennial flowers to grow.

When, Where, and How to Plant
While many species of tickseed are hardy throughout New England, some species will be only short-lived. Plant seeds indoors under grow lights 6 to 8 weeks before your last frost date and transplant outdoors after all danger of frost has passed. You can also purchase transplants from the local garden center or obtain divisions from a friend's garden. Plant from spring to early fall in a full or part sun location in well-drained soil. Space them 1 foot apart.

Growing Tips
Water new plants well. Once established, tickseed needs little care and is drought tolerant. Mulch plants with bark mulch to keep the soil moist and the weeds away.

Regional Advice and Care
During periods of wet summer weather, the soil must be well drained or the plant can develop crown rot. Tickseed can self-sow readily. Weed out self-sown seedlings in spring. Taller varieties can tend to sprawl and may need support to keep from flopping over. Generally tickseed doesn't have problems with insects and diseases. Divide plants every three to four years to rejuvenate the mother plant and produce more transplants for planting elsewhere in the garden or giving away. Cut back the plants to the ground in fall after a frost.

Companion Planting and Design
Plant tickseed flowers with coneflowers, blazing star, rudbeckia, and gaillardia. Grow taller varieties in meadows and wildflower plantings. Tickseed is a favorite of butterflies. Plant some close to the house or deck to enjoy the butterflies.

Try These
'Moonbeam' is a popular, pale yellow variety that only grows 1 foot tall with small, fernlike leaves. 'Creme Brulee' is similar looking to 'Moonbeam', but is a more vigorous growing plant. 'Early Sunrise' grows 16 to 20 inches tall and has semidouble flowers. However, it can be short-lived in our climate. 'Flying Saucers' has sterile yellow flowers that won't self-sow. It's a stronger plant, returns more reliably each year, and won't spread as much as other varieties. 'American Dream' is a pink variety that grows 8 to 16 inches tall, but may need protection in colder parts of our climate.

Veronica

Veronica spp. and hybrids

Botanical Pronunciation
ver-RON-ni-ka

Other Name
Speedwell

Bloom Period and Seasonal Color
Early to late summer; white, blue, violet, and pink

Mature Height × Spread
6 to 36 inches × 12 to 24 inches

Veronica is a standard cottage garden flower that is best known for its spires of blue, white, or pink flowers that bloom for many months in summer. Many gardeners believe the blue varieties produce some of the truest blues of any flower in the perennial garden. But veronica is more than just a traditional, spiky, English cottage garden perennial. Low-growing varieties make excellent groundcovers, and some have cup-shaped flowers. Butterflies and hummingbirds are attracted to all veronica flowers, and the blooms of tall varieties also make great cut flowers. The tall varieties of veronica grow in clumps, so they are well behaved in the flower garden, while groundcovers will spread and fill in an area.

When, Where, and How to Plant
Most varieties of veronica are hardy throughout our region. Check the hardiness zone before planting your varieties. Purchase plants from a local garden center or ask a friend for some divisions from their garden. Plant from spring to early fall in a full or part sun location in well-drained soil. Plants will be smaller and less floriferous when they're grown in part sun. Space plants 1 to 2 feet apart, depending on the size of the variety.

Growing Tips
Keep young plants well watered. Once established, older plants are somewhat drought tolerant. Veronica doesn't need any special fertilization other than a light layer of compost in spring.

Regional Advice and Care
Deadhead spent blossoms to encourage more blooms and extend the flowering time. When deadheading, cut back the flower head to a side branch to create a sturdier stem. Divide veronica in spring every few years to rejuvenate the plants and to produce new plants to replant elsewhere or give away. Cut back the plants to the ground in fall after a frost and compost the tops. Veronica can get powdery mildew disease if crowded or grown during humid summers. If powdery mildew is a problem, space plants farther apart or spray with an organic fungicide.

Companion Planting and Design
Grow tall varieties of veronica with other cottage garden plants, such as salvia, coreopsis, and sedum. Grow creeping varieties in the front of a perennial flower border or in a rock garden to cascade over a wall.

Try These
For taller varieties, try 'Sunny Border Blue', which has dark violet-blue flowers and grows 20 inches tall. 'Royal Candles' produces dark blue flowers on disease-resistant plants. 'White Icicles' is a white-flowered, spiky variety. 'Red Fox' has pink flowers. 'Crater Lake Blue' is a creeping variety that grows less than 12 inches tall with spikes of cup-shaped, blue flowers. 'Georgia Blue' is another creeping variety with cup-shaped flowers and white centers. 'Georgia Blue' may need winter protection in colder parts of our region.

Yarrow

Achillea spp. and hybrids

Botanical Pronunciation
ack-ih-LEE-uh

Other Name
Common yarrow

Bloom Period and Seasonal Color
Early to late summer; yellow, gold, red, rose, salmon, and white

Mature Height × Spread
6 inches to 3 feet × 2 to 3 feet

Yarrow is a commonly grown native perennial that has soft, fernlike foliage and flat clusters of colorful flowers that bloom on and off all summer. Yarrow is a common wildflower plant, but it also looks great in perennial flower borders. Low-growing varieties make great edging and groundcover plants. Yarrow is a clump-forming plant, but does spread by underground rhizomes. Care should be given where it's planted so it doesn't become invasive. Its aromatic flowers attract butterflies and beneficial insects that help keep a good ecological balance in the garden. Yarrow is good for cutting and drying for flower arrangements. Once established, yarrow is salt-spray tolerant, so is a good seaside plant.

When, Where, and How to Plant
Yarrow is hardy throughout our region. Sow seeds indoors under grow lights 8 to 10 weeks before your last frost. You can also sow seeds directly in the garden, but the plants may not fill out and flower well until their second year. For small plantings, consider purchasing transplants from a local garden center or ask for divisions from a friend's garden. Plant from spring to early fall in full sun in well-drained soil. Yarrow is tolerant of poor fertility soils. Space plants 1 to 2 feet apart.

Growing Tips
Yarrow is drought tolerant so only newly planted transplants or seedlings need water to get established. Yarrow needs little additional fertilizer once established; just spread a light layer of compost on plants in spring.

Regional Advice and Care
Deadhead spent flower heads starting in early summer to promote more flowering the rest of the summer. Cut back plants by one-half to stimulate new shoots and blooms. Thin spreading plants in spring to keep them from becoming invasive. Divide these plants and replant in a new location or give them away. Cut plants to the ground in fall after a frost and compost the foliage. Space plants farther apart or spray with an organic fungicide if powdery mildew is a problem.

Companion Planting and Design
Pair tall yarrow varieties with summer-blooming perennial flowers, such as balloon flowers, daylilies, and lavender. Grow low-growing varieties in rock gardens and as an edging plant along a wall or in front of a flower border. Of course, yarrow is a standard in many wildflower mixes and spreads quickly throughout an untended area.

Try These
Some good tall-growing varieties include 'Moonshine', with its soft yellow flowers. 'Paprika' has bright orange-red flowers whose color deepens as they age. 'Coronation Gold' is a popular golden variety that's widely adapted. 'Pearl' is an unusual white variety with double, buttonlike, white pom-pom flowers and lance-shaped leaves. A good low-growing variety is woolly yarrow (*A. tomentosa*) with yellow flowers that only grows 6 inches tall.

PERENNIAL VINES

FOR NEW ENGLAND

Perennial vines can be a blessing. They're fast growers that can cover an unsightly fence, wall, or building quickly. They make a perfect shade covering for your arbor or pergola. Some perennial vines, such as clematis and wisteria, have amazing flowers. And these flowers often have a sweet scent that turns your yard into a perfume factory when the vines are in bloom. Some vines are grown mostly for their fall foliage. There's nothing more stately than a Boston ivy vine with its red fall leaves creeping up the outside of a historic brick or stone building. Still others are grown for their evergreen leaves that add interest even in winter. Winter creeper vines can be used to block unsightly views or add a green backdrop to a garden.

Virginia creeper

Know Your Vine

The first step to deciding which perennial vine to grow is to understand its growth habit. Some vines, such as Boston ivy and Virginia creeper, can cover huge walls over time. Other strong climbers, such as wisteria, can scale trees and swallow houses whole! Well, maybe that's an exaggeration, but I did see a wisteria vine in full flower one spring in Philadelphia that was topping a 50-foot-high telephone pole. If you have a large wall or structure to cover and it's sturdy enough to support this kind of growth, these vines are worth trying. While we mostly think of perennial vines growing up, you can also grow Virginia creeper and winter creeper to crawl along the ground, cover a bank, or cascade over a stone wall.

Some perennial vines are tamer, comparatively, in their growth. Clematis can get large, depending on your selection, but many types are perfectly fine growing on a small arbor, trellis, or in among, other shrubs. The beauty of clematis is you can grow small- or large-flowered types and some that bloom in spring, summer, or even early fall. All types have interesting seedpods that add even more interest to this vine.

Different Types of Climbing

Once you've decided where it will grow and how large a vine you need, you'll need to know something about how it climbs. Some climbers, such as climbing hydrangea, Boston ivy, and Virginia creeper, have suction cup-like holdfasts on their branches that attach themselves to stone, wood, vinyl, or whatever material they're growing on. This makes it easy for them to climb and quickly become a visual statement in your yard. It also can be a curse. If you ever need

Clematis 'Madame Julia Correvon'

to paint or replace wooden siding, these holdfasts are hard to remove. Plus, they trap moisture next to the wood and vinyl, making rot and mold more likely. It's best to grow this type of vine on a wooden structure away from the building or against brick or stone structures.

Another type of vine twines to climb. Wisteria, climbing honeysuckle, and clematis wrap themselves around poles, fences, or trellises to grow vertically. You'll need strong structures to support their growth and places for them to attach. It's hard for them to climb up large pillars or flat smooth surfaces.

Some vines, such as trumpet vine, are just big and gangly, not really attaching themselves to any support. They need to the tied to a fence, trellis, or pergola to grow properly.

While most perennial vines grow and flower best in full sun, some, such as climbing hydrangea and winter creeper, are good choices for partly shaded areas to provide a screen. You'll have to be bold about using your pruners. Many of these vines not only need to be tamed in their growth every year, but actually flower better because of it.

Whatever perennial vine you grow, make sure the soil stays consistently cool and moist, has good fertility to grow, and has the right structure for the vine to grow on. Perennial vines are long-term propositions, which, if grown right, can be magnificent landscape features for years to come.

Boston Ivy

Parthenocissus tricuspidata

Botanical Pronunciation
par-the-no-SIS-us tri-kus-pi-DAY-ta

Other Name
Wall ivy

Bloom Period and Seasonal Color
Insignificant blooms; grown for bright red fall foliage

Mature Height × Spread
Up to 50 feet × 5 to 10 feet

This vigorous perennial vine is commonly found on the walls of brick buildings throughout New England. The "Ivy League" refers to the Boston ivy vines often found on buildings at Harvard, Yale, and Dartmouth colleges. The vines can eventually cover walls adhering to wood, wire, masonry, and stone with their sucker discs or holdfasts. They don't need any other support. The green vines produce insignificant flowers in early summer followed by black berries that birds enjoy. However, it's the fall color that is most important. The leaves turn red, orange, purple, or yellow, brightening up entire buildings with an autumn show. This deciduous vine can also be used as a groundcover to provide erosion control on slopes.

When, Where, and How to Plant
Boston ivy is hardy throughout our region. Plant vines purchased from a local garden center from spring to early fall in a part sun location for the best fall color. Boston ivy grows best in well-drained, loamy soils. To prevent leaf scorch in warmer areas, plant on an east-facing wall. Space plants 5 to 10 feet apart.

Growing Tips
Boston ivy should be well watered when planted, but is drought tolerant once established. Mulch to conserve soil moisture and prevent weed growth. Boston ivy doesn't need additional fertilization.

Regional Advice and Care
Control its growth by pruning in spring to reduce size. Prune to keep the ivy from clogging roof gutters and getting under and lifting up roof shingles. Boston ivy can become invasive, so dig out any self-sown vines or vines that root on the ground along the stems. Powdery mildew and leaf spot may form during wet summers; control by cleaning up leaves in fall and spraying with an organic fungicide. Scale insects are sometimes a problem and can be controlled with horticultural oil sprays.

Companion Planting and Design
If you're planting Boston ivy on a wall, be certain you want it as a permanent fixture. Once established and clinging to the wall, it is difficult to remove. Also, it's best to grow it up stone walls, chain-link fences, or masonry walls. Wooden walls will be hard to paint and may develop mold and rot due to Boston ivy's foliage holding moisture against the wood. Boston ivy is salt-spray tolerant so it's a good choice for coastal homes. Boston ivy can also be used to creep along a bank or waste area to provide some erosion cover and color.

Try These
'Veitchii' has small purplish leaves with deep serrations. 'Purpurea' has reddish purple leaves that turn bright red in fall. 'Fenway Park' is named after the famous baseball park in Boston close to where it was discovered. It features yellow leaves that turn green then a combination of red, orange, and yellow fall leaves.

Clematis

Clematis spp. and hybrids

Botanical Pronunciation
KLEM-uh-tiss

Other Name
Virgin's bower

Bloom Period and Seasonal Color
Spring to fall; white, pink, blue, red, yellow, and bicolors

Mature Height × Spread
6 to 20 feet × 2 to 5 feet

This romantic, fast-growing vine comes in a wide variety of flower colors, shapes, and sizes. Depending on the variety, you can have clematis blooming from spring to fall. The flowers can be small and delicate to large and gaudy-colored. I enjoy the seedpods, with their whorl of feathery tails, almost as much as the flowers. While it needs support to grow, clematis isn't choosy about scrambling over walls, up fences and trellises, or into shrubs, trees, and other perennials. Some varieties are quite tame in the landscape, while others can become large enough to serve as a screen or cover an unsightly object. The flowers are favorites of bees and butterflies, adding to the color and activity around these vines.

When, Where, and How to Plant

Many clematis species and varieties are hardy throughout New England. Purchase vines hardy for your area from a local garden center and plant in spring or summer. Most clematis varieties flower best in full sun. However, their roots like shaded, moist, well-drained, compost-amended soil conditions. Space plants 1 to 2 feet apart.

Growing Tips

Keep clematis roots consistently moist with a layer of bark mulch around their base. However, don't pile the mulch around the stems or it might lead to stem rot. Fertilize in spring with a layer of compost and monthly with an organic plant food.

Regional Advice and Care

Prune clematis varieties annually so they look and flower their best. How and when you prune depends on the type you are growing. Check with your local garden centers about specific instructions for pruning your clematis. Always deadhead clematis to promote more flowering later in the season, unless you want to enjoy the seedpods. Remove dead, broken, or diseased stems anytime. Provide a support structure, such as a trellis, arbor, or pole, for clematis to grow upon.

Companion Planting and Design

Clematis can be grown in many locations. Grow them up a trellis, arbor, or lamppost in the yard. Plant alongside a chain-link fence to make it more attractive. Plant clematis among shrubs, such as forsythia and lilacs, or other perennials, such as peonies, to provide flowers in summer when these plants aren't blooming. Plant clematis among roses to provide complementary colored flowers.

Try These

'Nelly Moser' is a large, pink- and white-pinwheel-flowered variety that grows well in full sun and part shade. It blooms in early summer and repeats blooms in fall. 'Henryi' produces large, white flowers and blooms from summer to fall. 'Niobe' produces large, red flowers and blooms from early to late summer. Sweet autumn clematis is an aggressive vine (take note) that will cascade over a pergola or arbor. It produces small, fragrant white flowers in fall. 'Patricia Ann Fretwell' has unusual double, frilly pink flowers. 'Blue Bell' has nodding, deep purple flowers that bloom from midsummer to fall.

Climbing Hydrangea

Hydrangea anomala petiolaris

Botanical Pronunciation
hye-DRAYN-jee-uh an-NOM-al-a pet-ee-ol-LAY-riss

Bloom Period and Seasonal Color
Spring to early summer; white

Mature Height × Spread
30 to 50 feet × 5 to 8 feet

This strong, woody deciduous vine has beautiful dark green, glossy leaves and large, white, flat flowers in early summer. Unlike many other vines, climbing hydrangea can flower in part shade. Like ivy, it attaches itself using holdfasts or small rootlets to a wall, fence, or building and can climb up to 50 feet tall. Climbing hydrangea can be a slow-growing vine at first, but once established it will take off and provide many years of beauty. Climbing hydrangea needs a strong structure to climb on or up. It can enliven the corner of a house or a north wall with its vigorous growth. An added attraction is the cinnamon-colored, exfoliating bark that adds interest in winter.

When, Where, and How to Plant

Climbing hydrangea is hardy to zone 5 and may need protection in colder parts of our region. Purchase plants from a local garden center in spring and plant after all danger of frost has passed. You can also plant in summer as long as the plant stays well watered. Plant in a full sun (cooler areas) to partly shaded location in well-drained, rich soil amended with compost. Avoid hot, dry locations. Climbing hydrangea will flower best with sun and will flower less in shade. Space plants 5 to 10 feet apart.

Growing Tips

Keep the soil around climbing hydrangea evenly moist with regular waterings and a layer of bark mulch. Fertilize in spring with a layer of compost and a small handful of an organic plant food.

Regional Advice and Care

Like Boston ivy, climbing hydrangea should be planted against a stone, brick, or masonry wall or against a wooden wall that is rot-resistant and which you won't have to paint. When grown against vinyl or common wood siding, the holdfasts will leave marks, and rot and mold can develop on the siding. If growing on a wooden or metal trellis near a building, place the trellis at least 3 feet from the structure. Prune climbing hydrangea after flowering to keep the growth inbounds. It is not as aggressive a spreader as the ivies. Be patient with the growth. Climbing hydrangea will often take three to five years to reach the flowering stage. As the old adage says about perennial vines, "first they sleep, then they creep, then they leap." There are no significant pests of climbing hydrangea, except deer.

Companion Planting and Design

Plant climbing hydrangea along a wall, building, or fence where it can become a permanent fixture. It's perfect for a forgotten north or east wall along a garage or the side of the house. Climbing hydrangea can also grow up trees, pergolas, and arbors. Just make sure the structures are strong enough to support the weight.

Try These

Most garden centers carry the white-flowered, green-leaved species. 'Miranda' is a variegated leaf variety with cream-and-green foliage and white flowers.

Climbing Honeysuckle

Lonicera sempervirens

Botanical Pronunciation
lon-ISS-er-a sem-per-VEYE-renz

Other Name
Trumpet honeysuckle

Bloom Period and Seasonal Color
Early to midsummer; red, orange, and yellow

Mature Height × Spread
10 to 20 feet × 3 to 6 feet

This climbing version of the widely grown native honeysuckle has the beauty and toughness of the bush honeysuckles, but with a climbing habit that makes it a great plant for pergolas, arbors, and walls. The small flowers often have two colors in one flower and bloom in early summer. They will repeat bloom throughout the growing season, especially if the plant is deadheaded. Some species of climbing honeysuckle are fragrant too. The small red fruit that emerge after flowering are favorites of birds. However, unlike Japanese honeysuckle (*L. japonica*), this vine isn't invasive. This fast-growing, twining vine is deciduous in our climate, but it's an evergreen in warmer locations of the country. It's an attractive plant for bees, butterflies, and hummingbirds as well.

When, Where, and How to Plant
Climbing honeysuckle is hardy in our region. Purchase plants from a local garden center in spring and plant after all danger of frost has passed right into early fall. Although climbing honeysuckle will grow and flower in part shade, the more sun the vine has, the more flowers you'll get. Plant these vines in well-drained, compost-amended soil. Space plants 3 to 5 feet apart.

Growing Tips
Keep climbing honeysuckle plants well watered and mulched with bark mulch to keep the soil consistently moist and to keep weeds away. Add a layer of compost and an organic plant food for fertilizer each spring.

Regional Advice and Care
Prune climbing honeysuckle after blooming to keep it inbounds and looking attractive. Climbing honeysuckle leaves can get ratty looking by midsummer, especially under hot, dry conditions and from insect and disease attacks. Plant in part sun and keep the vine well watered to prevent the leaves from dying back. Reduce the number of insects feeding on the leaves to keep them looking attractive in summer. Climbing honeysuckle is a haven for aphids, mealybugs, and powdery mildew disease. Control aphids and mealybugs with sprays of insecticidal soap. Control powdery mildew with proper pruning and sprays of organic fungicide.

Companion Planting and Design
Plant climbing honeysuckle to grow up an arbor, trellis, wall, or pergola. The vine twines so it will need something to wrap around, such as a pole, post, or wire. You can also grow climbing honeysuckle down a bank or rock wall, letting it cascade down the slope as well. It looks great as a backdrop to other tall perennials, such as peonies, coneflowers, and bee balm.

Try These
'Alabama Crimson' and 'Magnifica' are popular red varieties that flower throughout the summer. 'Cedar Lane' is a red variety that's more disease resistant. 'Blanche Sandman' is a vigorous orange-red variety. 'Sulphurea' has yellow flowers but is not as vigorous a vine as 'Blanche Sandman'. 'Gold Flame' is a yellow-flowered *Lonicera heckrottii* cross with fragrant flowers.

Trumpet Vine

Campsis radicans

Botanical Pronunciation
KAMP-sis RAH-di-kanz

Other Name
Trumpet creeper

Bloom Period and Seasonal Color
Midsummer to fall; red, orange, or yellow flowers

Mature Height × Spread
10 to 30 feet × 5 to 10 feet

This aggressive, woody vine produces large clusters of trumpet-shaped flowers prized by hummingbirds. The flowers give way to bean-shaped pods. It also has attractive, long dark green leaves made of 7, 9, or 11 leaflets. Trumpet vines are easy to grow. In fact, the problem with trumpet vine isn't growing it, but restraining it. It covered the deck at my old house after only a few years of growing. It needs yearly attention to pruning and supporting to keep the vine inbounds and growing vertically. The vine has aerial rootlets that climb on walls and structures, but since it is so heavy it may need other supports to keep it vertical. For that reason, it's a great addition to trellises, fences, and arbors.

When, Where, and How to Plant
Trumpet vines are hardy throughout New England, but may experience some winter dieback in colder regions. Purchase plants at a local garden center and plant from spring to early fall in full to part sun in well-drained, moist soil. Space plants 5 to 10 feet apart.

Growing Tips
Trumpet vines don't need additional fertilizer and actually thrive on only moderately fertile soil. Add a thin layer of compost in spring to keep the vine healthy. Trumpet vine does need moist soil, however, so water well and mulch with bark mulch each spring for moisture retention and weed prevention.

Regional Advice and Care
Trumpet vine is slow to leaf out in spring, so don't assume it has died if the branches are still bare while other shrubs have leaves or flowers. Trumpet vine can become too aggressive for its space and needs to be pruned back each spring. Prune out any dead, broken, or diseased branches first. The flowers form on new growth, so after it leafs out in spring, prune back wayward branches to the trunk and shorter structural branches. This will stimulate more new growth and potentially more flowers. Trumpet vine can be an invasive vine in New England, so remove spent flowers to prevent seed from forming and cut back any new shoots arising from the roots.

Companion Planting and Design
Grow trumpet vines up walls, arbors, pergolas, fences, and lampposts. It looks great as a backdrop to other tall perennial flowers, such as coneflowers and bee balm. It grows well in part shade, creating a dark green wall of foliage, but it won't flower as well as vines grown in full sun. Trumpet vine can also grow over walls or down banks to cover a slope.

Try These
'Crimson Trumpet' has deep red flowers. 'Indian Summer' has orange-red flowers and strong aerial roots. 'Flava' has yellow flowers. 'Variegata' has orange flowers with white-and-green leaves.

Virginia Creeper

Parthenocissus quinquefolia

Botanical Pronunciation
par-the-no-SIS-us kwin-kweff-FOL-lee-ah

Other Name
Woodbine

Bloom Period and Seasonal Color
Insignificant blooms; grown for colorful foliage
and berries

Mature Height × Spread
30 to 50 feet × 5 to 10 feet

This aggressive deciduous vine is similar to Boston ivy in that it's mostly grown for the colorful leaves in fall and the blue berries that form in summer. The biggest difference between Virginia creeper and Boston ivy is the shape and color of the leaves. The leaves turn a purple to reddish color in fall and drop earlier than Boston ivy leaves. The berries are favorites of birds. Since it's grown for its colorful fall leaves, Virginia creeper is a good choice for growing on a north wall or to brighten a dark area. The vines have holdfasts that attach to a wall or structure. They are best grown up masonry, stone, or a fence, since the holdfast can leave marks on wood and vinyl.

When, Where, and How to Plant
Virginia creeper is hardy throughout our region. Purchase plants from a local garden and plant from spring to early fall in well-drained, compost-amended soil. The leaves will have the best color if grown in part shade. Space plants 5 to 10 feet apart.

Growing Tips
Virginia creeper grows in a wide range of soils as long as they stay moist. Water plants well and mulch with bark mulch. Virginia creeper doesn't need additional fertilizer other than a thin layer of compost each spring around its roots.

Regional Advice and Care
Like Boston ivy, once Virginia creeper attaches itself to a wall or building it will be hard to remove or to paint the wall. Plant where it can grow unimpeded for many years. Virginia creeper can become invasive in our region so, if possible, remove berries to stop it from self-sowing. Prune vines in spring to keep it inbounds. Virginia creeper does strongly resemble poison ivy. The difference is Virginia creeper has five leaflet leaves, while poison ivy has three leaflet leaves ("leaves of three, let them be"). Be careful not to confuse the two vines. Virginia creeper doesn't have any significant pests and diseases.

Companion Planting and Design
Grow Virginia creeper up a wall, building, or fence where it can remain for years. It's best planted on surfaces other than wood since the lush growth can cause the wood to mold and rot over time. If you're growing it against a wooden house, consider building a trellis 3 feet away from the building so plenty of air can flow behind the vine to keep the wood dry. Virginia creeper can also be grown over walls or on banks to cover a slope. You can often see it rambling in wild areas over other trees and shrubs.

Try These
'Engelman' is a strong grower that clings to structures, such as trellises, more easily than the regular species. 'Moham' or 'Star Showers' is a newer variety of Virginia creeper that features variegated green-and-white leaves.

Winter Creeper

Euonymous fortunei

Botanical Pronunciation
u-ON-i-mus for-TU-ne-i

Other Name Climbing euonymous

Bloom Period and Seasonal Color
Insignificant blooms; grown for the colorful variegated white, yellow, and green with tinges of purple foliage

Mature Height × Spread
1 to 2 feet × 2 to 4 feet

Winter creeper is a versatile plant. It can be trained into an attractive low-growing groundcover, mounded shrub, or a vertical vine. It's semi-evergreen so winter creeper is a good choice to cover a low wall, structure, or unsightly object. I grew it once to cover part of the foundation on my home. While the white flowers in spring are insignificant, the succulent foliage can be very colorful. Varieties often have variegated green, white, and yellow leaves, sometimes with a tinge of red or purple. The leaves turn a reddish purple in fall with cold weather and will stay evergreen in all but the coldest parts of our region.

When, Where, and How to Plant

Winter creeper is hardy in the warmer parts of zone 4. In colder areas it will need winter protection to survive. It may drop its leaves in colder areas, but still survive and regrow in spring. Purchase transplants and plant from spring to early fall in well-drained, compost-amended soil. Winter creeper grows in almost any type of soil as long as it doesn't stay permanently wet. Growth will be more vigorous in full to part sun locations. Space 2 to 4 feet apart.

Growing Tips

Keep the soil around winter creeper uniformly moist with regular waterings and by adding a layer of bark mulch. Fertilize in spring with a layer of compost and an organic plant food.

Regional Advice and Care

When growing winter creeper as a vine, support the stems with a trellis or arbor. The stems won't attach themselves, so they will need to be tied to the supporting structure. In spring prune back any dead, diseased, or broken branches and train the plant to fit the area. When grown as a groundcover, creeping stems root wherever they touch the ground, so annual pruning may be needed to keep it in place. Winter creeper may get euonymous scale insects. Control by spraying horticultural oil or Neem oil. This vine has been known to set lots of seed and can become invasive in some areas of our region. Prune regularly to remove seedpods and select variegated cultivars that are not as invasive.

Companion Planting and Design

While winter creeper makes a good groundcover to cascade over a wall or bank, or a nice mounded shrub if pruned regularly, it is also an excellent vertical screen. Plant it to hide the foundation around your house, a utility box, or an old stump.

Try These

'Emerald N' Gold' is low growing, with lustrous green leaves edged with yellow. 'Ivory Jade' is a 3-foot-tall variety with deep green leaves sporting a white margin. 'Sarcoxie' is an upright form that grows to 4 feet tall without training, but it sets lots of seeds, so it may become invasive. 'Emerald Beauty' grows to 6 feet and has dark green foliage year-round.

Wisteria

Wisteria floribunda

Botanical Pronunciation
wiss-TEER-ee-uh flore-ih-BUN-duh

Other Name
Japanese wisteria

Bloom Period and Seasonal Color
Spring; pink, purple, white, and lilac

Mature Height × Spread
20 to 35 feet × 2 to 5 feet

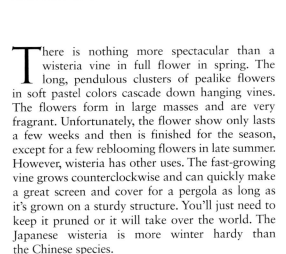

There is nothing more spectacular than a wisteria vine in full flower in spring. The long, pendulous clusters of pealike flowers in soft pastel colors cascade down hanging vines. The flowers form in large masses and are very fragrant. Unfortunately, the flower show only lasts a few weeks and then is finished for the season, except for a few reblooming flowers in late summer. However, wisteria has other uses. The fast-growing vine grows counterclockwise and can quickly make a great screen and cover for a pergola as long as it's grown on a sturdy structure. You'll just need to keep it pruned or it will take over the world. The Japanese wisteria is more winter hardy than the Chinese species.

When, Where, and How to Plant
Wisteria is hardy in warmer parts of zone 4, so it will grow in many areas of our region. It may grow and survive the colder parts of New England, but may not reliably bloom each spring. Purchase plants from a local garden center and plant in spring after all danger of frost has passed or in summer in well-drained, compost-amended soil. Wisteria needs full sun to reliably flower and doesn't grow well in dry soils. Space plants 5 feet apart but close to the posts or trellis where it will climb.

Growing Tips
Water well and mulch with bark to keep the soil evenly moist and reduce competition from weeds. Fertilize in spring with an organic plant food.

Regional Advice and Care
Wisteria's biggest problems are lack of flowers and growing too large. Prune in late winter to reduce the size and promote better flowering. Check with your local garden center or Master Gardener group for details on pruning wisteria vines. Grow named varieties that are hardy in your area to ensure you get spring blooms. Seedlings may take many years to grow to the flowering stage. Grow the vine on a strong supporting structure or pole since the vine can get very heavy when older. Although various insects and diseases may attack the leaves, none are a significant problem. Wisteria can become invasive in our region. Deadhead to prevent the seeds from spreading.

Companion Planting and Design
Grow wisteria vines up a pillar, arbor, pergola, or strong fence. It makes a great cover for a shade structure. Plant it in the back of a perennial border behind shrubs and perennial flowers, such as roses, hydrangeas, and bee balm. Wisteria can also be trained up an old tree to give the appearance of new life.

Try These
'Alba' is a white-flowering variety. 'Rosea' is a pinkish white variety with a strong fragrance. 'Lavender Falls' is a fragrant blue variety that readily reblooms. 'Blue Moon' is a Kentucky wisteria (*W. macrostachya*) that is less aggressive than the Japanese wisteria and has better hardiness than other varieties.

SHRUBS

FOR NEW ENGLAND

Shrubs are so common in many yards that we take them for granted. They often are planted around houses to block the foundation or grouped into hedges or islands to block views or objects, such as a utility box. We really appreciate shrubs, though, when they flower. Man, they can put on a show. Shrubs can knock you over with their beauty when blooming, and there is a flowering shrub for every season.

Shrubs Mark the Seasons

In New England, we anxiously await a harbinger of spring and know warmer weather is coming soon when the forsythia starts to bloom. There is nothing like a lilac shrub in full bloom with its fragrant flowers to tell us summer is right around the corner. Summer-blooming beauties, such as pepperbush and hydrangea, keep the flower power flowing. And fall is punctuated with autumn colors from the rose of Sharon.

Dogwood

But shrubs aren't just about flowers. When deciding on a shrub for your landscape, it's important to first follow the "right plant for the right place" rule. All too often I see yews, junipers, and spireas hacked into geometric shapes along the front of a home only because they were growing too large for the space provided, and the owner had to do something. It's best to choose a shrub that will fit that space when it's full grown. It may look a little small at first, but the beauty of many shrubs is that they grow fast.

Also, consider the sun, soil, and weather conditions. Some shrubs, such as rhododendrons and azaleas, love the shade and acidic soil conditions. Other shrubs, such as roses, flower best in full sun. Some shrubs, such as cotoneaster and hydrangea, do well with salt spray and may be good choices for coastal areas. Most shrubs like well-drained soil, so consider growing them on raised beds or amending the soil heavily with organic matter if you have clay soil. Consider the hardiness zone of your shrub and where you live. You certainly can push the envelope by protecting shrubs with burlap in winter or growing in a microclimate. Just don't let the burlap touch the foliage or stems in winter, or it may contribute to the leaves and branches drying out by wicking moisture away from the plant.

Boxwood hedge surrounded by daylilies, crocosmia, zinnias, and lobelia.

What Part Will Shrubs Play?

Then consider the role your shrub will play in the landscape. Will it play nice with other shrubs in a border and not sucker and spread? Do you need it to block a view or create a boundary with your neighbor's property? Are you looking for it to provide three to four seasons of interest in the yard? Is it something you want to attract wildlife and birds to your property? Needless to say, there is a shrub for every situation.

Some of my favorite shrubs are those that keep giving in the landscape. Shrubs such as ninebark have colorful flowers, beautiful berries, and interesting bark. We often overlook berries and bark, but many times these will be the most attractive aspects to the shrub. Viburnums, dogwoods, and hollies are some of the shrubs that provide this fall and winter interest. Plus, the berries on some shrubs, such as elderberry and blueberry, are edible for us too. So you get a double bonus.

You have a window of time to work with. You can plant deciduous shrubs from spring until early fall. Evergreen shrubs can also be planted during this period, but in colder areas try to plant before fall so the shrub has enough time to get established before winter. Dig a hole twice as wide as the rootball and as deep. Amend the soil if you need to change the pH or have very poor soil. Otherwise, use the native soil to backfill the hole and keep the shrub well watered.

If planted the right way and in the right place, your shrub can provide joy and beauty for years to come.

Blueberry

Vaccinium spp.

Botanical Pronunciation
vak-SIN-ee-um

Other Name
Highbush blueberry

Bloom Period and Seasonal Color
Spring with white flowers

Mature Height × Spread
1 to 6 feet × 2 to 5 feet

Blueberries are best known as a delicious edible crop, but they also make an excellent landscape plant. I think they are underused as an edible landscape plant. There are three different types of blueberries you can grow in your yard. Highbush blueberries grow to 6 feet tall and produce the most fruit. Lowbush blueberries only grow 1 foot tall and are best used as groundcovers. Half high blueberries are a cross between the highbush and lowbush types; they grow 2 to 4 feet tall. All blueberries have attractive white flowers in spring, colorful blue or pink berries in summer, and magnificent red fall foliage in autumn. These plants are hardy, easy to grow, and a *great* alternative to burning bushes (*Euonymus alatus*).

When, Where, and How to Plant

Blueberries are hardy throughout New England. Purchase plants from a local garden center and plant from spring to summer. Sites in full sun are best for fruit production and fall leaf color. Blueberries need an acidic soil to grow their best. Plant in well-drained, fertile soils amended with compost. If needed, lower the pH in the soil to below 5.0 with additions of sulfur before planting. Space plants 2 to 6 feet apart depending on the type of blueberry you're growing.

Growing Tips

Blueberries have shallow root systems. Keep the soil evenly watered and mulched with wood chips, sawdust, or bark mulch to reduce weed competition and keep the soil moist. Fertilize in spring with a balanced organic plant food for blueberries. Add sulfur in fall to reduce the soil pH (if needed).

Regional Advice and Care

Blueberries are low-care, long-lived plants once established and once you've made the soil acidic. My in-laws in New Hampshire have productive bushes that are forty years old. They don't need pruning until they are five years old. Protect the plants from deer and rabbit browsing with tall fencing or cages around individual plants. Protect the fruits from birds with netting placed over plants before the berries turn blue (or pink, depending on your type).

Companion Planting and Design

Grow blueberries together in groups in a shrub border. Plant early-, mid- and late-season varieties to extend the berry production season. Although they're self-pollinating, for best fruiting, plant at least two different varieties. Also, grow blueberries as a foundation planting around your house. Plant half high blueberries under windows and highbush varieties along foundations where they can grow tall. Blueberries grow well with other acid-loving deciduous shrubs, such as rhododendrons.

Try These

'Bluecrop', 'Blueray', 'Patriot', and 'Jersey' are all highbush varieties that grow well here. 'Northsky' is a half high variety that only grows 1 to 2 feet tall. 'Northcountry' is a half high variety that grows 2 to 3 feet tall. 'Pink Lemonade' is a new highbush variety that grows 4 to 5 feet tall and features *pink* fruits.

Boxwood

Buxus spp.

Botanical Pronunciation
BUK-sus

Other Name
Common box

Bloom Period and Seasonal Color
Insignificant spring blooms; grown for evergreen foliage

Mature Height × Spread
4 to 15 feet × 4 to 15 feet

Boxwood is a standard evergreen shrub that is often used in formal gardens throughout England and Europe. We certainly can grow boxwoods in New England too. It's best grown in a formal hedge to define a space or used to create a knot garden. It's also a good shrub for foundation plantings and to mix in a perennial flower border to add a green backdrop for other flowers. The broad, evergreen leaves can be sheared multiple times during a growing season to create a formal look, or the plant can be pruned more informally to have a more natural appearance. If it's not pruned regularly, though, it can become large and will need drastic pruning to bring it back into shape.

When, Where, and How to Plant
Boxwood is hardy to zone 5, so in colder parts of New England it may need winter protection to survive. Purchase boxwood plants from a local garden center. Plant from spring to summer in full to part sun in well-drained, compost-amended soil. Boxwood will not grow well in poorly drained soils. Space plants 2 to 6 feet apart.

Growing Tips
Boxwood grows best in cool, moist, fertile soils. Water regularly and mulch with bark mulch to keep the soil evenly moist and keep weeds at bay. Be careful weeding since boxwoods have shallow root systems. Fertilize in spring with a layer of compost and a handful of an organic fertilizer.

Regional Advice and Care
Boxwood can be marginally hardy in our region, and the evergreen leaves can turn bronze if exposed to winter winds and cold. Choose winter hardy varieties, plant them in a protected spot away from winter winds, and protect their evergreen leaves by wrapping burlap around four stakes placed around the plant so the burlap doesn't touch the boxwood foliage. Shear boxwoods regularly starting in early summer to keep them in shape. Boxwoods also make good topiary shrubs pruned into geometric shapes. If they get overgrown, they can be severely pruned and they will regrow.

Companion Planting and Design
Plant boxwood shrubs in a low hedge to outline a formal herb or flower garden, as a specimen plant in a border, or along a house's foundation. Boxwood creates a green backdrop for colorful perennial flowers, such as salvia, black-eyed Susan, and veronica, and annual flowers, such as zinnias, cosmos, and cleome. Mix and match flowering shrubs, such as potentilla and dwarf spirea, with boxwoods.

Try These
The Korean boxwood (*B. microphylla*) is considered the most cold hardy. The hybrids 'Green Gem' and 'Green Velvet' grow 3 feet tall and wide in a rounded form. 'Winter Beauty' has dark green foliage in a 4-foot-tall and -wide rounded form. 'Green Mountain' can grow to 6 feet tall and wide and has good cold hardiness.

Cotoneaster

Cotoneaster spp.

Botanical Pronunciation
ko-to-ne-AS-ter

Other Name
Rockspray cotoneaster

Bloom Period and Seasonal Color
Spring pink flowers; red berries and colorful fall foliage

Mature Height × Spread
2 to 3 feet × 5 to 8 feet

Cotoneaster is a low-growing, colorful shrub with attractive small flowers, berries, and fall foliage color. The long spreading branches look particularly attractive when grown to cascade down a wall or bank. It can also be used as a groundcover in front of a perennial flower or shrub border. Bees favor the pink flowers in spring. I really have never noticed this, but some people believe the flowers have an offensive smell. The plant remains nondescript until red berries and red-colored fall foliage form in autumn. The berries are favored by birds and can remain on the plants for months. Cotoneaster is a good choice for seaside homes since the plant is salt-spray tolerant.

When, Where, and How to Plant

Depending on the species, cotoneaster is hardy to zone 4 in New England; deciduous species are the hardiest for New England. Purchase plants from a local garden center and plant from spring to early fall in well-drained, fertile soil, amended with compost. Cotoneaster isn't fussy about the soil type, but grows better in loose soil. Cotoneaster has a small root system, so carefully remove it from its container to plant. Plant at the same depth as the shrub was in the container, spacing plants 3 to 5 feet apart.

Growing Tips

Keep young plants well watered. Once roots are established, the plants are drought tolerant. Apply mulch, such as bark mulch or wood chips, in spring to preserve soil moisture and keep weeds away.

Fertilize monthly with a handful of an organic plant food.

Regional Advice and Care

Prune errant vertical branches to shape the shrub in spring and early summer. Mulch newly planted cotoneasters with bark mulch in late fall to protect them from winter damage due to freezing and thawing cycles. Older shrubs should be cold tolerant and won't need mulch. Branches may root where they touch the ground, allowing you to create new plants from the mother plant. Scale insects can attack cotoneaster. Spray plants with a horticultural oil to prevent damage.

Companion Planting and Design

Plant cotoneaster in rock gardens and perennial borders as a groundcover. They also look good in front of taller shrubs, such as lilacs and spireas. Cotoneaster can be grown to cover a slope or cascade over a rock wall.

Try These

Cranberry cotoneaster (*C. apiculatus*) is a popular species version. 'Peking' cotoneaster is an erect version that can grow to 4 feet tall if not pruned. It has black berries and red foliage in fall. 'Tom Thumb' is a low-growing variety that stays dwarf and has glossy dark green leaves that turn a vibrant red in fall. 'Hessei' grows 18 inches tall, spreads horizontally, and has good resistance to insects and diseases.

Daphne

Daphne × burkwoodii

Botanical Pronunciation
DAF-nee burk-WOOD-ee-eye

Other Name
Burkwood daphne

Bloom Period and Seasonal Color
Spring (may rebloom in early fall); pale pink

Mature Height × Spread
2 to 3 feet × 3 to 5 feet

This spring-blooming shrub has small, pale pink flowers that grow in clusters on the stem ends. While the flowers are attractive, what you will notice is the intense sweet fragrance they emit. Daphne is an evergreen in warmer parts of our region depending on the winter. In colder areas it will lose its leaves in winter, but survive. The naturally rounded plant is an attractive landscape shrub. Some varieties have variegated yellow and green leaves giving this shrub interest even when not in bloom. It can be a finicky plant to care for in colder parts of New England, with branch dieback a problem. But, with a little winter protection, it will be a showpiece in your landscape for years.

When, Where, and How to Plant
Daphne is hardy to zone 4 in New England, but will not be evergreen in cold areas. Purchase plants from a local garden center and plant from spring to early fall in well-drained soil with moderate fertility. Consider building a raised bed because poorly drained soil is a daphne killer. Plant daphne where it will be protected from cold winds in winter and shaded during midday summer sun. Daphne doesn't like to be moved, so choose your location wisely. Space plants 3 to 5 feet apart depending on the variety.

Growing Tips
Daphne grows best in a humusy soil that's kept cool and moist. Apply mulch, such as bark mulch or wood chips, to maintain soil moisture levels. Fertilize in spring with a layer of compost. Add lime to raise the soil pH around daphne to neutral pH (if needed).

Regional Advice and Care
With all its beauty in the landscape, daphne can be a temperamental plant. Branches may suddenly die back, seemingly without cause. Daphne can get various diseases, such as canker and crown rot, and insects, such as aphids and scale. Proper soil drainage helps avoid the diseases. Sprays of insecticidal soap and Neem oil help with the insects. Prune plants to shape and remove errant branches after flowering. Prune back to a side branch or trunk and avoid trimming just the branch ends.

Companion Planting and Design
Daphne looks good planted in a mixed shrub border or with tall-growing perennials, such as peonies and baptisia. You can also plant daphne near walkways, windows, and patios to enjoy the sweet fragrance in spring. Daphne is also an attractive woodland plant when grown in filtered light under tall deciduous trees. Often woodland plantings are more protected from winter winds as well as the intense summer sun.

Try These
'Carol Mackie' is a vigorously growing variety with creamy yellow leaf margins around green leaves. 'Silveredge' has white margins around green leaves. 'Briggs Moonlight' is not as vigorous a grower as other daphnes, but it has white fragrant flowers and yellow leaves with green edges.

Deciduous Azalea

Rhododendron spp. and hybrids

Botanical Pronunciation
roh-doh-DEN-dron

Other Name
Flowering azalea

Bloom Period and Seasonal Color
Early spring; pink, salmon, yellow, white, rose, and bicolors

Mature Height × Spread
4 to 8 feet × 4 to 8 feet

Azaleas are in the *Rhododendron* family but are usually distinguished from other rhododendrons by their smaller plant size. There are deciduous and evergreen azaleas. Evergreen azaleas are not as hardy as deciduous types; you'll find these growing well in more southern climates but they are not reliable throughout New England. Deciduous azaleas are more winter hardy. Before the leaves emerge, they flower in early spring, with brilliant flower colors turning a woodland or landscape into a flower show. Deciduous azaleas look best grouped together as understory plants or planted in a partly shaded area of your yard. After the amazing spring flower show the dark green foliage makes an excellent backdrop for other flowering shrubs and perennials.

When, Where, and How to Plant

Deciduous azaleas are hardy to zone 4, so they grow well in most parts of New England. Purchase plants from a local garden center and plant from spring to early fall in a partly shaded location in well-drained, humus-rich soil with a low pH. Space plants 4 to 6 feet apart.

Growing Tips

Deciduous azaleas are shallow-rooted and need an acidic soil, high in organic matter, to grow and flower best. Amend the soil with sulfur in spring to lower the pH to around 5 (if needed). Keep plants well watered and mulch with pine needles, peat moss, or bark mulch to keep the soil cool and moist and to keep the pH low. Fertilize in spring with an azalea or rhododendron plant food. Don't fertilize after July 1 or it may delay dormancy, which may lead to winter injury.

Regional Advice and Care

Deciduous azaleas can grow well in a sunny location in northern areas (as long as they have consistently moist soil). In colder areas or along the coast, they need protection from the cold winter winds; place four stakes around plants and wrap burlap around the stakes. Prune after blooming to shape plants. Remove dead or diseased branches anytime. Deciduous azaleas can be attacked by scale insects. Spray a dormant oil spray on branches in late winter before the flowers emerge to kill overwintering insect eggs.

Companion Planting and Design

Plant deciduous azaleas grouped in a woodland setting with filtered light, such as that grown under high-canopied oaks or maples or in a landscape. Azaleas pair well with evergreens, such as rhododendrons and cedars, and with other spring-flowering shrubs such as forsythia.

Try These

'Exbury Hybrid' deciduous azaleas are probably the most common type in New England. They have an upright, vase shape and bloom in a variety of warm colors, such as orange, red, and peach. Some varieties have bicolored blooms. 'Northern Lights' azaleas were bred in Minnesota so they are very hardy. They are more compact shrubs with bloom colors, such as pink, white, gold, and salmon.

Dogwood

Cornus spp.

Botanical Pronunciation
KORE-nus

Other Name
Shrub dogwood

Bloom Period and Seasonal Color
Spring; white or yellow flowers; colorful summer berries and fall foliage and bark color

Mature Height × Spread
3 to 10 feet × 3 to 6 feet

Shrub dogwoods are in the same family as the flowering tree dogwoods that are common throughout southern parts of New England. These deciduous shrubs don't have the same stature as the flowering tree dogwood (which I'll cover in the tree section of this book). But they're native, tough plants that offer many other benefits. The clusters of white or yellow flowers bloom in spring followed by colorful blue or white berries that birds love. In fall the foliage turns a purplish red. Some varieties have colorful bark that contrasts well against the white snow in winter, giving your garden some color in this bleaker time. The shrubs are as equally suited as a wildlife planting as they are a specimen in a mixed shrub border.

When, Where, and How to Plant
Dogwoods are hardy throughout New England. Purchase plants from a local garden center and plant from spring to early fall in well-drained, compost-amended soil. Shrub dogwoods grow well in wet soils as long as it's not in standing water. They can grow in full sun to partly shaded locations, but have the best fruiting and stem color in sunny spots. Depending on the variety and usage, space plants 4 to 8 feet apart. For hedges, plant closer together; for specimen plantings, farther apart.

Growing Tips
Shrub dogwoods need little care once established. Keep them well watered the first year. Mulch with wood chips or bark mulch to keep weeds away and keep the soil evenly moist. Fertilize annually with a thin layer of compost around the drip line of the shrub.

Regional Advice and Care
Prune brightly colored bark varieties in spring to promote more 1-year old growth. The younger stems tend to have the best winter color. Prune to remove dead, diseased, and broken branches anytime.

Companion Planting and Design
Shrub dogwoods grow well on a bank to prevent erosion and cover an area. They are a good shrub for wildlife hedges to provide food and shelter for birds and other animals. Since they tolerate moist soils, plant them along a stream or pond. Plant the brightly colored bark varieties where they can be viewed in winter from a window. Plant varieties with good fall foliage color with other fall foliage shrubs, such as fothergilla and viburnum. Compact types look great in a mixed shrub border or along your foundation.

Try These
The red twig dogwood (*C. sericea*) grows 8 to 10 feet tall and wide with bright red stems in winter. There is a yellow twig version as well. 'Ivory Halo' is another red twig variety, but this one has variegated white-and-green leaves, giving it more interest in summer. 'Arctic Fire' is a red twig dogwood that only grows 3 to 5 feet tall. Silky dogwoods grow 6 to 8 feet tall with blueberries; they're particularly adapted to poorly drained soils.

Elderberry

Sambucus spp. and hybrids

Botanical Pronunciation
sam-BEW-kus

Other Name
Elder

Bloom Period and Seasonal Color
Spring; white or pink flowers; red or black berries

Mature Height × Spread
5 to 12 feet × 5 to 10 feet

Elderberries are common shrubs often found growing wild in meadows, abandoned fields, and roadside ditches. They grow well in wet sites making them versatile in the landscape. This native plant is prized by bees and insects for its flat clusters of white or pink flowers, and, by birds for their clusters of berries in summer. They are one of my favorite edible landscape shrubs. While some elderberry varieties feature large berries for eating, this edible landscape shrub also has newer varieties with a more ornamental plant form. Some varieties feature cut leaves that look like a Japanese maple while others have jet black, yellow, or variegated foliage that make for interesting contrasts with other shrubs and flowers in the garden.

When, Where, and How to Plant
Elderberries are hardy throughout New England. Purchase plants from a local garden center and plant from spring to early fall in well-drained, fertile soil. Elderberries need constant moisture to grow and fruit their best. They grow well in wet areas, as long as there is no standing water. Plant in groups, spacing plants 5 to 8 feet apart.

Growing Tips
Keep plants well watered. Fertilize elderberries in spring with a layer of compost and a small handful of an organic plant food. Mulch with wood chips or bark to reduce competition from grasses and weeds and keep the soil moist.

Regional Advice and Care
Elderberries grow in a vase shape. Canes older than three years old will often be brittle and not leaf out, or flower and fruit as well. Prune these old canes to the ground in early spring to stimulate new growth. Cover plants in early summer with bird netting if you're growing the plants for their black fruits. The fruits make good jams, juice, and wine. The flowers can be used to make champagne.

Companion Planting and Design
Grow elderberries for fruit on the edge of your vegetable garden or in an area with other edible shrubs, such as currants and gooseberries. Grow more ornamental varieties in a mixed shrub border or in the perennial flower garden. Place black-foliaged varieties in back of brightly colored flowers, such as phlox and bee balm, to highlight those flowers. Plant wild species in wet areas as wildlife plantings. Elderberry will spread by suckers.

Try These
'York' and 'Adams' are American varieties (*S. canadensis*) bred for their large, black berries. Grow these if you are looking for fruit production. For more ornamental varieties try the European species (*S. nigra*) and cultivars, such as 'Black Lace' with its cut leaves and small stature. 'Black Beauty' has full-sized black leaves with pink flowers. 'Aurea' features greenish yellow leaves. 'Marginata' has variegated yellow and green leaves and black fruits. The red-berried species (*S. racemosa*) blooms earlier than black-fruited varieties, but the berries are not edible raw.

Firethorn

Pyracantha coccinea

Botanical Pronunciation
pi-ra-CAN-tha cok-SIN-i-a

Other Name
Scarlet firethorn

Bloom Period and Seasonal Color
Spring; white flowers; fall, orange or red berries

Mature Height × Spread
6 to 12 feet × 6 to 8 feet

This large shrub is semi-evergreen where it's hardy in New England. In colder areas it may lose its leaves during cold winters. When you do plant it, you'll be treated to white flowers in spring and brilliant orange or red berries in summer. The berries are ornamental and birds love them as well. The "fire" part of its name comes from this brilliant berry display. The second part of its name refers to the sharp thorns on the branches. So, while firethorn can be difficult to prune and work with without getting pricked by the thorns, on the plus side, it makes an impenetrable hedge to keep wildlife out of your garden.

When, Where, and How to Plant

Firethorn is hardy only to zone 5, so check your hardiness zones before planting. Plant varieties purchased from a local garden center in spring after all danger of frost has passed or in summer. A location in full sun is the best for flower and berry production in well-drained, compost-amended soil. Firethorn is tolerant of dry soils once established. Firethorn shrubs can't be transplanted easily, so choose your original planting site well. Space plants 6 to 8 feet apart. Plant closer together, if creating a hedge.

Growing Tips

Water newly planted firethorn shrubs well in spring. Apply mulch, such as bark mulch, to conserve soil moisture and keep weeds away. Fertilize in spring with a layer of compost and an organic plant food.

Regional Advice and Care

Since firethorn shrubs are marginally hardy in many parts of New England, plant the hardiest varieties in a spot protected from winter winds. Prune firethorn carefully—because of the thorns—in late spring after flowering to thin out crowded growth and remove dead, diseased, or damaged branches. Firethorn can also be shaped into topiary and as espalier. Firethorn is susceptible to diseases, such as fireblight and scab. Grow resistant varieties, if possible. Prune infected branches to control fireblight and spray to control scab disease.

Companion Planting and Design

Plant firethorn shrubs along your home's foundation or in a border planting mixed with other shrubs. Firethorn looks good combined with shrubs with attractive fall leaf colors, such as fothergilla and viburnum. Espalier (meaning to train to a form) firethorn along a wall or trellis. Or plant a hedge of firethorn as a barrier against deer and other wildlife in your yard.

Try These

'Chadwickii' grows 6 feet tall with brilliant orange berries. 'Lalandei' is a popular 12-foot-tall variety with orange berries; however, it is very susceptible to scab disease. 'Monon' grows 6 to 8 feet tall and is considered one of the hardiest varieties. 'Mohave' is fire blight and scab resistant, but is only hardy to zone 6. It's best grown along southern coastal areas of New England.

Flowering Quince

Chaenomeles speciosa

Botanical Pronunciation
kee-NOM-uh-leez spee-see-OH-suh

Other Name
Japanese quince

Bloom Period and Seasonal Color
Early spring; white, pink, coral, orange, and red

Mature Height × Spread
3 to 8 feet × 3 to 8 feet

This spring-blooming, easy-to-grow deciduous shrub is a showstopper when it's in full bloom. It grabs your attention partly because it blooms before the leaves emerge and so early in the spring when little else is flowering. Also, the colorful flowers are borne in abundance along the stems in single or double forms literally covering the plant. After blooming, older varieties may produce edible fruits, which can be used to make preserves when they're harvested in fall (though newer hybrids may not have fruit). The shrub has dark green leaves all summer making it a perfect backdrop for other colorful summer- and fall-blooming flowers and shrubs. The branches can have thorns making flowering quince a potential barrier plant to keep wildlife out of an area.

When, Where, and How to Plant
Flowering quince is hardy to zone 4, but it may need winter protection in the colder parts of New England. Purchase varieties hardy for your area from a local garden center and plant from spring to summer in a full to part sun location in well-drained soil. Note that plants flower best in full sun. Space plants 3 to 6 feet apart depending on the variety.

Growing Tips
Water new plants well. Once established flowering quince is drought tolerant. Fertilize in spring with a layer of compost and a handful of an organic plant food.

Regional Advice and Care
Flowering quince produces multiple branches and can get too dense and crowded over time. However, it can take a severe pruning and grow back well. Flowers are borne on older wood, so prune after flowering to remove crowded, dead, or broken branches and to rejuvenate the shrub. Scab disease can cause leaves to yellow and drop in summer. Spray with an organic fungicide in spring and after rains to reduce this disease. Aphids, mites, and scale can attack the branches and leaves. Spray in winter with a dormant oil before flowering to control scale. In summer, spray insecticidal soap to control mites and aphids.

Companion Planting and Design
Plant flowering quince in a mixed shrub border with summer-blooming shrubs, such as lilac, spirea, and weigela. Once it's finished blooming, flowering quince doesn't have much appeal other than as a green backdrop plant. It can be planted in an edible hedgerow with gooseberries and currants, used as a barrier plant, or planted *en masse* in seldom-used areas for a surprising splash of spring color.

Try These
'Cameo' is a popular low-growing, double-flowered, pink quince variety that's disease resistant and has few thorns. 'Jet Trail' has masses of single white flowers on 3- to 4-foot-tall shrubs. 'Spitfire' has double bright red blossoms. 'Texas Scarlet' is an older variety with orange-red single blooms. 'Toyo-Nishiki' has unusual pink, white, and red flowers and produces tasty fruits.

Forsythia

Forsythia × intermedia

Botanical Pronunciation
for-SYE-thee-uh in-tur-MEE-dee-uh

Other Name
Border forsythia

Bloom Period and Seasonal Color
Spring; yellow

Mature Height × Spread
6 to 10 feet × 6 to 10 feet

One of the most noteworthy flowering shrubs in spring, forsythia is a widely grown plant throughout our region. The brilliant yellow blooms appear before the leaves emerge creating a yellow snowstorm of color. It is certainly an amazing site, but unfortunately, it may bloom sporadically in colder regions and after flowering is over, forsythia simply is a nondescript green shrub in the landscape. It is commonly grown because of its ease of growing. This shrub is cold tolerant, grows in most soils, and easily propagates itself by rooting its stems along the ground. If it gets out of hand forsythia can readily be severely pruned back to regrow and still bloom again the following year.

When, Where, and How to Plant

Forsythia shrubs are hardy throughout New England, but the flower buds may not be hardy. If you live in colder parts of our region, select varieties known to have cold hardy flower buds or all you'll get in spring is green leafy growth. Purchase shrubs from local garden centers and plant from spring to early fall. Plant in full sun for best flowering, in well-drained, compost-amended soil. Space plants 6 to 10 feet apart. Grow them closer together if you're forming a hedge.

Growing Tips

Water new plants well. Once established, forsythia can be drought tolerant. Apply mulch, such as wood chips or bark mulch, to suppress competing weeds. Fertilize lightly in spring with compost.

Regional Advice and Care

Forsythia seems to be *everywhere* in spring in our region. Unfortunately, unless the flower buds were protected by snow or we had a mild winter, they often don't flower well. This plant can also get unruly without periodic pruning. Prune after flowering to thin out the branches and reduce the height but avoid shearing the plant. You can also cut the whole plant back severely to bring it under control and rejuvenate it. Forsythia has few pest problems.

Companion Planting and Design

In a mixed shrub border plant forsythia with other flowering shrubs that bloom later, such as lilac and spirea. Consider planting spring-flowering bulbs, such as tulips, crocus, and hyacinth, in front of forsythia for the complementary colors. Plant forsythia as a visual screen in a hedge or to block an unsightly view. To give the corner of your yard a splash of spring, plant forsythia in groups in out of the way locations or plant it as a groundcover to cascade over a wall.

Try These

'Lynwood' is a popular variety with tall upright growth and purple-tinged fall foliage. 'Arnold Dwarf' is a low-growing, 3-foot-tall variety that grows well as a groundcover, but which doesn't flower as profusely as taller varieties. 'Meadowlark' and 'Northern Sun' possess good flower bud tolerance to cold temperatures and are more likely to flower in northern landscapes.

Fothergilla

Fothergilla spp.

Botanical Pronunciation
foth-er-GIL-a-

Other Name
Large fothergilla

Bloom Period and Seasonal Color
Spring; white; yellow fall foliage

Mature Height × Spread
2 to 8 feet × 2 to 6 feet

Fothergilla is an attractive, spring-flowering shrub that grows to a low-to-medium size, depending on the species. I think it is underused and should be grown more in our region. It is part shade tolerant, but flowers best in full sun. The white, bottlebrush-like flowers have a sweet, honey scent. They appear in spring before the leaves emerge. After flowering, the attractive blue-green foliage fills out the shrub for summer. In fall the large leaves turn a brilliant yellow-orange-red color combination. Fothergilla has few pest problems and grows in any well-drained, slightly acidic soil. Fothergilla will sucker and fill in a hedge with new plants, or it can naturalize in an area with filtered sun.

When, Where, and How to Plant

Fothergilla is hardy to zone 4 depending on the species. Gardeners in colder parts should look for the hardiest varieties and protect them in winter. Fothergilla grows best in a site in full sun in moist soils. Purchase plants from local garden centers and plant from spring to early fall in well-drained, slightly acidic soil that has been amended with peat moss and compost. Space 2 to 4 feet apart.

Growing Tips

Keep plants watered well and mulched with pine needles or bark mulch in spring to maintain the soil moisture levels and prevent weeds. Fertilize in spring with an acidifying fertilizer that you would use for rhododendrons.

Regional Advice and Care

This carefree shrub only needs occasional pruning after flowering in spring to remove older branches that are not flowering or growing strongly. Prune to shape the shrub removing any errant, dead, diseased, and broken branches whenever you see them. Protect more tender species of fothergilla from cold winters by driving four stakes in the ground around a shrub and wrapping burlap around the stakes to block the winter winds.

Companion Planting and Design

Plant fothergilla as a specimen shrub along the house foundation or in front of a mixed shrub border. The low-growing versions are perfect for growing under windows without eventually blocking the view. Fothergillas grow well near azaleas and rhododendrons because of their similar soil needs and tolerance to part shade. They look good planted in front of evergreens or dark green foliaged shrubs, such as flowering quince. Dark foliage shows off fothergilla's bright fall leaf color well.

Try These

'Mt. Airy' has large flowers, blue-green foliage, and vivid fall foliage color on a 6-foot-tall and -wide shrub. 'Jane Platt' is smaller, growing to 3 feet tall and wide; it does not have as strong a fall color show. 'Blue Shadow' is similar to 'Mt. Airy', but has powdery blue leaves that stand out all summer. 'Blue Mist' has similar colorful blue leaves on a dwarf plant, but it's not as colorful in fall as 'Blue Shadow'.

Holly

Ilex spp. and hybrids

Botanical Pronunciation
EYE-lex

Other Name
Common holly

Bloom Period and Seasonal Color
Evergreen foliage; often grown for bright red, orange, and yellow berries

Mature Height × Spread
6 to 20 feet × 3 to 6 feet

Hollies are a broad group of deciduous and evergreen shrubs. Some grow as small as 2 to 3 feet while others look like trees, sometimes reaching above 20 feet. The hollies most commonly grown here and which are hardy in New England tend to be small- to medium-sized shrubs. While the flowers are insignificant on most holly species, the berries can be bright and colorful, offering interest in fall and winter. Plants are either male or female, with only the females having berries. The evergreen varieties are hardy in warmer parts of our region. Their glossy green leaves keep gardens looking lively in winter. Deciduous varieties are more winter hardy and can grow in wet soil areas. Both types are attractive plants to birds.

When, Where, and How to Plant

Depending on the species, deciduous hollies are hardy to zone 4 and evergreen varieties are hardy to zone 5. Select varieties that are hardy for your area. Purchase plants from a local garden center. Plant hollies from spring to summer in a full sun to part shade location in well-drained, slightly acidic soil. Hollies fruit (produce berries) best in full sun. Space 5 to 15 feet apart depending on the variety.

Growing Tips

Keep the soil evenly moist and slightly acidic by watering hollies well after transplanting and mulching with pine needles, bark mulch, or wood chips. Apply an acidifying fertilizer in spring.

Regional Advice and Care

Plant evergreen hollies in a spot protected from winter and drive four stakes around bushes and wrap burlap around the stakes to protect them from winter winds. Deciduous hollies are tougher and need less protection. Prune both types of hollies in spring to remove dead, damaged, and diseased growth and to shape the plant. Don't prune after flowering; you may remove the current year's berry crop.

Companion Planting and Design

Plant a male pollinator variety within 300 feet of a female variety to produce berries. Plant evergreen hollies as foundation plants or specimen plants in a mixed shrub border with other acidic soil-loving plants, such as rhododendrons, azaleas, and fothergillas. Plant deciduous hollies with shrub dogwoods and viburnums. Hollies tend to sucker and spread on their own. Both types of hollies can be planted as hedges or barrier plants and used to attract birds.

Try These

For evergreen hollies try 'China Boy' and 'China Girl' for their 8- to 10-foot-tall habit, glossy leaves, and hardiness. 'Blue Prince' and 'Blue Princess' stand 12 to 15 feet tall and have very dark blue-green leaves with red berries. For deciduous varieties try 'Winter Red' and 'Winter Gold' with red or gold berries on 8-foot-tall plants. 'Apollo' is a good male pollinator for those two females. 'Cacapon' has red berries on dwarf 5-foot-tall shrubs and can be pollinated by the early blooming 'Jim Dandy'.

Hydrangea

Hydrangea spp. and cultivars

Botanical Pronunciation hy-DRAIN-juh

Other Name Hortensia

Bloom Period and Seasonal Color
Mid- to late summer; white, pink, red, and blue

Mature Height × Spread
3 to 15 feet × 3 to 12 feet

Hydrangeas have been making a comeback. They were popular Victorian flowers but then fell out of grace for years. They are mostly grown for their large flowers that bloom from midsummer to fall. This group is diverse from the native, smooth-leaf hydrangea (*H. arborescens*) with flowers so large they tend to flop over in midsummer to the tall, stately paniculata hydrangeas (*H. paniculata*) that look like small trees. The oak leaf (*H. quercifolia*) hydrangea has oaklike leaves. Probably the most highly prized are the colorful, big leaf hydrangeas (*H. macrophylla*) with their red, pink, or blue flowers. Hydrangeas are showy plants in the landscape, growing in full sun to part shade. They tolerate salt-air conditions and so are common seaside plants.

When, Where, and How to Plant

Many hydrangea species are hardy throughout New England. Choose hydrangeas based on your hardiness zone. The big leaf hydrangea and oak leaf types are less hardy than the smooth leaf and paniculata types. Purchase plants from a local garden center and plant from spring to early fall in well-drained, moist, slightly acidic soil. Space plants 4 to 10 feet apart.

Growing Tips

Hydrangea roots don't like to dry out. Water plants well and mulch with pine needles or bark mulch to preserve the soil moisture, keep the soil slightly acidic, and prevent weed growth. Fertilize in spring or fall with an acidifying plant food similar to what you'd use for rhododendrons. To change the flower color on big leaf varieties to blue, lower the pH by applying sulfur to the soil. To change the flower color to pink, raise the pH by applying lime.

Regional Advice and Care

Prune smooth leaf varieties to a few feet tall in late winter to stimulate new growth. Prune tall, paniculata-type hydrangeas in late winter to remove dead and diseased branches and to shape the plant. Prune smooth-leaf hydrangeas after flowering so the stems are a few feet off the ground. Depending on the variety they will bloom on old wood and/or new wood next year.

Companion Planting and Design

Plant hydrangeas as foundation or specimen plantings along your house or garage. Lower-growing hydrangeas can be planted in a perennial flower garden. Plant large varieties in island beds with other deciduous shrubs, such as fothergilla.

Try These

'PeeGee' hydrangea is a famous paniculata type with white flowers that turn pink with age. 'Limelight' is a newer selection with lime green flowers. 'Endless Summer' is a popular big leaf hydrangea that flowers on old and new wood; it has blue blossoms. It's good for cold areas because even if old growth dies to the ground, new growth emerging in spring will flower in late summer. 'Forever Pink' and 'Forever Red' are two compact pink and red versions. 'Annabelle' is a popular smooth-leaf variety with large, 12-inch-diameter blossoms.

Japanese Andromeda

Pieris japonica

Botanical Pronunciation PY-er-is ja-PON-i-ka

Other Name Lily of the valley plant

Bloom Period and Seasonal Color
Spring; white (some varieties have red buds)

Mature Height × Spread
4 to 8 feet × 3 to 6 feet

Japanese andromeda is a broadleaf evergreen that is a staple in southern New England gardens. My mother's house in Connecticut has one that's over forty years old and it's still thriving. It's generally hardy to zone 5, so it isn't appropriate for colder parts of our region. The beautiful young leaves often have a reddish glow. The leaves eventually turn dark green, with some varieties having variegated leaves. The "necklaces" of white or pink flowers bloom in spring. Japanese andromeda stays attractive all summer and adds some greenery to the landscape in winter. This slow-growing shrub is similar to rhododendron in that it grows well in part shade and in acidic soils.

When, Where, and How to Plant
Purchase plants at a local garden center and plant from spring to summer in a full sun to part shade location. Japanese andromeda grows best in well-drained, humus-rich, acidic soil. Space plants 3 to 8 feet apart, depending on the selection.

Growing Tips
Water new plants well. Mulch the base of plants well with bark mulch, pine needles, or wood chips to keep the soil consistently moist and reduce weed competition. Fertilize in spring with an acid-based plant food similar to what you'd use for rhododendrons.

Regional Advice and Care
Japanese andromeda leaves and flower buds can dry out easily in winter and die due to cold winds. Protect plants by planting in a protected location and driving four stakes around each andromeda and wrapping burlap around the stakes in late fall. Prune in spring to remove dead, diseased, and broken branches and to shape the plant. Lacebugs can attack the foliage causing holes in the leaves especially during dry periods. Spray insecticidal soap or Neem oil to control this pest.

Companion Planting and Design
Since Japanese andromeda grows well in sun or partly shaded locations on acidic soil, it's a good match with rhododendrons, azaleas, and fothergillas. It's a formal plant in the landscape, so looks best planted against a foundation or in a mixed shrub border. Low-growing compact varieties fit well under windows and in small spaces. The evergreen leaves make a nice backdrop to lower-growing flowering shrubs, such as potentilla, cotoneaster, and dwarf spirea. Some Japanese andromeda varieties are popular as bonsai plants as well.

Try These
'Mountain Fire' is a very popular, newer variety that has bright orange-red new growth in spring with white flowers. 'Valley Valentine' is a popular pink-flowered variety with deep red buds. It grows up to 8 feet tall. 'Dorothy Wycoff' is a compact, yet vigorously growing variety, with pink flowers. Its foliage can turn bronze in winter. 'Pygmaea' is a compact variety that only grows 2 feet tall. 'Variegated' features variegated white-and-green leaves and grows 6 feet tall.

Juniper

Juniperus spp. and hybrids

Botanical Pronunciation
ju-NIP-er-us

Other Name
Common juniper

Bloom Period and Seasonal Color
Evergreen; green, gold, and blue

Mature Height × Spread
1 to 40 feet × 5 to 20 feet

You see them *everywhere* in New England. Junipers are common evergreen plants in many landscapes. This group is huge and varied. They all have attractive green or blue-green needles and blue berries that add winter interest to a garden. There are creeping types that grow no more than a few feet tall, but spread like a carpet. Many small- to medium-sized junipers make great landscape shrubs in borders and alongside houses. Large shrub types can be used as visual screens or barriers in the landscape. Tall, columnar varieties look like small trees. All these junipers are hardy and tough plants that even deer avoid. They have bristly needles that can be scratchy. Junipers are often good candidates for topiaries.

When, Where, and How to Plant
Junipers are generally hardy throughout New England. Purchase plants from a local garden center and plant from spring to summer in a full sun location in well-drained, humus-rich soil. Junipers can adapt to many soil types. Space plants depending on their ultimate mature size.

Growing Tips
Water young shrubs well and mulch with pine needles or bark mulch to keep the soil evenly moist and weeds at bay. Fertilize in spring with a layer of compost and an organic plant food formulated for evergreens.

Regional Advice and Care
Prune junipers in spring after a spurt of new growth to shape the plant and remove dead, broken, or diseased branches. Wear gloves and a long-sleeved shirt since the needles are scratchy. Overgrown junipers can be pruned back severely, but it will take many years for the shrubs to fill back in again. Some selections may be susceptible to diseases, such as cedar-apple rust and stem dieback, and to insects, such as bagworms. Select resistant varieties.

Companion Planting and Design
Plant low-growing junipers in front of a shrub border, along a wall, in a rock garden, or creeping down a bank. Plant small- to medium-sized selections as foundation plants or in a mixed shrub border. Plant tall, columnar junipers on the corner of a home or in back of a shrub planting. For mass plantings, grow large-sized varieties. These also can form an informal hedge to block a view or utility box.

Try These
For low-growing junipers, try 'Blue Rug', 'Blue Prince', and 'Bar Harbor'. These grow 6 to 12 inches tall, have a creeping form, and blue-green foliage that can turn blue to purple in winter. For a low-growing mounded variety, try 'Nana'. The 'Sargent' juniper is a popular 3-foot-tall and 7-foot-wide variety that is disease resistant. 'Old Gold' is a golden-colored shrub that's 2 to 3 feet tall and 4 to 5 feet wide. Pfitzeriana types are small shrubs that can have golden, blue-green, or variegated needles depending on the variety. 'Burkii' and 'Emerald Sentinel' are tall, columnar-shaped juniper cultivars.

Kerria

Kerria japonica

Botanical Pronunciation
KAIR-ee-uh juh-PON-ih-kuh

Other Name
Japanese rose

Bloom Period and Seasonal Color
Spring (sometimes reblooms in late summer); yellow

Mature Height × Spread
6 to 10 feet × 6 to 8 feet

Kerria is a Japanese native with arched branches that produce a bountiful display of yellow flowers in spring. The deciduous shrub can also rebloom in late summer. The golden flowers are single or double and are produced on old wood. They are particularly nice in the landscape because, depending on the weather, they can bloom for up to 6 weeks. Kerria is also part shade tolerant, making it a rare choice for a flowering shrub in a shadier location. The color of the flowers is deeper in part shade than full sun. Its arching branches radiate off main stems making for an interesting, cascading pattern. The stems are a greenish yellow color that makes them good choices to add interest to a winter landscape.

When, Where, and How to Plant
Kerria is hardy to zone 4, but may need protection from the winter weather in colder areas of New England. Purchase plants from a local garden center and plant from spring to summer in a well-drained, humus-rich soil location that stays evenly moist. Kerria isn't fussy about the fertility of the soil. Space plants 6 to 8 feet apart.

Growing Tips
Keep kerria well watered for best growth and flowering. Mulch in spring with bark mulch to maintain soil moisture and keep weeds away. Fertilize in spring with a layer of compost. Don't fertilize kerria too heavily or you'll get too much young growth and fewer flowers.

Regional Advice and Care
Prune kerria plants after flowering in spring to shape the shrub. Kerria can have many dead branches after a hard winter. Remove dead, diseased, or broken branches at any time. If the kerria shrub gets overgrown or isn't growing strongly, you can cut it to the ground to rejuvenate the plant. Kerria sends up suckers from their roots and can spread aggressively. Protect kerria shrubs from winter temperatures in colder areas by driving four stakes around the shrubs and wrapping with burlap around the stakes in late fall.

Companion Planting and Design
Plant kerria shrubs along your home's foundation in a location where their stems can naturally arch. Kerria makes a nice informal hedge because the suckers will fill the space between plants quickly. Because of this shrub's shade tolerance, consider planting in a woodland setting or at the edge of a forest to add some spring color. Kerria's branch patterns look interesting against the snow, so plant in a mixed shrub hedge with rhododendrons and mountain laurel to highlight the branches.

Try These
'Pleniflora' is a popular double-flowered variety that features pom-pom-like blossoms. 'Shannon' is another large-flowered variety that grows to 6 feet tall. 'Picta' is a variegated form that only grows to 4 feet tall, but is not as strong a bloomer as other varieties.

Lilac

Syringa vulgaris and hybrids

Botanical Pronunciation
si-RING-ga vul-GAY-ris

Other Name
Common lilac

Bloom Period and Seasonal Color
Spring; blue, purple, red, pink, and white

Mature Height × Spread
5 to 15 feet × 6 to 12 feet

One of the signature shrubs of New England is the lilac. Spring in New England wouldn't be the same without its fragrant, colorful, single or double flowers that bloom in May. Some varieties will rebloom again in late summer. When grown *en masse*, such as at the Arnold Arboretum in Boston, they put on quite an amazing display. The scented blooms make great cut flowers for the indoors. These tough shrubs are one of the hardiest in New England. They can grow into large shrubs if not pruned; there is even a tree form (*S. reticulata*) that's a popular street tree. There are also more naturally dwarf, rounded species that make great foundation plants because they don't get out of control.

When, Where, and How to Plant
Purchase plants from local garden centers or root suckers from a friend's or neighbor's plant. Plant from spring to early fall in a full sun location for best flowering. Lilacs need a well-drained soil to survive. They grow best in fertile, slightly alkaline soil that's been amended with compost. Space plants 6 feet apart.

Growing Tips
Keep young plants well watered and mulched with wood chips or bark mulch to preserve the soil moisture and reduce weed competition. Once established, lilac plants are drought tolerant. Each spring add compost and an organic plant food. Overfeeding plants may delay their flowering.

Regional Advice and Care
Lilacs won't bloom well due to poor soil water drainage or too much shade. Prune lilacs after flowering to remove dead blossoms and to keep the plant inbounds. If your lilac gets overgrown, prune back one-third of the branches to the ground each year, letting the suckers grow from the base, until the whole plant has been rejuvenated. Thin weak suckers each spring. Lilacs can get scale on their leaves and bark. Spray horticultural oil to control scale. Powdery mildew can make lilacs drop their leaves early. Spray an organic fungicide to control it.

Companion Planting and Design
Lilacs make a great informal hedge. Select varieties that sucker freely. Plant the more formal French hybrids as specimens on the corner of your house or in a mixed shrub border with other sun-loving shrubs such as viburnum and spirea. Plant rounded species, such the Meyer lilac, as a foundation plant. Plant the Japanese tree lilac as a street tree or specimen in the yard.

Try These
There are hundreds of lilacs varieties. Choose yours based on plant size, flower color, and fragrance. 'President Lincoln' is a classic, blue-flowering variety. 'Charles Joly' has magenta flowers. 'Belle of Nancy' is a double pink form. 'Ludwig Spaeth' is considered one of the best purple-flowered varieties. 'Miss Ellen Willmott' is a classic, double-white form. 'Sensation' has unique purple flowers edged in white and 'Primrose' is an unusual yellow-flowered variety.

Mock Orange

Philadelphus × *virginalis*

Botanical Pronunciation
fil-a-DEL-fus × ver-jin-AY-lis

Other Name
Virginal mock orange

Bloom Period and Seasonal Color
Late spring to early summer; shades of white

Mature Height × Spread
6 to 10 feet × 8 to 10 feet

This large shrub is a prized late-spring bloomer with its single- or double-petaled white flowers. Its claim to fame is the sweet, orangelike scent of the flowers that bees and butterflies love as well as people! When in flower, this fast-growing shrub is outstanding, but it is nondescript the rest of the growing season. The old-fashioned varieties can be a bit more fragrant than the modern types. Mock orange blooms make great cut flowers in bouquets indoors, scenting the whole house. In the garden its large size makes it a good addition to shrub borders, informal hedges, and specimen plantings. Mock orange looks like a bridal wreath spirea in appearance, but with stiffer branches and less arching stems.

When, Where, and How to Plant
Mock orange is hardy throughout New England. Purchase plants from a local garden center and plant from spring to early fall in well-drained soil amended with compost. It's very adaptable to many types of soil conditions. Mock orange flowers best in full sun. Space plants 6 to 8 feet apart.

Growing Tips
Keep young plants well watered. Established mock orange plants are drought tolerant. Mulch with wood chips or bark mulch to preserve soil moisture and suppress weeds. Fertilize in spring with a layer of compost and an organic plant food. Avoid overfertilizing or the shrub may be slow to flower.

Regional Advice and Care
Prune out dead, diseased, and broken branches in spring. Prune to shape this shrub after flowering. Mock orange can get overgrown and may need rejuvenation pruning periodically. To rejuvenate, prune the shrub back severely after flowering to stimulate new growth and to bring it inbounds. But it may take a few years to grow back to its former shape. Mock orange has few severe insect or disease problems.

Companion Planting and Design
Since mock orange tends to be a large plant and looks best when allowed to grow to its full proportions, plant it on the corner of a house or building where it can grown large but won't block windows or views. Mock orange also looks good mixed with forsythia, viburnums, and lilacs in an informal hedgerow or an island planting in the lawn. In the back of a perennial flower border, plant smaller varieties. Plant lower-growing perennial flowers in front of mock orange to hide the bottom of the shrub that tends to look bare with little foliage.

Try These
'Virginal' is an old-fashioned, double variety that grows to 10 feet tall and the flowers have an intense fragrance. 'Minnesota Snowflake' is a popular double variety with less fragrance, but it only grows to 6 feet tall. 'Snow Dwarf' is a compact version that grows only 3 feet tall. ''Starbright' is a newer tall variety with fragrant flowers and purple-bronze new leaves.

Mountain Laurel

Kalmia latifolia

Botanical Pronunciation
KAL-mee-uh lat-if-FOH-lee-a

Other Name
Calico bush

Bloom Period and Seasonal Color
Spring; white, pink, red, and bicolors

Mature Height × Spread
5 to 12 feet × 5 to 6 feet

Mountain laurel is a broadleaf evergreen that grows and flowers well in full sun to part shade, making it a versatile shrub in the landscape. The broad, dark green leaves provide interest all year long. In spring, clusters of cup-shaped flowers open in shades of white, pink, and red. It's a favorite of bees and butterflies. The shrub grows naturally in the filtered light under tall deciduous trees, such as oak and maple, especially near a wet, swampy area. I remember playing among mountain laurel groves as a child in Connecticut. It flowers best, though, with more sun in an open landscape, but the leaves may turn a yellow-green color in full sun.

When, Where, and How to Plant
Mountain laurel is hardy to zone 5. In colder areas of New England, it will need to be protected in winter with burlap barriers to block the winter wind. Purchase plants from your local garden center and look for the hardiest varieties for cold areas. Plant shrubs from spring, after all danger of frost has passed, into summer in well-drained, moist, acidic, cool soils. Avoid windy areas, if possible. Space plants 4 to 6 feet apart.

Growing Tips
Keep young shrubs well watered. Keep the soil evenly moist and acidic with a layer of wood chips or evergreen bark mulch. Fertilize mountain laurel in spring with a plant food for acidic-loving plants, such as you'd use for rhododendrons.

Regional Advice and Care
Mountain laurel will get spindly, develop leaf spots, and have few flowers if it's grown in too much shade. Look for leaf spot resistant varieties if growing under these conditions. It also doesn't grow well in poorly drained soils. It's a slow grower that should only be pruned to shape the plant in spring after flowering. Dead, diseased, and broken branches can be taken out at any time. Mountain laurel doesn't have many pest problems.

Companion Planting and Design
Plant mountain laurel in a part shade location as a foundation plant, out of direct winds. Group it with other broadleaf evergreens, such as rhododendrons and pieris. Plant mountain laurel in a woodland setting under tall deciduous trees or at the forest's edge.

Try These
Breeders at the University of Connecticut have created many varieties of mountain laurel suited for New England. 'Olympic Fire' is an older variety with reddish pink flower buds and waxy leaf spot resistant foliage. 'Pink Surprise' has pink flowers with reddish purple new foliage growth in spring, on an open plant habit. 'Raspberry Glow' features burgundy-red flower buds that open to pink. It develops good flower color even in shade. 'Snowdrift' has pure white flowers with dark green, leathery leaves. 'Elf' is a compact variety only growing 3 to 5 feet tall with pink-changing-to-white flowers.

Ninebark

Physocarpus opulifolius

Botanical Pronunciation
fy-so-KAR-pus op-yoo-lih-FOH-lee-us

Other Name
Atlantic ninebark

Bloom Period and Seasonal Color
Late spring and early summer; whitish pink
flowers; reddish fruits in fall; reddish peeling bark

Mature Height × Spread
5 to 10 feet × 6 to 8 feet

This attractive, native, deciduous shrub gets its common name from extreme peeling of the bark that is said to have nine layers. The plant itself is an easy-to-grow, hardy, large shrub with cascading branches and dark green leaves. Newer varieties have light green or even dark burgundy-colored leaves making this an interesting shrub even when it's not flowering. I like how the bright red flowers of my rose campion look contrasted with the dark ninebark foliage. The flowers emerge in late spring in clusters of white or pink.

The bright red fruit adds color in fall as well and are favorites for birds. With its reddish, peeling bark this shrub looks attractive every season of the year.

When, Where, and How to Plant
Ninebark is hardy throughout New England. Purchase plants from a local garden center and plant from spring to early fall in a full to part sun location on a well-drained, fertile soil, amended with compost. It's adapted to wet soils, but does best with good water drainage. Space plants 4 to 6 feet apart.

Growing Tips
Keep new plantings well watered; older plantings are more drought tolerant. Add a layer of bark mulch or wood chips in spring to preserve soil moisture and keep weeds away. Fertilize in spring with a layer of compost and an organic plant food.

Regional Advice and Care
Ninebark is an adaptable shrub that grows well under many conditions. It flowers and fruits best in full sun. Varieties with different colored leaves make this a good choice for part shade locations too. It has few pest problems, but individual limbs may die back over time and need to be removed at the base of the plant. The whole shrub may need rejuvenation pruning periodically to encourage new, younger branches with better leaves and flowers.

Companion Planting and Design
Plant ninebark as a foundation shrub where it won't grow to block a window or walkway. Give it enough space to grow in its naturally arching branch pattern for the best look. In a mixed shrub border, plant ninebark with other deciduous shrubs, such as lilacs and spireas. Use different-colored ninebarks in the back of a perennial flower border to show off the brightly colored perennials, such as coneflowers and bee balm.

Try These
'Snowfall' has dark green leaves on a 7-foot-tall shrub with showy flowers and berries. 'Diablo' has dark purple leaves that contrast well with the flowers and berries. In shade the leaves are not as deeply colored. 'Dart's Gold' and 'Nugget' feature yellow foliage on 5- to 6-foot-tall shrubs. The foliage turns greener in shade. 'Coppertina' has orange copper-colored foliage. 'Center Glow' has burgundy leaves with a golden center.

Pepperbush

Clethra alnifolia

Botanical Pronunciation
KLETH-ruh al-ni-FO-lee-uh

Other Name
Summersweet

Bloom Period and Seasonal Color
Mid- to late summer; white or pink flowers; yellow fall foliage

Mature Height × Spread
5 to 8 feet × 4 to 6 feet

This common native shrub is often found in moist woodland areas because it tolerates part shade and moist soils well. Pepperbush is a multistemmed, rounded shrub that is slow to leaf out in spring. Often gardeners will think it has died, only to see their pepperbush covered with leaves a week or so later. One thing I like about pepperbush is it blooms in mid- to late summer when few other shrubs are flowering. And the white or pink flowers are shaped like candles and are very fragrant. It's a great shrub to grow close to a deck, patio, or window to enjoy the scent. In fall the foliage turns a golden color adding to the multiseason interest.

When, Where, and How to Plant
Pepperbush is hardy throughout New England. Purchase plants from a local garden center or take divisions from a neighbor's or friend's plant. Plant shrubs from spring to early fall in well-drained, moist soil in a part sun or shade location. Pepperbush grows best in humus-rich, slightly acidic soils that don't dry out. Space plants 4 to 6 feet apart.

Growing Tips
Keep pepperbush soil moist by watering regularly and mulching with pine needles or evergreen bark mulch (which will also keep the soil slightly acidic). Fertilize in spring with an organic plant food.

Regional Advice and Care
Pepperbush may have some twig dieback after the first winter, but otherwise it grows well in our climate. Pepperbush forms flowers on new growth so prune the shrub in spring to promote new growth and to shape the plant. Remove dead, diseased, and damaged branches at any time. Pepperbush suckers freely. Prune out crowded new growth or dig up and divide the main bush to create new shrubs. Pepperbush has few pests. Protect plants from deer and rabbit browsing by erecting a barrier of burlap, wire, or wood in late fall.

Companion Planting and Design
Plant pepperbush as a foundation plant where it won't block a window, door, or walkway. Plant it close to the house and windows so you can enjoy the fragrant flowers in summer. Pepperbush also looks great in a mixed shrub border with earlier blooming potentilla and dwarf spirea or in a hedgerow where it will sucker freely and fill in the space. To add color in midsummer, plant pepperbush in the back of a perennial flower border with other midsummer bloomers, such as daylilies and bee balm. Pepperbush is tolerant of salt spray so can be planted near the ocean.

Try These
'Hummingbird' grows 3 to 4 feet tall and wide and has good fall foliage color. 'Ruby Spice' has dark pink flower buds that open to light pink and don't fade. It also has dark glossy foliage. 'Creel's Calico' grows 5 feet tall with variegated white-and-green leaves.

Potentilla

Potentilla fruticosa

Botanical Pronunciation
poh-ten-TIL-a froo-ti-KOH-sa

Other Name
Shrubby cinquefoil

Bloom Period and Seasonal Color
Midsummer until frost; yellow, white, pink, and orange

Mature Height × Spread
2 to 4 feet × 2 to 4 feet

Potentilla is a native, small, rounded shrub that is a beauty in a small garden. What's really special about this shrub is, unlike many other deciduous shrubs, potentilla blooms in waves from midsummer until frost. The small, buttercup-like flowers are traditionally yellow- or golden-colored, but newer varieties feature white, pink, and even orange-colored options. The finely textured, small leaves give this shrub a delicate look, and its slow growth rate makes it a popular choice to pair with perennials in the flower garden. But it is also a tough shrub that doesn't have many soil requirements and fits in many locations in the landscape as long as it has enough sun to flower well.

When, Where, and How to Plant
Potentilla is hardy throughout New England. Purchase plants from a local garden center and plant from spring to early fall in well-drained soil amended with compost. Potentilla will grow on any soil as long as it's not too wet. Space plants 3 to 6 feet apart.

Growing Tips
Water newly transplanted potentilla plants well and mulch with wood chips or bark mulch to keep the soil evenly moist and prevent weed growth. Fertilize in spring with a layer of compost and an organic plant food.

Regional Advice and Care
Potentilla is a relatively easy plant to grow. However, there will be some winter dieback in cold areas.

Prune out dead, diseased, and broken branches in spring. Prune periodically during the summer to shape the plant. Remove suckers to prevent the shrub from becoming overcrowded. Potentilla can be cut back severely, if necessary, to rejuvenate the shrub. Avoid planting in hot/dry conditions or spider mites may become a problem. Spray the plants with insecticidal soap to kill the mites.

Companion Planting and Design
Plant potentilla under windows along the foundation or mixed in a shrub or perennial flower border. The yellow-flowered varieties look attractive planted next to blue-flowering baptisia, salvia, and catmint. They also can be grown as a low hedge or around a formal herb garden. Mix and match other colored varieties with perennial flowers and low-growing shrubs, such as cotoneaster and dwarf spirea.

Try These
'Abbotswood' is a popular white-flowered variety that grows to 3 feet tall and wide. 'Abbotswood Silver' is a white-and-green variegated leaf form. 'Gold Drop' and 'Gold Finger' are common varieties that have bright yellow flowers that bloom for long periods. 'Pink Beauty' has pink flowers on 2-foot-tall and -wide shrubs. 'Snowbird' has double-petaled, white flowers. 'Tangerine' has yellow flowers flushed with orange on a 2-foot-tall and -wide shrub. 'Sunset' is a 16-inch-tall newer variety with yellow flowers that have red hues.

Privet

Ligustrum vulgare

Botanical Pronunciation
li-GUS-trum vol-GAY-ree

Other Name
Common privet

Bloom Period and Seasonal Color
Spring; white

Mature Height × Spread
5 to 15 feet × 5 to 15 feet

Privet is a popular, small-leaved hedge plant that grows quickly. Privet can be evergreen in warmer climates, but is mostly a deciduous plant in New England. The individual plant is nondescript, but when grown together it makes a good hedgerow plant. Because of its fast growth, it can be sheared frequently to create a formal-looking, dense hedge that can grow tall and be used to block views or define garden rooms in your landscape. Privet has small fragrant flowers. However, some people don't like the strong scent and avoid the plant for this reason. Privet also produces black berries and these berries are eaten by birds and spread throughout the landscape, making this an invasive plant in some areas.

When, Where, and How to Plant
Privet is hardy to zone 4. It may need some winter protection in colder parts of New England. Purchase plants from a local garden center. Plant from spring to summer in a full to part sun location in well-drained, compost-amended soil. Privet tolerates different types of soils, but grows best if the soil is kept moist. Space plants 4 to 6 feet apart.

Growing Tips
Water young privet plants regularly. Once established, it is drought tolerant. Mulch to maintain soil moisture and prevent weed growth. Fertilize in spring with a layer of compost and an organic plant food.

Regional Advice and Care
Privet should be pruned regularly to remove dead, diseased, and broken branches and to maintain its shape. Shear the plants three to four times a year starting after flowering and continue whenever the new growth gets long. Prune tall hedges so that the top of the hedge is slightly narrower than the bottom. This will allow light to reach the bottom of the hedge and prevent the lower branches from dying off due to shading. Privet plants are attacked by a number of diseases, such as blight and powdery mildew. Look for disease-resistant varieties. Aphids, spider mites, and whiteflies can also attack these shrubs. Spray plants with insecticidal soap to control these pests.

Companion Planting and Design
Privet is mostly used grouped together as a hedge plant to define a neighbor's boundary, block an unsightly view, or provide structure to a garden. Low-growing privet hedges can be used as borders for formal rose, perennial, or tea gardens. Privet hedges are traditionally used in knot gardens as well. Individual plants can be shaped into almost any form, such as a mound or box, making them useful as formal plants in a foundation planting.

Try These
'Cheyenne' is a common privet variety with multiple stems and dark green leaves. 'Amur River North' is a tall privet variety that produces 2-inch-long panicles of white flowers. 'Pyramidal' has a natural upright shape making it easier to prune.

Rhododendron

Rhododendron spp. and hybrids

Botanical Pronunciation
ro-do-DEN-drun

Other Name
Common rhododendron

Bloom Period and Seasonal Color
Spring; white, pink, red, purple, and yellow

Mature Height × Spread
3 to 10 feet × 3 to 10 feet

Rhododendrons are stalwarts in the New England shrub border. They are one of the few broadleaf evergreen shrubs that have brilliant, spring-blooming flowers and are hardy in your climate. I talked about deciduous azaleas (also in the Rhododendron family) in a previous entry. The bright flowers come in a broad range of colors, such as purple, pink, and red. They are generally, grouped as large-leaved (and -sized) and small-leaved (and sized) types. In our climate they grow well in full sun as well as part shade. The dark evergreen leaves provide color in winter to contrast the predominant browns and whites of that season. Some varieties have large, almost tropical plant-sized leaves, while others have small leaves that turn a brilliant, reddish fall color.

When, Where, and How to Plant

Rhododendrons can be hardy to zone 4 or 5. Select varieties hardy for your area. Purchase plants from a local garden center. Plant in spring to summer in moist, well-drained, humus-rich, acidic soil. Rhododendron flowers best in a site of filtered light. Avoid hot, dry, windy sites. They may need some winter protection if grown in windy locations. Space plants 3 to 6 feet apart.

Growing Tips

Keep rhododendron plants well watered. Apply mulch, such as pine needles, wood chips, or peat moss, to keep the soil acidic, cool, and moist. Fertilize in spring to lower the pH to 5.0 with an acidifying fertilizer meant for rhododendrons.

Regional Advice and Care

Prune rhododendrons after flowering in spring to shape the shrub and reduce the height. Don't prune into old wood; rhododendrons are slow to recover from severe pruning. Remove dead, diseased, or broken branches at any time. Protect exposed plants in cold climates by driving four stakes around the shrub and wrapping burlap around the stakes to buffer winter's drying winds. Don't let the burlap touch the foliage or it may dry the leaves out.

Companion Planting and Design

In a mixed shrub border, plant large-leaved rhododendrons, which are also large plants, with other evergreens, such as mountain laurel. Plant these large shrubs on the corner of a building so they don't block a view from a window. They grow well on the north side of garages and buildings. Plant the smaller-sized and -leafed varieties as foundation plants or in a mixed shade border with hostas, astilbe, and ornamental grasses.

Try These

For large-leaved varieties that can grow to 10 feet tall, try the lilac-purple 'Grandiflora', white-flowered 'Catawba White', or red-flowered 'Roseum Elegans'. For small-leaved varieties the 'PJM' is probably the most popular. This shrub grows 3 to 6 feet tall and wide with light purple flowers and nice fall foliage color. Variations include 'Olga', which has pink flowers, and 'Molly Fordham', which has white flowers. These variations may not be as hardy as the traditional 'PJM'.

Rose of Sharon

Hibiscus syriacus

Botanical Pronunciation
hi-BIS-kus si-ri-A-kus

Other Name
Shrub althea

Bloom Period and Seasonal Color
Midsummer to fall; white, pink, blue, lilac, red, and bicolors

Mature Height × Spread
8 to 10 feet × 6 to 8 feet

Rose of Sharon is a rare shrub because it blooms from mid- to late summer to fall when few other shrubs are in flower. It has beautiful, large, single or double cup-shaped flowers in a range of bright colors. The large, vase-shaped shrub is quick growing and has many vertical stems that are often covered with flowers in late summer, making for a striking show. Rose of Sharon is a low-maintenance shrub that leafs out late in spring, so don't worry if it's still bare when other shrubs are growing. Since its big show is late in the growing season, rose of Sharon is often paired with other earlier blooming, full sun-loving shrubs to provide continuous color.

When, Where, and How to Plant
Rose of Sharon is hardy to zone 5, so it will need winter protection in colder areas. Purchase plants from local garden centers and plant from spring to early fall in well-drained, fertile soil. Rose of Sharon is tolerant of many soil types. The sunniest and hottest locations produce the most flowers. Space plants 4 to 6 feet apart.

Growing Tips
Water plants well and mulch with wood chips or bark to keep the soil moist and weed-free. Fertilize in spring with a layer of compost and an organic plant food.

Regional Advice and Care
Rose of Sharon blooms on new shoots formed in spring. Prune in spring to remove dead, diseased, broken, or winter-injured branches. Prune to shape the shrub and encourage more new growth. In colder areas, drive four stakes around the shrub and wrap burlap around the stakes to break the drying winds. Protect the plant from insects, such as spider mites and aphids, with sprays of insecticidal soap and from diseases by mulching around the plant and cleaning up fallen leaves well in autumn. Rose of Sharon can spread by seed so is considered invasive in some areas. Consider purchasing varieties with sterile seed.

Companion Planting and Design
Rose of Sharon looks great planted in a shrub border with forsythia, lilac, viburnum, and other shrubs with complementary bloom times. It also can be planted in a hedgerow to block an unsightly view. Avoid planting it as a specimen plant in the lawn since it will have little interest for much of the summer.

Try These
'Aphrodite' has a pink flower with a dark red eyespot in the center and doesn't produce viable seeds. 'Bluebird' is an older variety with blue flowers with a reddish base. 'Diana' produces large white flowers that don't produce viable seeds. 'Tricolor' has unusual double, pink, red, and purple flowers on the same plant. 'Minerva' is a heavy blooming lavender-colored variety with a pink eye. The shrub is smaller than many other varieties, only growing to 5 to 8 feet tall.

Shrub Rose

Rosa spp. and hybrids

Botanical Pronunciation
ROE-zuh

Other Name
Landscape rose

Bloom Period and Seasonal Color
Summer; white, pink, red, yellow, purple, and salmon

Mature Height × Spread
2 to 5 feet × 2 to 5 feet

Roses are a *huge* group of plants, and many types of roses grow well in New England. However, some gardeners have shied away from growing varieties due to their reputation for requiring high maintenance, attracting lots of pests, and lacking hardiness. A relatively new group of roses is on the market that aims to make rose growing much easier. The shrub roses are hardy, low-maintenance varieties that grow to 6 feet tall and bloom all season. They come in single- or double-flowered forms in a multitude of color shades. This group of roses grows well next to other low-growing shrubs or in a perennial flower border. Some varieties have fragrant flowers while others produce colorful hips in fall.

When, Where, and How to Plant

Shrub roses are hardy in New England, but may need protection in zone 4 areas. Purchase plants from a local garden center and plant from spring to summer in well-drained soil amended with compost. Shrub roses flower best in full sun (although some can take a little bit less). Space plants 2 to 5 feet apart.

Growing Tips

Keep roses well watered and mulch to conserve soil moisture and prevent weed growth. Fertilize monthly with an organic plant food.

Regional Advice and Care

Prune shrub roses anytime to remove dead, diseased, and broken branches. Prune in late winter to remove winter-injured branches and to shape the roses. If plants are struggling or have gotten out of control, prune shrub roses severely, and they will regrow from the crown well. However, on grafted varieties, *don't* prune below the graft union (the area with a bulge on the stem) on the main stem or you will remove the desired variety. Shrub roses have less insect and disease problems than other roses, but you still may have to control Japanese beetles by handpicking, trapping, or spraying them.

Companion Planting and Design

Plant shrub roses in a perennial flower border to add summer-long color. Many of the pink and red varieties look particularly beautiful near blue-colored perennials, such as salvia and clematis. In a hedgerow, plant shrub roses to add beauty to a boundary line of your property. Shrub roses can even be grown in containers. Protect the container roses in winter, bringing them into a garage or unheated basement.

Try These

'Bonica' produces clusters of pink-colored flowers and orange hips in fall. The 'Meidiland' series features shrub roses in pink, red, or white with good disease resistance and strong growth. Knockout roses are another series with single- and double-petaled roses in a range of colors. 'John Cabot' is a Canadian Explorer series shrub rose with great winter hardiness and fragrant, fuchsia-pink blooms. The Carefree series features disease-resistant plants and varieties, such as 'Carefree Wonder' (pink), 'Carefree Spirit' (red), and 'Carefree Sunshine' (yellow).

Smokebush

Cotinus coggygria

Botanical Pronunciation
koe-TYE-nus koe-GUY-gree-uh

Other Name
Smoketree

Bloom Period and Seasonal Color
Early summer; yellow flowers; cream, pink, or purple plumes

Mature Height × Spread
12 to 15 feet × 10 to 12 feet

Smokebush is a large deciduous shrub with attractive oval leaves that are green or burgundy depending on the variety. This is a specimen shrub in the landscape or it can be used in a hedgerow. The common name refers to the plumelike hairs, which look like cotton candy, that erupt from the small yellow flowers. I know gardeners who swear the whole bush looks like it's engulfed in smoke when it's in full "bloom." These plumes can last for weeks and actually darken in color over time. The shrub is easy to grow, adapted to many soil and weather conditions, and it particularly does well in hot, dry soils. Some varieties also feature attractive orange fall leaves.

When, Where, and How to Plant

Smokebush is hardy to zone 4 when planted in a protected location. Purchase plants from a local garden center and plant from spring to early fall in well-drained soil. Smokebush isn't fussy about the soil type or fertility as long as it's well drained. Space plants 12 to 15 feet apart.

Growing Tips

Water young smokebush plants well. Once established, smokebushes are drought tolerant. Mulch with wood chips or bark mulch to keep weeds away and to keep the soil moist. Fertilize in spring with a layer of compost. If the shrub isn't growing strongly, feed some organic plant food annually.

Regional Advice and Care

Prune in spring to rejuvenate the shrub, bringing it back inbounds, or remove any winter-injured branches. Prune anytime to remove dead, diseased, and broken branches. Some gardeners consider the flowers messy and not all that attractive. If you want just the colorful foliage, prune smokebushes heavily in spring to remove flowering wood. Smokebushes are mostly trouble-free shrubs. However, they can die back due to wilt diseases if they're grown on poorly drained soils.

Companion Planting and Design

Since smokebushes grow into large shrubs, care should be given about where they are planted. Locate them on the corner of a building or along a windowless structure, such as a garage, so there's room for the bush to grow but where it won't block a view from a window. In a mixed shrub hedgerow, plant smokebush as a "smoke"-screen with other large shrubs that bloom earlier in the season, such as lilacs, viburnums, and spireas. Smokebush can tolerate dry, poor soil conditions where other shrubs might struggle.

Try These

'Daydream' grows 10 feet tall and wide with dense, creamy white blooms. 'Nordine' is a purple-leafed version that's very hardy and has yellow-orange fall foliage color. 'Royal Purple' has purple foliage and plumes, but isn't as hardy as 'Nordine'. 'Velvet Cloak' is another purple-leafed variety with good fall color. 'Golden Spirit' produces light golden foliage that fades to lime green in summer and turns orange-red in fall.

Spirea

Spirea spp.

Botanical Pronunciation
spy-REE-a

Other Name
Steeplebush

Bloom Period and Seasonal Color
Midsummer; pink, rose, and white

Mature Height × Spread
3 to 8 feet × 3 to 5 feet

Spirea is a broad group of durable, deciduous plants that are well adapted to our New England climate. There are a number of different species available, and they all feature small leaves on thin stems with colorful pink, red, or white flower clusters. Depending on the species, the stems can be long and cascading, creating a stunning visual when in full bloom. There is nothing like the look of a bridalwreath spirea in full bloom. Other species have more compact growth and are able to fit neatly into a foundation planting or perennial flower border in the landscape. Newer varieties have yellow-green leaves that offer a nice contrast to the flower colors. Some varieties have nice fall color as well.

When, Where, and How to Plant
Spireas are hardy throughout New England. Purchase plants from your local garden center and plant from spring to early fall in full to part sun in well-drained soil. Spireas aren't picky about the type of soil as long as it's well drained. Space plants 3 to 6 feet apart.

Growing Tips
Once established, spireas are drought tolerant but keep young plants well watered. Add a layer of wood chips or bark mulch in spring to maintain soil moisture and to suppress weed growth. Add a layer of compost and an organic plant food in spring to promote new growth.

Regional Advice and Care
Since spirea blooms on new wood, prune the tips of the stems in spring to promote more flowering.

Some spireas sucker freely so they should be thinned vigorously. Because of this aggressive growth, they can become invasive. Prune after flowering, removing individual stems to the ground. Spirea can also be pruned severely to rejuvenate the shrub. Deadhead spent flowers to keep the plant looking tidy. Spireas can get powdery mildew disease on the leaves. Space plants farther apart and spray an organic fungicide to control it.

Companion Planting and Design
Plant large, cascading spireas where they won't block a view from a window, such as alongside a garage or on the corner of your foundation. Shorter, more compact varieties fit well in a mixed shrub border with other deciduous shrubs, such as forsythia, daphne, and clethra. Compact varieties with attractive foliage also make good anchoring shrubs in a perennial flower border, providing visual interest all summer.

Try These
'Bridalwreath' or 'Vanhoutte' spirea is the classic, large, flowing, white-flowered spirea with cascading branches. 'Snowmound' is a 7-foot-tall version that has less disease. 'Anthony Waterer' is a popular 4- to 5-foot-tall and -wide spirea with pink-rose-colored blooms and reddish fall foliage color. 'Goldflame' is a gold leaf spirea with light pink blooms. It grows 3 feet tall and wide. 'Goldmound' is a similar gold leaf version, but the leaves are less likely to fade in full sun and during hot weather.

Viburnum

Viburnum spp. and hybrids

Botanical Pronunciation vy-BER-num

Other Name Sweet viburnum

Bloom Period and Seasonal Color
Spring; pink, white, and red; colorful fruits and fall foliage

Mature Height × Spread
6 to 12 feet × 6 to 10 feet

Viburnums form a diverse group of easy-to-grow, native, deciduous shrubs that work well in many places in the landscape. You'll see wild plants naturally growing, but newer selections have improved growth habits. Their clusters of white flowers bloom in mid-spring. Some viburnums have flat flowers, while others have snowball-shaped blooms. A few viburnums have fragrant flowers, making them excellent choices for planting under windows or near decks. For many other viburnums, it's the late summer and fall berry production and fall foliage color that make this plant shine. Berries come in colors such as red, white, and blue-black. Viburnums make excellent wildlife shrubs; birds love the berries and some of the berries make an excellent jam or jelly. Fall foliage color can be reddish purple.

When, Where, and How to Plant
Viburnums grow throughout New England. Purchase plants from a local garden center and plant from spring to early fall in well-drained, compost-amended, moist soil. You'll get the most fruit production and best fall color when it's planted in full sun, but part sun locations will do. Space plants 6 to 10 feet apart.

Growing Tips
Viburnum likes a moist soil, so keep plants well watered and add a layer of wood chips or bark mulch each spring to maintain soil moisture and keep weeds away. Fertilize in spring with a layer of compost and an organic plant food.

Regional Advice and Care
Some viburnums can grow into large shrubs that may need rejuvenation pruning periodically to keep them inbounds. Prune after flowering to shape. Remove any dead, diseased, or broken branches anytime. Viburnums generally don't have many insect or disease problems. The viburnum leaf beetle may defoliate certain species, such as the arrowwood viburnum (*V. dentatum*). Control this insect with an appropriate pesticide spray in spring.

Companion Planting and Design
Viburnums are versatile plants. Plant lower-growing types, such as the Korean spice viburnum (*V. carlesii*), near windows or patios to enjoy their fragrance. Plant large shrubs, such as the American cranberry bush (*V. trilobum*) or snowball viburnum (*V. opulus*) in a mixed shrub hedgerow with other large shrubs, such as lilacs and forsythia. Plant easy-to-grow natives, such as the nannyberry (*V. lentago*) and black haw viburnum (*V. prunifolium*), along a forest's edge to provide food for wildlife, or plant in an abandoned area to fill in a space.

Try These
'Wentworth' is a good American cranberry viburnum with excellent fruit production. 'Compactum' is a 6-foot dwarf version. 'Morton' is an arrowwood viburnum with large black-berries and deep red fall foliage colors on a 12-foot-tall shrub. 'Blue Muffin' is a 4-foot-tall dwarf arrowwood viburnum. 'Roseum' is a famous snowball viburnum, with large, round white flowers. 'Mariesii' is a classic doublefile viburnum (*V. plicatum*) with horizontal branching. 'Cayuga' is a variety of the Koreanspice viburnum that features fragrant white flowers on 5-foot-tall plants.

Weigela

Weigela florida

Botanical Pronunciation
wy-GEE-la FLOR-i-da

Other Name Old-fashioned weigela

Bloom Period and Seasonal Color
Late spring to early summer; white, pink, and red

Mature Height × Spread
2 to 10 feet × 4 to 12 feet

Weigela is an old-fashioned shrub that has undergone a bit of a renaissance. While the traditional form of weigela is a large shrub with arching stems, green leaves, and pink or red flowers, newer varieties have more compact growth and offer a variety of flower and leaf colors. This has broadened the use of weigelas in the landscape and piqued interest in this plant. No longer are they the "one trick shrub pony" that is nondescript after flowering. With interesting leaf patterns and colors, weigelas can be a star in your shrub border or even mixed in with flowers in a foundation planting. Some forms are even small enough to grow in containers, as long as they are protected in winter.

When, Where, and How to Plant
Weigela are hardy to zone 5, so they may need some winter protection in colder areas. Purchase plants from a local garden center and plant from spring to early fall in well-drained, compost-amended soil. Space plants 3 to 6 feet apart.

Growing Tips
Weigela is adaptable to most soils, but grows best on well-drained soils that stay consistently moist. Keep well watered and mulch with wood chips or bark mulch to keep weeds away and soil moist. In spring, feed these shrubs by topdressing a layer of compost and feeding an organic plant food.

Regional Advice and Care
Weigela branches can suffer some winter dieback, especially in windy sites and cold areas. Prune out dead, diseased, or damaged branches in spring and prune to shape the shrub after flowering. In cold areas, consider driving four stakes around young shrubs and wrapping burlap around the stakes to protect the plants from winter winds. Older plants are more winter tolerant. Weigela doesn't have any significant pest problems.

Companion Planting and Design
In a hedgerow, plant tall weigela varieties with other large shrubs, such as lilacs and viburnums, or on the corner of a building so as not to block a view. In a mixed shrub border, plant compact varieties with interesting foliage in with perennial flowers or along the foundation. Since weigela branches aren't attractive when they're bare, consider mixing this shrub with evergreens, such as mounded cedars, to block some of the bare branches from view in winter.

Try These
'Bristol Snowflake' is a tall, vigorous, white-flowering variety. 'Wine and Roses' and 'Minuet' are 3- to 4-foot-tall varieties with rose-pink blooms and purple-tinged green leaves. 'My Monet' is a 2-foot-tall dwarf shrub with pink flowers and white, pink, and green leaves. 'Midnight Wine' only grows 2 feet tall with dark burgundy-colored leaves and pink flowers. These dwarf cultivars can be grown in a container. 'Variegata Dwarf' grows only 3 feet tall with pink flowers and white edged with green leaves. 'Rubridor' grow 7 feet tall with yellow-green leaves and rose-colored blooms.

Witchhazel

Hamamelis spp.

Botanical Pronunciation
ham-a-MEE-lis

Other Name
Common witchhazel

Bloom Period and Seasonal Color
Fall or late winter; yellow, orange, or red;
colorful fall foliage

Mature Height × Spread
10 to 15 feet × 10 to 15 feet

Witchhazel is an unusual plant in the shrub world, and I'm always pleasantly surprised by it. Depending on the species you're growing it will bloom either in late fall after all the leaves of deciduous plants have dropped or late winter before any other shrubs have leafed out. The spiderlike flowers are small, but noticeable, since they cover the shrub, and there are no leaves to interfere with viewing them. The flowers come in yellow to almost red colors and have a slight fragrance. Witchhazel also has beautiful golden fall foliage making it a good choice in the autumn garden. This large, woody shrub is shade tolerant, so it is a good plant for working into woodland settings.

When, Where, and How to Plant
While some species of witchhazel are native to our area, there are species that are marginally hardy in colder parts of New England. Check your hardiness zone before purchasing. Purchase plants from a local garden center and plant from spring to early fall in well-drained, moist, slightly acidic soil. Space plants 10 to 12 feet apart.

Growing Tips
Water witchhazel well and mulch with pine needles or wood chips to keep the soil consistently moist and slightly acidic. In spring, add a layer of compost and an acidifying fertilizer to keep the plant growing healthy.

Regional Advice and Care
The native witchhazel (*H. virginiana*) needs little care. Prune to remove dead, diseased, and damaged branches in spring and to shape the shrub. Prune to remove suckers from the base of the plant if they start crowding the branches. Witchhazel can be slow to grow, so give it plenty of room to fill in. For marginally hardy witchhazels, consider driving four stakes around the shrub and wrapping burlap around the stakes to protect the plant from winter winds. Place the burlap up after flowering in fall or remove the burlap early enough in late winter to enjoy the flowers.

Companion Planting and Design
In a mixed-shrub border, plant witchhazel with other large deciduous shrubs, such as weigelas, lilacs, and viburnums. Plant in a location where it can grow to its full size and where you can enjoy the flowers in late fall or winter. Consider planting in groups in a woodland setting under tall deciduous trees, such as oaks.

Try These
'Arnold Promise' is a popular yellow-flowering variety that blooms in late winter. 'Primavera' has very fragrant yellow flowers in late winter and attractive golden leaves in fall. 'Diane' has red-copper colored, late-winter flowers. The common witchhazel (*H. virginiana*) blooms in late fall with yellow flowers. 'Coombe Wood' is a Chinese witchhazel (*H. mollis*) that has golden late-winter blooms and a large, broad growth habit. However, it is the least hardy of the witchhazels.

Yew

Taxus spp.

Botanical Pronunciation
TAKS-us

Other Name
Common yew

Bloom Period and Seasonal Color
Grown for dark evergreen needles

Mature Height × Spread
2 to 40 feet × 2 to 20 feet

Yew is a standard evergreen shrub found around many homes in New England. They vary widely in size, but most have the trademark dark green needles. Some even have golden needles. Yews mostly are grouped as upright plants (pyramidal or columnar) or low-growing, spreading plants depending on the variety. Some produce bright red berries that aren't necessarily ornamental, but which can spread seeds, making some forms of yews invasive. While the classic English and Irish yews (*T. baccata*) grow into large trees and may only be hardy in warmer parts of our region, there are many other smaller species that grow well here. Yews can be allowed to grow in their natural form or be tightly trimmed into a formal hedge or screen plant.

When, Where, and How to Plant
Some types of yews are hardy to zone 4, while others are hardy only to zone 6. Select varieties based on your region and the hardiness zone of your plants. Purchase plants from a local garden center and plant from spring to summer in well-drained, sandy, fertile soil. Space plants 2 to 20 feet apart, depending on the variety.

Growing Tips
Keep young yews well watered. Once established, yews are drought tolerant. Yews grow best in humus-rich soil that has excellent drainage. Fertilize yews in spring with a layer of compost and an evergreen shrub fertilizer.

Regional Advice and Care
Select the right yew for your location to avoid having to hack it back when it's older and overgrown (a too common sight in many yards). Yews don't respond well to pruning into old wood, so never prune below the green needles. Remove dead, diseased, and broken branches anytime. Trim in early summer to shape the shrub and keep it inbounds. Trim again every few weeks if growing yews as a formal hedge. Yews are generally insect and disease free, but the needles may yellow in windswept locations.

Companion Planting and Design
Plant smaller yews as a foundation plant along a house near other evergreens, such as rhododendrons, or to highlight a walkway or entrance. Use these yews as a formal hedge around an herb or flower garden. Yews make good substitutes for boxwoods in formal gardens in cold areas. Plant taller yews as a hedgerow to block a view or mark a boundary line.

Try These
'Capitata' is a common pyramidal form that can grow large, but which can be kept well pruned and tamed. 'Aurescens' is a slow-growing 3-foot-tall and -wide variety that has yellow needles when they are young. 'Densiformis' is a standard yew that's wider (8 feet) than tall (4 feet) and can be sheared easily. 'Hicksii' is an upright yew that grows 20 feet tall and 12 feet wide. 'Viridis' is a columnar yew that grows 12 feet tall and has pale yellow-green, young needles.

TREES
FOR NEW ENGLAND

There is no other plant in your landscape that says you'll be around for a while like a tree. Like kids, trees are long-term commitments. It's no wonder we debate the merits of planting them in our yard. But there is a tree to fit any yard. And although large shade trees may take many years to turn into that majestic tree you imagine, many of the smaller trees will grow quickly into a beautiful landscape feature.

How to Pick?

Deciding on which tree to plant is much like deciding on which shrub. First, you'll need to think about the role the tree will have in your yard. Are you planting a tree for shade, flowers, fall foliage, berries, an informal hedge, winter interest? Some trees will combine many of these features. Do you want an evergreen or deciduous tree? Do you need a tree that tolerates pollution in the city? Do a quick assessment of the spaces you have available for trees. Is the area for your tree in full sun and have well-drained soil? The most important factor is having the adequate room to grow the tree of your dreams. I've seen too many beautiful trees be deformed by utility companies pruning trees that have grown into power lines. I've also seen mature trees removed from yards because their roots are interfering with septic lines, sidewalks, and driveways.

Once you know how much space you have and the size tree that will fit that area, then it's time to decide what qualities you want. For small flowering trees, it's hard to beat redbuds, crabapples, and dogwoods. For large shade trees, maples and oaks are the standards, but less widely grown trees, such as sweetgum and tulip tree, provide shade and great fall color. For city trees, lindens tolerate the conditions in urban

River birch (*Betula nigra* 'Heritage')

areas well. If you find a large tree you love, but don't have the room, often there are dwarf or weeping versions that can fit in a small space.

While we often grow trees for shade, flowers, and fall color, don't forget the winter. We have a long winter in New England, so any way to brighten up the landscape is welcome. Growing trees with interesting bark colors and textures is a great way to make the yard look alive. Large trees, such as sycamore and zelkova, and smaller trees, such as the birches and paperbark maples, offer beautiful bark colors that can be enjoyed right to spring.

Picking the Right Tree

When selecting the tree from a local nursery, look for a container or balled-and-burlapped tree that doesn't have damage to the trunk, has branches evenly spaced around the trunk, and has been kept well watered. In containers, check to see if roots are growing out the drainage holes. This is a sign the tree is rootbound and may be slow to recover once it's planted. For balled-and-burlapped trees, rock the tree trunk back

Flowering cherry *Prunus yedoensis*

and forth. The root-ball should move with the trunk. If it moves independently, the roots haven't gotten established in the rootball and this tree may not transplant well.

Once you bring your prize home, dig a hole twice the diameter of the rootball and as deep. Only amend the soil with compost if you have very poor soil fertility. Water it well. Stake the tree only in windy locations and only for the first year. The gentle rocking of the trunk in the breeze actually helps tree roots get firmly established. Create a mulch ring around the tree and mulch with organic matter each year to keep the soil evenly moist and weed free. Water regularly the first year. Often trees have 90 percent of their roots removed or damaged in the transplanting process from tree farm to garden center so that they'll need some pampering. Once established, your tree will thrive with little care to become that permanent fixture in your yard.

American Elm

Ulmus americana

Botanical Pronunciation
ULL-mus uh-mer-ee-KAHN-ah

Other Name Elm

Bloom Period and Seasonal Color
Not grown for color; grown for its vase shape

Mature Height × Spread
60 to 90 feet × 30 × 70 feet

The American elm was the quintessential, deciduous street tree throughout many towns and cities in New England until Dutch elm disease wiped out many of the trees in the early 1900s. You can easily see why this was such a prized tree. The large trunk grows up to 90 feet tall and has a huge, vase-shaped top, making it perfect to provide shade, but also not so much of a space hog on the ground level. Through breeding and selection, there are now American elms on the market with improved resistance to the Dutch elm disease, so this tree is starting to be seen again in landscapes. Because of its size, make sure you have a large enough space to accommodate this beautiful tree in your yard.

When, Where, and How to Plant

American elms are hardy to zone 3 and are found throughout New England. Purchase disease-resistant trees from a local garden center or nursery. Plant in spring to early fall in a full sun location. Elms in the wild grow well near streams and wetlands, so make sure the soil in your location is consistently moist. The tree tolerates salty soils, making them suitable for coastal sites.

Growing Tips

Keep young trees well watered and mulched with bark mulch to maintain soil moisture and reduce competition from lawn grass and weeds. Fertilize in spring with a layer of compost and an organic plant food sprinkled around the tree's drip line.

Regional Advice and Care

Even though they're medium-fast growers, it will take many years to grow a sizable elm tree in your yard. Keep the tree healthy by removing dead, diseased, or broken branches in fall, keeping it well watered and fed regularly. Protect young trees from elm beetles and deer browsing.

Companion Planting and Design

You can plant American elms in lawn areas, abandoned meadows, or as street trees. They make good shade trees. Elms are striking in the landscape, so plant where you can enjoy the full view of the tree's structure. Keep a large mulch ring around the tree to reduce grass competition and prevent damage from lawn mowers and string trimmers.

Try These

Dutch elm disease is still present, so it's important to choose newer varieties that are reportedly more resistant. One of the best is 'Valley Forge'. It has the classic, tall vase shape with green leaves that turn yellow in autumn. 'Princeton' grows only 70 feet tall and has also shown good disease resistance. 'Jefferson' is a hybrid that grows 50 feet tall and wide with good arching branches. 'Liberty' is a widely touted variety, but its disease resistance isn't as good as others, and it's also susceptible to other diseases beyond Dutch elm. Chinese elm (*U. parvifolia*) is a smaller tree than the American types, but is resistant to this disease and is often used to create disease-resistant hybrids.

American Tamarack

Larix laricina

Botanical Pronunciation LAR-iks lar-ih-SEE-nah

Other Name Larch

Bloom Period and Seasonal Color
Year-round; bluish green needles; turns bright yellow in autumn

Mature Height × Spread
50 to 80 feet × 20 to 30 feet

This native tree of eastern North America is unique. It has needles like other evergreens, such as spruce and pine, but it's deciduous. The bluish green needles are attractive in summer and turn golden yellow in late fall, making American tamarack one of the last trees to turn color in autumn. I often see wild stands of tamaracks in late fall with brilliant golden foliage, standing out in an otherwise defoliated deciduous forest. However, the needles then drop for winter. Tamarack trees have a slow to medium growth rate. They are best grown in groves for the most dramatic effect, but dwarf and weeping versions (some standing less than 10 feet tall) look great in gardens. Tamaracks do produce cones, but they are small, egg-shaped, and not particularly ornamental.

When, Where, and How to Plant
American tamarack is very hardy throughout New England. Purchase trees from a local nursery and plant in spring or summer in well-drained, acidic, moist soils. American tamarack grows well in wet sites. Space trees 20 to 30 feet apart.

Growing Tips
American tamarack needs cool, moist soils to thrive. Plant trees near streams or in wet areas. American tamarack is most suited to a naturalized setting. Fertilize young trees with compost and an acidifying fertilizer. Once established, they should grow fine without additional plant foods.

Regional Advice and Care
American tamarack trees don't grow well in lawn settings, in the shade, near air or water pollution, or on hot sites. European larch (*L. decidua*) is more tolerant of these conditions. It really is a native tree that thrives in its natural environment. Birds and other wildlife enjoy these trees for food and shelter. Remove dead limbs anytime. Aphids can be a problem on new growth. Spray insecticidal soap to kill them on young trees. On tall, mature trees invite ladybugs and other predators come to feed on the aphids.

Companion Planting and Design
Plant in a woodland setting, abandoned meadows, wetland areas, and generally in any location where wild American tamaracks would thrive. Plant in groups or groves for the most dramatic fall color effect. Dwarf versions of these trees in the garden serve as an unusual specimen tree. Weeping tamarack has a cascading growth pattern that makes for an interesting small tree in a garden. American tamarack is also commonly used as a bonsai tree.

Try These
Most nurseries only carry the native species of American tamarack. 'Blue Sparkler' is an improved selection with very blue needles. 'Deborah Waxman' is a dwarf selection that grows only 4 feet tall and wide. 'Newport Beauty' barely reaches 2 feet tall and is a slow grower. 'Pendula' is a weeping form of American tamarack; it grows 12 feet tall and 10 feet wide with a cascading growth habit. 'Puli' is another weeping form that has a narrow, upright growth.

Ash

Fraxinus spp.

Botanical Pronunciation
FRAK-si-nus

Bloom Period and Seasonal Color
Fall; yellow to purple (depending on species);
grown mostly for its height

Mature Height × Spread
60 to 70 feet × 30 to 40 feet

This tall, native tree is a common sight in New England forests and makes an excellent landscape, park, street, or shade tree. It's mostly grown for its tall rounded crown and evenly distributed branches. Some species have particularly attractive fall foliage color turning yellow or even purplish-colored in autumn. The female trees produce seedpods, called samaras, that may become a nuisance in a more formal setting when they drop. They litter the ground and may produce many new seedlings that will require weeding out. Look for seedless varieties if this is a concern. Next time you're at Fenway Park for a baseball game, think of this tree with every ball that's hit. Ash wood has been traditionally used to make baseball bats.

When, Where, and How to Plant

Ash trees are hardy throughout New England depending on the species. White ash (*F. americana*) and green ash (*F. pennsylvanica*) are considered the hardiest. Purchase trees from a local nursery and plant from spring to early fall in deep, fertile soils. Ash trees, however, are tolerant of poorly drained soils too. Space trees 30 to 40 feet apart.

Growing Tips

Keep young trees well watered and mulched in a lawn, park, or garden setting with a layer of bark mulch. Refresh the mulch each year and keep a mulch ring around trees to prevent the trunk from getting injured by lawn mowers or string trimmers. Feed an organic plant food around the drip line of young trees. Established ash trees don't need fertilizer.

Regional Advice and Care

Ash trees need little care to keep growing strong. They are bothered, though, by insects and diseases. Ash yellows is a disease that stunts and kills trees in a few years. The emerald ash borer is a new, widespread insect concern in all New England states because it can spread fast and quickly kill healthy trees. To reduce the spread of diseased or insect-ridden wood, cut down infected trees, do not transport ash wood to other locations, and report any signs of emerald ash borers to your local forestry officials.

Companion Planting and Design

Grow ash trees in wide-open areas, such as a large yard, park, school campus, or forest. Plant where the tree has plenty of room to expand and won't interfere with overhead power lines or nearby buildings. They make excellent shade trees in a lawn.

Try These

'Autumn Applause' is a popular 50-foot-tall white ash tree that has deep red fall foliage color. 'Greenspire' is a 40-foot-tall white ash with orange fall foliage color. 'Jungiger' is a 50-foot-tall white ash that is seedless and produces purple fall foliage. 'Patmore' and 'Summit' are seedless green ash varieties that grow 50 feet tall and have yellow fall color. 'Bergeson' is one of the hardiest ash varieties available that's seedless with fall yellow color.

Beech

Fagus spp.

Botanical Pronunciation
FA-gus

Other Name
Common beech

Bloom Period and Seasonal Color
Fall; bronze or yellow foliage; grown mostly for its height, colorful leaves, attractive bark

Mature Height × Spread
50 to 70 feet × 100 feet

The beech tree is a staple in New England forests. Its large spread, attractive light gray, smooth bark, and brilliant fall foliage color make it an excellent woodland or specimen tree. The branches of mature beech trees can arch downward, touching the ground, creating an amazing sight of foliage from ground to sky. I've seen some great examples of these planted around the mansions in Newport, Rhode Island. There is more variety in beech trees than you would think. Some varieties have attractive purple leaves, and some have weeping forms that fit nicely in a garden or small space yard. Some beech varieties can also be trimmed severely into a hedge for use in a formal garden. The beech nuts are prized food for bears and squirrels.

When, Where, and How to Plant
Beech trees are hardy throughout New England. Purchase trees from a local nursery. Plant from spring to early fall in well-drained, slightly acidic, moist soil. Beech trees don't grow well on wet sites. They also have shallow root systems, so plant where mowers and other vehicles won't be driving over the roots. Space trees 40 to 50 feet apart.

Growing Tips
Keep young trees well watered. Because beech trees are shallow rooted, mulch around the trunks to prevent damage to their roots from lawn machinery. Spread compost around newly planted trees; older trees don't need plant food.

Regional Advice and Care
Beech trees have few major pest problems. Fruit drop can be a litter problem in or near formal gardens. Beech trees can sucker freely sending up new trees and become overcrowded. Prune in early summer to clear out these trees as needed.

Companion Planting and Design
Beeches are amazing specimen trees in yards and great forest trees. But take note that grass won't grow well under mature beech trees due to their cascading growth habits. Dwarf and weeping versions fit well in gardens planted with perennials and small shrubs. Plant purple-leaved weeping beech trees as a backdrop to more brightly colored, large shrubs, such as lilac and weigela. Because of the natural cascading branch habit, beech trees create a sheltered area around the trunk that becomes a secret location for kids and adults. Some formal gardeners will trim beeches heavily to create a formal hedge.

Try These
'Riversii', 'Rohanii', and 'Spaethiana' are common varieties of the classic American beech (*F. grandifolia*) or copper beech. They have deep purple-colored leaves, and the tree grows 50 feet tall. 'Dawyck' is a tall, narrow tree that comes in yellow or purple leaf forms. 'Pendula' is a common cascading beech with branches that grow downward quickly after extending outward. There are purple- and yellow-leaved versions. 'Tricolor' has white, pink, and green variegated leaves and only grows 30 feet tall. 'Tortuosa' only grows 15 feet tall with contorted branches and trunk. 'Asplenifolia' has fernlike leaves with yellow fall color.

Birch

Betula spp.

Botanical Pronunciation
BET-you-luh

Other Name
American birch

Bloom Period and Seasonal Color
Fall; yellow; green catkins in spring; grown for
the arching shape, colorful bark, and fall color

Mature Height × Spread
30 to 40 feet × 12 to 15 feet

This native, deciduous North American tree is commonly found in New England forests, but it also makes a great landscape tree in the yard. Birch trees are one of New England poet Robert Frost's favorites for their arching shape, beautiful fall foliage color, and attractive bark. When grown in groves or groups, they make a striking statement. Some birch, such as yellow (*B. alleghaniensis*) and white birch (*B. papyrifera*), are large trees used for shade, while smaller birch species, such as river birch (*B. nigra*) and weeping birch (*B. pendula*), are often grown as clumps and make excellent garden plants. The leaves on many species turn a brilliant gold in fall. The colorful and textured bark looks stunning, especially after the leaves drop.

When, Where, and How to Plant
Birch trees are hardy throughout New England. Purchase trees from a local nursery. Plant from spring through early fall in well-drained, slightly acidic soils. Birch grows best in cool sites and in full sun. Space most trees 30 to 40 feet apart; space weeping and shorter forms closer together.

Growing Tips
Keep young trees well watered. In lawn settings, build a mulch ring around the drip line and mulch to protect the roots and trunk from mower damage. Fertilize young trees in spring with a tree fertilizer. Older trees generally don't need fertilization.

Regional Advice and Care
Prune in summer to remove crossing or competing branches. Don't prune from late winter to spring because the sap will flow, creating the opportunity for diseases to attack. Some birch trees will come under fire by insects, such as the bronze birch borer. Plant resistant species if borers are a problem. The white birch, in particular, can suffer branch breaking during ice and snowstorms.

Companion Planting and Design
Plant large birch trees as specimens in the yard or along a forest edge. Plant weeping forms and smaller trees in the garden as accent plants or in a mixed tree and shrub border. Locate those birches with attractive bark, such as the white, paper, and river birches, where you can look outside the house and enjoy a view of the trees in winter.

Try These
River birches are widely grown because of their easy-to-grow nature, bronze borer insect resistance, beautiful golden fall foliage, and cinnamon-colored peeling bark. 'Heritage' is a large river birch that looks great in a yard. 'Summer Cascade' and 'Fox Valley' river birch only grow 15 feet tall. White birch varieties include some with colorful leaves. 'Purple Splendor' has purple leaves that contrast nicely with the white bark. 'Youngsii' is a weeping form that only grows only 15 feet tall and wide with nice golden fall foliage. 'Whitespire' has pure white bark that doesn't peel, nice fall foliage color, and resists bronze borer. 'Snowy' is a borer-resistant variety of paper birch.

Canadian Hemlock

Tsuga canadensis

Botanical Pronunciation
TSOO-ga ka-na-DEN-sis

Other Name
Eastern hemlock

Bloom Period and Seasonal Color
Year-round; green needles

Mature Height × Spread
40 to 70 feet × 25 to 35 feet

Canadian hemlock is an evergreen native tree that is often found in New England forests. This beautiful tree can be seen growing along streams and wet areas in the woods providing a quiet place for rest and contemplation. But this isn't just a fine specimen tree. You'll be amazed at the different forms of this native tree. Hemlocks can be trimmed into beautiful, large hedges. Also, there are creeping forms that act like groundcovers, weeping forms that make interesting additions to gardens and dwarf forms that mix well in a small tree and shrub border. Unlike many other needled evergreens, hemlocks can tolerate shade, making them good choices for hedges and shrubs around shady yards.

When, Where, and How to Plant
Canadian hemlock is hardy throughout New England. Purchase plants from a local nursery. Plant in spring or summer in well-drained, moist soils. Avoid hot, dry windy locations and areas where there is air pollution and salt spray, such as close to a road. Space plants 30 to 40 feet apart closer for dwarf forms or if you're growing hemlocks in a hedge.

Growing Tips
Keep trees well watered. Mulch annually with pine needles, bark, or wood chips to maintain soil moisture conditions, creating a mulch ring to avoid trunk damage due to lawn mowers or string trimmers. Fertilize in spring with an evergreen tree plant food.

Regional Advice and Care
If you're growing hemlock as a specimen tree, only prune off dead branches. When growing as a hedge plant, trim in spring when the new growth appears. Shear the hedge so that the top is narrower than the bottom to prevent bottom branches from dying off due to lack of light. Avoid planting Canadian hemlock in areas where the woolly adelgid insect is present. This pest can kill a tree in a few years. Protect young trees from deer browsing with a fence or repellent sprays.

Companion Planting and Design
Canadian hemlocks look very natural planted in a wooded area or near streams. Grow them as hedges to block a view or mark a boundary line. Grow shorter, shrub forms as foundation plants along the shady part of your home near other shade lovers, such as rhododendrons. Plant weeping forms as focal points in a mixed shrub border. Plant creeping forms in a rock garden or to cascade over a wall.

Try These
For large trees and hedges, look for the species form of Canadian hemlock. 'Pendula' is a popular weeping form that grows 15 feet tall and wide. 'Horsford Contorted' is a dwarf, contorted form with twisted branches. 'Cole's Prostrate' is a good creeping form that grows only 1 foot tall. 'Jeddeloh' is a shrub form similar to the popular bird's nest spruce. 'Aurea Compacta' is a dwarf shrub with yellow needles.

Cedar

Thuja occidentalis

Botanical Pronunciation
THEW-ya ok-si-den-TAY-lis

Other Name Arbovitae

Bloom Period and Seasonal Color
Year-round; evergreen foliage

Mature Height × Spread
12 to 15 feet × 3 to 5 feet

Cedar is native to New England and is an all-purpose evergreen. You often see it grown as a foundation plant around houses, as a specimen in mixed-shrub borders, or as hedge plants to block a view or define a boundary line. The species doesn't have the same dense foliage as the cultivated varieties. These are best grown into a hedge to provide a windbreak or screen. Cultivated varieties have more attractive foliage with a denser pattern and look best in more formal plantings near a house or in a shrub border. This low-maintenance evergreen is hardy and tough, withstanding New England's winter cold and winds, and can grow quickly to mature size. The foliage and wood is prized for that classic cedar scent.

When, Where, and How to Plant

Purchase cedar shrubs at a local garden center and plant from spring to early fall in well-drained, fertile soil. Cedar grows best in slightly acidic, moist soil. Space plants 3 to 5 feet apart, depending on the type of cedar. Plant it so that the crown of the plant is a few inches above the soil line.

Growing Tips

Keep young plants well watered and weed-free. Established plants are more drought tolerant. Mulch plants with bark mulch or wood chips to maintain even soil moisture conditions. Fertilize cedars in spring with compost.

Regional Advice and Care

Cedars can be pruned into geometric shapes or allowed to grow into their natural form. Most selections are naturally rounded, pyramidal, or columnar. Prune once new growth appears in early summer and again in midsummer to keep them inbounds and looking tidy. If you prune overgrown cedars back into the old wood, it will take a number of years for it to regrow into its original form. Prune hedges so that the bottom is wider than the top so that the bottom branches will get enough sun and not die off over time. The biggest pest of cedars is deer. Protect young plants with deer repellent sprays or fencing.

Companion Planting and Design

Cedars are best used as a backdrop to other flowering shrubs, such as spireas, rhododendrons, and roses. You can also grow flowering vines, such as clematis, to twine into the evergreen foliage. Cedars make excellent hedges when planted in rows.

Try These

'Emerald Green' is a newer variety with a narrow, upright form and dark green foliage that holds its color well even in winter. 'Little Gem' is a rounded version that only grows 3 feet tall and wide, making it a good choice as a foundation plant under a window. 'Rheingold' is a 5-foot-tall and -wide rounded cedar with unusual orange-yellow foliage that deepens in color in winter. 'Hetz Wintergreen' is a tall pyramidal form that grows to 20 feet with dark green foliage. It's more shade tolerant than other cedars.

Colorado Blue Spruce

Picea pungens

Botanical Pronunciation
pi-CEE-a PUN-gens

Other Name Colorado spruce

Bloom Period and Seasonal Color
Year-round; blue-green needles

Mature Height × Spread
30 to 50 feet × 10 to 20 feet

This classic evergreen tree is a standard for Christmas trees, but also makes an excellent large specimen in the yard and a great informal hedge. There are also dwarf, weeping, and creeping forms that look beautiful combined with other shrubs and flowers. The horizontal, stiff branches hold their shape well and the attractive blue needles make this tree noteworthy, especially in winter. The blueness of the needles varies depending on the tree you select. It grows slowly into a conical shape and produces small cones. The needles are stiff and sharp, making this also a good tree to plant in hedges to keep wildlife out. It makes a nice living Christmas tree, as long as it's planted into the ground right after the holiday.

When, Where, and How to Plant
Colorado blue spruce is hardy in our region. Purchase trees from a local nursery or garden center. Plant trees in full sun from spring to summer in well-drained, slightly acidic, humus-rich, moist ground. Space specimen trees 20 to 30 feet apart. Plant weeping, creeping, and dwarf forms closer together.

Growing Tips
Although blue spruce trees are more drought tolerant than other types of spruce, keep trees well watered. In a lawn setting, create a mulch ring around trees and add bark mulch, pine needles, or wood chips to keep the soil moist and protect the trees from damage due to string trimmers and lawn mowers.

Regional Advice and Care
Colorado blue spruce grows naturally into a beautiful, pyramidal shape. You can prune the growth tips on branches in spring to shape the tree even more if desired. They usually form branches to the ground when grown in full sun. Insects, such as the spruce gall aphid, can cause growth tips to die back and deform individual branches. Spider mites can cause poor growth on new branches. Spray insecticidal soap to control this pest. Colorado blue spruces are tolerant of salt spray, so they can be planted along roads or near the ocean.

Companion Planting and Design
Plant Colorado blue spruce as a specimen tree in a large yard. Mix it with other large evergreens, such as fir trees, to create an informal hedge to block a view. Birds and other wildlife will appreciate the winter cover these trees provide. Plant dwarf forms in a mixed-shrub border with other evergreens. Plant weeping tree types in the garden as a focal point plant. Plant creeping types on a bank or cascading over a wall.

Try These
'Thompsen' and 'Hoopsii' are two common large, pyramidal varieties with good needle color and plant shape. 'Fat Albert' is a dwarf blue spruce that grows 20 feet tall with good blue needle color. 'Glauca Pendula' is a creeping or weeping variety, depending on the selection. 'Glauca Globosa' is a shrub form that grows 4 feet tall and wide.

Crabapple

Malus spp. and hybrids

Botanical Pronunciation
MAY-lus

Other Name
Flowering crabapple

Bloom Period and Seasonal Color
Spring; white, pink, and rose; yellow fall foliage

Mature Height × Spread
6 to 25 feet × 6 to 20 feet

Crabapples are probably one of the most popular flowering landscape and street trees in New England. Some would say they are actually overused as they seem to be everywhere from private developments to industrial complexes. But there's a reason for this popularity. Crabapples are hardy, tough trees that flower reliably each spring with an amazing show of color. Trees can be covered in white, pink, or red blooms. Some varieties have colorful leaves as well. There are many different tree shapes too. This tree can grow into a medium-sized shade tree or be a small dwarf depending on the selection. In fall, the crabapples are edible and colorful for birds and people. Plus, some varieties have great fall color. No wonder they're everywhere!

When, Where, and How to Plant

Crabapples are hardy throughout New England. Purchase trees from a local garden center. Plant from spring to early fall in full sun in well-drained, fertile, loamy soil. Depending on the selection, space trees 10 to 20 feet apart.

Growing Tips

Water young crabapple trees well. Create a mulch ring around trees grown in the lawn with wood chips or bark mulch, and replenish the mulch each spring to keep the soil moist and to create a barrier to reduce trunk damage from string trimmers and mowers. Fertilize in spring with a tree plant food.

Regional Advice and Care

Prune crabapples to remove dead, broken, or diseased branches anytime. Prune to remove suckers and watersprouts, crowded branches in the tree's center, and twiggy growth that doesn't flower well in late winter. Protect the trunk of young trees from mice and voles with tree guards in fall. Apple scab, rust, and powdery mildew diseases can plague crabapples. Select resistant varieties or spray an organic fungicide in spring.

Companion Planting and Design

Large varieties of crabapples make great focal points in your yard. Plant shade-loving annual flowers, such as impatiens, or perennials, such as lamium, under a crabapple tree for added color. Select dwarf trees to anchor a perennial flower garden. Plant crabapple trees in a mixed-tree hedgerow as a wildlife planting with other berry-producing shrubs and trees, such as viburnum and serviceberry.

Try These

The key to selecting crabapple varieties is getting the right size and shape tree and one with good disease resistance. 'Sargent' crabapple grows 6 to 8 feet tall and wide with pink buds and white flowers. 'Sargent Tina' is similar, but only grows 5 feet tall. 'Donald Wyman' grows 20 feet tall with white flowers and bright red crabapples in fall. 'Prairie Fire' grows 20 feet tall and wide with dark red flowers, dark red fruits, and cherrylike bark. 'Purple Prince' is similar to 'Prairie Fire' but has burgundy colored foliage. 'Golden Raindrops' grows 20 feet tall with white flowers and small, yellow fruits.

Dogwood

Cornus spp. and hybrids

Botanical Pronunciation
KORE-nus

Other Name
Flowering dogwood

Bloom Period and Seasonal Color
Spring; white or pink; red fall foliage

Mature Height × Spread
20 to 30 feet × 20 to 30 feet

There is no small, deciduous tree more outstanding when in full flower than the dogwood. The large white or pink blooms are larger than the flowers on many other trees. But the color show doesn't end there. Dogwoods produce colorful fruit during the summer that birds enjoy. In fall they have a reddish purple fall foliage color to brighten a landscape. In winter the grayish brown, alligator-skinlike bark is revealed. Because it is a native tree that naturally grows on the forest's edge, dogwoods are versatile in the landscape as specimen trees in yards to forest trees growing in part sun. Some types are small trees that barely reach 10 feet tall, while other types have interesting horizontal branching patterns.

When, Where, and How to Plant
Dogwoods are hardy to zone 5 (and some to zone 4), depending on the selection. Purchase trees from your local garden center and plant from spring to early fall in full to part sun in well-drained, slightly acidic soil, rich in organic matter. Dogwoods aren't tolerant of salt spray, pollution, heat, or drought. Depending on the selection's mature size, space trees 10 to 20 feet apart.

Growing Tips
Water young trees well and create a mulch ring around trees in the lawn with wood chips, pine needles, or bark mulch to keep the soil moist and protect the trunks from lawn mowers and string trimmers. Fertilize in spring with a tree plant food.

Regional Advice and Care
Dogwoods are slow growing. Prune trees in spring only to remove dead, diseased, or broken branches. Too much pruning can create the opportunity for diseases, such as dogwood anthracnose, and insects, such as dogwood borer, to attack. Plant resistant varieties and keep trees healthy to avoid these problems.

Companion Planting and Design
Dogwood trees look great planted as specimen trees in a lawn with flowering annuals, such as impatiens, or perennials, such as lamium, planted underneath the tree. Plant dogwoods at the corner of your house or along the forest edge.

Try These
The flowering dogwood (*C. florida*) is the most popular and best flowering type. The Cherokee series features selections with white, pink, or pinkish red flowers on disease-resistant trees. 'Cherokee Sunset' features variegated pink-and-yellow leaves. 'Rubra' is a common pink-flowered selection. 'Pendula' is a weeping form. Kousa dogwoods (*C. kousa*) can have better disease resistance, hardiness, and drought tolerance than the flowering dogwood. 'Venus' grows 20 feet tall with white flowers. 'Santomi' is a dwarf selection only growing to 8 feet tall. Pagoda dogwood (*C. alternifolia*) is a tough-growing native that features white flowers, blue berries, and a horizontal branching pattern making it interesting in winter as well. Cornelian cherry (*C. mas*) has attractive, but not as showy, yellow flowers early in spring and edible red fruits on hardy trees.

Eastern Redbud

Cercis canadensis

Botanical Pronunciation SER-sis kan-a-DEN-sis

Other Name Redbud

Bloom Period and Seasonal Color
Early spring; red, purplish pink, and white;
yellow fall foliage

Mature Height × Spread
20 to 30 feet × 25 to 35 feet

This small, native, deciduous tree is mostly grown for its jaw-dropping spring flower show. In early spring, before the leaves emerge, redbuds produce fluorescent red, purple, magenta, or white pealike flowers that fill a tree's branches. Because it is one of the first trees to bloom, it is very noticeable in the landscape. It's also a nicely sized tree for most landscapes, and some dwarf forms are available. The heart-shaped leaves are attractive in summer and the fall foliage color can be a brilliant yellow depending on the variety. This tree is marginally hardy in some parts of New England and may suffer some winter dieback. But when it's grown in a protected location, it can become a focal point in the yard or garden.

When, Where, and How to Plant
Eastern redbud is hardy to zone 5. Some varieties are hardy to zone 4 with protection. Purchase trees from a local nursery and plant from spring to early fall in a moist, well-drained soil in a full or part sun location. Space trees 20 feet apart.

Growing Tips
Keep eastern redbuds well watered. Create a mulch ring around the base of the trees planted in lawn and mulch with wood chips or bark mulch to keep the soil moist, weed free, and to protect the trunk from lawn mowers and string trimmers. Fertilize in spring with tree plant food.

Regional Advice and Care
Eastern redbud can be a short-lived tree if it's exposed to chronic diseases and winter damage. Plant in a location protected from cold northern and western winter winds, especially if you're growing in zone 4. Prune after flowering in spring to remove dead, broken, or diseased branches and reduce any branch crowding in the middle of the tree.

Companion Planting and Design
Plant eastern redbuds as a specimen tree in a small yard or mix and match the tree with other smaller flowering trees, such as crabapples and serviceberries. Because eastern redbud can be a dwarf tree, consider growing it in a small yard as a patio tree or even working it into the foundation plantings in a spot that won't block a view of the rest of the garden. Redbuds will flower best in full sun, but can also be planted in a woodland or along the forest's edge where it will be growing in part sun.

Try These
'Forest Pansy' features rosy-pink flowers and reddish purple spring foliage that turns green in summer. It also has reddish purple fall foliage color. 'Covey' and 'Pink Heartbreaker' are weeping dwarf redbuds that only grow 8 feet tall and feature pink flowers and yellow fall foliage color. 'Silver Cloud' is a green-and-white variegated leaf redbud with pink flowers, but it doesn't flower heavily. 'Hearts of Gold' is the first gold-leaved redbud. The leaves emerge red, then turn golden. The flowers are lavender-purple-colored.

Eastern White Pine

Pinus strobus

Botanical Pronunciation
PYE-nus STROE-buss

Other Name Northern white pine

Bloom Period and Seasonal Color
Year-round; evergreen needles

Mature Height × Spread
50 to 80 feet × 30 to 50 feet

This large, evergreen tree is a common site in many New England forests. The long, soft evergreen needles give a velvety appearance to the tree as they wave in the breeze. This fast-growing evergreen produces 6- to 8-inch-long cones that are great food for wildlife and decorations for the holidays. Like many other large evergreens, there are now many dwarf versions of the original. Some types have golden-colored needles while others have blue-green needles. Because of the varieties of forms and colored needles, eastern white pine has become a versatile plant in the landscape. It can be grown as anything from a large shade tree in the yard to a unique weeping shrub in a flower garden.

When, Where, and How to Plant

Eastern white pines are hardy throughout New England. Purchase trees from a local nursery. Plant in spring or summer in full sun in moist, well-drained, acidic soil. Eastern white pines often prefer light loamy or sandy soils. Space large trees 20 to 30 feet apart. Space dwarf trees closer, depending on the selection.

Growing Tips

Keep Eastern white pine trees well watered, especially when they're young. Create a mulch ring around the base of trees planted in lawns using pine needles or wood chips. This will help maintain the soil moisture, keep the soil slightly acidic, and minimize trunk damage from mowers and string trimmers. Fertilize in spring with a plant food for evergreen trees.

Regional Advice and Care

Eastern white pines have brittle branches that break easily in ice, wind, or snowstorms. Unfortunately, once a branch breaks, a new one will not grow in that spot, and the tree will be permanently deformed. Eastern white pines also can't tolerate salt spray or air pollution, so they are not good choices along the coast or near roads. Prune broken branches back to the trunk and remove dead and diseased branches anytime. Eastern white pines can be attacked by insects, such as the white pine weevil that bore into the pine tree leader and cause it to dieback. The tree usually recovers, however.

Companion Planting and Design

Plant Eastern white pines in the yard to create a shady grove. Plant dwarf and different colored needle trees in the garden as interesting focal points. Eastern white pines also make a great informal hedge. They can be sheared, but not as close or as often as cedar or false cypress.

Try These

The most common variety is the large species form. However, there are many dwarf forms. The words "Nana" or "Compacta" are general terms given to any mounded or dwarf types. 'Blue Shag' is a popular compact form with blue-green needles. 'Contorta' has twisted and curled branches. 'Fastigiata' is a tall, columnar form with blue-green needles. 'Pendula' is a weeping form. 'Aurea' has yellow needles.

False Cypress

Chamaecyparis spp.

Botanical Pronunciation
kam-ee-SIPP-ur-iss

Other Name
Cypress

Bloom Period and Seasonal Color
Year-round; evergreen foliage

Mature Height × Spread
50 to 70 feet × 10 to 20 feet

False cypress can become a large evergreen tree in the landscape (though there are dwarf forms available). However, like other evergreens, such as cedars, there are many variations on the theme. There are many slow-growing shrub versions of false cypress and some dwarf tree types. Most false cypress trees have a tall, conical shape. These look striking against a large building. The foliage is arranged in an upward facing, horizontal pattern around the trunk giving it an interesting form. Some needles are blue-green or golden in color. I think this carefree evergreen is underused in our yards. It's a good choice for those looking for alternatives to the regular spruce, cedar, and pine trees for a hedge or mixed evergreen border.

When, Where, and How to Plant

False cypress is hardy to zones 4 or 5, depending on the selection. Look for the hardiest varieties if you're growing it in colder parts of New England. Purchase your trees from a local nursery. Plant from spring to early fall in moist, compost-amended, well-drained soil in full to part sun. Depending on the selection's mature size, space trees 5 to 20 feet apart.

Growing Tips

Keep false cypress trees (and shrubs) well watered. Create a mulch ring around plants grown in lawns to keep the soils moist and prevent damage from string trimmers and lawn mowers. Fertilize in spring with a plant food formulated for evergreens.

Regional Advice and Care

Large false cypress trees are best grown in their natural, unpruned form, unless you're using them for a hedge. Shrub versions can be sheared by pruning in spring after a flush of new young growth. If growing false cypress as a hedge, shear the plants regularly in summer, being sure the top of the hedge is narrower than the bottom to prevent the lower branches from dying due to lack of sun.

Companion Planting and Design

Plant full-sized false cypress trees in an open area where they can grow unimpeded by power lines or buildings. False cypress is useful as a hedge plant to block a view or create privacy. Plant dwarf and shrub versions as foundation plantings and in a mixed evergreen border with dwarf spruce and cedar. Some are so dwarf they can be used in containers or a rock garden.

Try These

'Filifera' is a Japanese false cypress (*C. pisifera*) that grows 25 feet tall and has stringlike, graceful, cascading branches. 'Filifera Aurea' is a golden foliaged version. 'Golden Spangle' and 'Aurea Nana' are slow-growing, rounded, dwarf versions that only grow 4 feet tall. 'Soft Serve' is a slow-growing conical Japanese false cypress that grows 8 to 10 feet tall. Hinoki false cypress (*C. obtusa*) normally grows 70 feet tall. However, the most popular Hinoki cypress is 'Nana Gracilis' that grows 6 to 10 feet tall with dark green, wavy branches.

Flowering Cherry

Prunus spp. and hybrids

Botanical Pronunciation
PROO-nus

Other Name
Ornamental cherry

Bloom Period and Seasonal Color
Spring; pink or white; red or yellow fall color

Mature Height × Spread
20 to 50 feet × 20 to 50 feet

Flowering cherry trees are beautiful additions to the landscape in the yard or as a specialty tree around the house. There are many variations of flowering cherry, but three main types grow best in New England. The Oriental cherry (*P. serrulata*) is the classic flowering cherry of Japanese fame. Selections grow 20 to 30 feet tall at maturity with tons of single or double pink and white flowers, but no fruits. The weeping Higan cherry (*P. subhirtella*) is a large tree, growing 20 to 40 feet tall, but has a weeping shape with pink flowers, and again, it has no fruits. The purple leaf sand cherry (*P. cistena*) is a smaller tree with attractive purple leaves and fragrant, white flowers. Some dwarf forms of flowering cherry are available.

When, Where, and How to Plant
Flowering cherries are hardy to zone 5; sand cherries can grow in zone 4. Purchase trees from a local nursery and plant from spring to early fall in well-drained, fertile soil and in full sun. Flowering cherries don't demand highly fertile soils. Space plants 20 to 30 feet apart, closer for smaller species.

Growing Tips
Keep young trees well watered. Create a mulch ring around trees grown in the lawn and cover it with wood chips or bark mulch. This will keep the soil evenly moist, prevent weed growth, and protect the trunks from lawn mowers and string trimmers. Fertilize in spring with a tree plant food.

Regional Advice and Care
Flowering cherries can be attacked by a number of insects and diseases. Prune in spring after flowering to remove black knot fungal galls on branches. Protect trees from powdery mildew and fire blight with an organic spray. Be on watch for aphids, borers, tent caterpillars, and Japanese beetles. Handpick or spray with the appropriate organic sprays to control these pests.

Companion Planting and Design
Plant large flowering cherry trees in your lawn as a shade or specimen tree or even plant them along the road. Site the tree where future growth won't grow into power lines or buildings. Plant weeping flower cherries and dwarf versions in foundation plantings, small spaced yards, or in mixed tree and shrub borders. These are easier to manage for insect and disease control.

Try These
'Kwanzan' is the most popular Oriental flowering cherry. This double-flowered pink selection is one of the hardest of Oriental types and has orange fall foliage color. 'Royal Burgundy' is similar to 'Kwanzan', but has reddish purple leaves. 'Mt. Fuji' produces double, white flowers and has a slightly weeping habit. 'Pendula' is a single white-flowered Higan cherry that grows to 25 feet tall. 'Snow Fountain' and 'White Fountain' produce white flowers and only grow 10 feet tall and wide with golden fall foliage. 'Big Cis' is a purpleleaf sand cherry that grows to 15 feet tall with pink flowers and dark purple foliage.

Flowering Pear

Pyrus calleryana

Botanical Pronunciation
PY-rus kal-er-ee-AY-na

Other Name
Callery pear

Bloom Period and Seasonal Color
Spring; white; yellow, orange, and red fall foliage

Mature Height × Spread
30 to 50 feet × 15 to 20 feet

The flowering pear is a widely used (and some may say overused) ornamental tree for good reason. The tree grows quickly to 30 to 40 feet tall in a narrow, teardrop shape. It's loaded with fragrant, white flowers in spring, produces only small, nonedible fruits in summer, and has an attractive range of yellow, orange, and red colors in fall. It's very adapted to hot and dry conditions, withstands air pollution, and is resistant to the fire blight disease that ravages other pear trees. It's a great tree in the lawn, in a small yard, or along the street. Its one drawback is that on older trees the branches may split, but newer selections have better branch angles and less splitting.

When, Where, and How to Plant
Flowering pears are hardy to zone 5, so are best grown in southern parts of our region. Purchase trees from a local nursery and plant from spring to early fall in well-drained, fertile soils. However, flowering pears are adaptable to many soil conditions. Space trees 10 to 20 feet apart.

Growing Tips
Keep young trees well watered. Create a mulch ring covered with wood chips or bark mulch around trees grown in lawns. This will keep the soil evenly moist, prevent weed growth, and protect the trunks from damage from lawn mowers and string trimmers. Fertilize in spring with a tree plant food.

Regional Advice and Care
Because of their strong, upright growth, flowering pears may have narrow crotch angles and split easily during high winds, ice, or snowstorms. This can quickly deform a tree beyond repair. Select varieties with wider crotch angles. Flowering pears don't have any major insect or disease problems. Remove dead, diseased, and broken branches anytime, and prune after flowering in spring to remove suckers, watersprouts, and crowded growth in the center of a tree.

Companion Planting and Design
Plant flowering pears as a street tree, in a lawn area, or to line a property boundary. Because of their propensity to split branches, plant where they will be protected from high winds to minimize the damage. You can also protect them by planting in groups with other medium-sized trees, such as crabapples and flowering cherries.

Try These
'Bradford' pear is the most commonly planted flowering pear, but it should be avoided due to its narrow branch crotch angles and propensity to split branches. Newer selections are better trees and should be planted instead. 'Cleveland Select' (aka 'Chanticleer' and 'Stone Hill') grows 35 feet tall in a pyramidal shape. It has wide branch angles, good disease resistance, and is long lived. 'Jack' and 'Jill' are newer selections that only grow 20 feet tall and have a round growth habit with dense foliage growth.

Ginkgo

Ginkgo biloba

Botanical Pronunciation
GINK-oh bye-LOBE-ah

Other Name
Maidenhair tree

Bloom Period and Seasonal Color
Fall; golden foliage; also grown for unique growth habit

Mature Height × Spread
30 to 50 feet × 30 to 50 feet

Ginkgos are ancient trees. These trees are the last of its species to survive prehistoric times, and you can almost imagine a dinosaur munching on its leaves. This tree can grow more than 50 feet tall in an irregular pyramidal shape. The fan-shaped leaves remind you of quaking aspens, and this tree is actually a good, longer-lived substitute for aspens in our landscapes. Unlike many other trees, ginkgo trees can be male or female— pick male trees. While their shape is unique, it is known for its brilliant golden fall foliage color. It's a tough tree that can withstand heat, drought, sandy soils, pests, salt spray, and air pollution! This makes it an excellent urban and coastal tree. Ginkgo leaf extracts are also used as a medicinal herb; I can't remember what for.

When, Where, and How to Plant
Ginkgo trees are hardy throughout New England. Purchase trees from a local nursery and plant from spring to early fall in extremely well-drained soils. Ginkgos like a sandy, deeply dug hole to grow well. They don't tolerate poor water drainage. Space trees 30 to 50 feet apart.

Growing Tips
Keep young trees well watered. Once established, older trees are drought tolerant. Create a mulch ring covered with wood chips or bark mulch around the trees being grown in lawns. This will keep the soil evenly moist, prevent weed growth, and protect the trunks from damage from lawn mowers and string trimmers. Fertilize young trees in spring with a tree plant food. Older trees usually don't need fertilization.

Regional Advice and Care
Young ginkgo trees should be pruned to a central leader system. Remove small twiggy growth along the trunk and any competing branches in late winter. Select only known male varieties. Although it may take twenty years, female trees produce malodorous fruits that drop and cause a mess under the tree. Ginkgo trees are pest-free trees.

Companion Planting and Design
Ginkgoes can eventually become a large tree in the landscape. Plant them in a yard as a shade tree where they can grow unimpeded without interfering with nearby power lines or buildings. Although they grow well in urban settings, they need enough room to grow to their full glory. Ginkgo trees are also frequently used in bonsai.

Try These
'Autumn Gold' and 'Magyar' are common male varieties with symmetrical, conical forms, good fall foliage color, and medium growth rate. 'Princeton Sentry' grows narrow, up to 60 feet tall, but only is 25 feet wide, making it a good candidate as a street tree. 'Jade Butterfly' is a dwarf ginkgo, growing only 10 to 20 feet tall. 'Pendula' is a weeping form that grows 12 feet tall and has horizontal branches with a slight drooping arch.

Goldenrain Tree

Koelreuteria paniculata

Botanical Pronunciation
kol-ru-TEE-ri-a pan-ik-u-LA-ta

Other Name
Pride of India tree

Bloom Period and Seasonal Color
Summer; yellow; orange-yellow fall foliage

Mature Height × Spread
20 to 40 feet × 20 to 40 feet

I f you're looking for a different type of tree for your yard consider the goldenrain tree. This medium- to large-sized, rounded, deciduous shade tree brightens up the summer landscape with its golden flowers. This tree produces large, 1- to 2-foot-long clusters of golden-colored flowers in early summer. The flowers are followed by attractive seedpods covered with papery husks similar to Chinese lantern plants. Golderain trees also can have attractive fall foliage, with its leaves turning an orange-yellow color. This tree is tolerant of adverse conditions including heat, drought, air pollution, and heavy wind. It grows well in a variety of soils, but has been noted to be invasive in some areas.

When, Where, and How to Plant

Goldenrain tree is hardy to USDA zone 5, so is marginally hardy in colder parts of New England. Purchase trees for a local nursery and plant in spring after all danger of frost has passed. Plant trees in full sun in well-drained, moist soil. Space trees 30 feet apart.

Growing Tips

Goldenrain tree grows best in moist soils, so water young trees well. Goldenrain tree has thin bark and is easily damaged. Create a mulch ring covered with wood chips or bark mulch around trees grown in lawns and to keep the soil evenly moist and the trunk protected from damage due to lawn mowers or string trimmers. Fertilize in spring with a plant food made for trees.

Regional Advice and Care

Goldenrain tree needs little care once it's established. Prune out dead, diseased, or broken branches at any time. Young trees tend to have few branches. Prune young trees to a central leader system to develop proper branch angles. The limbs of a goldenrain tree tend to droop, so plant this tree where there's enough room to work around the branches to prune. Goldenrain tree seeds can self-sow and become invasive. Weed out seedlings in spring.

Companion Planting and Design

Goldenrain tree makes a great specimen tree in the landscape or a shade tree in a large outdoor, patio area. It doesn't get so large to overwhelm a small yard. Although goldenrain tree is resistant to winds, the brittle branches may still break and cause a mess. It also doesn't tolerate salt spray and isn't a good coastal tree. Because of its tolerance to air pollution and adaptability to various soils, though, goldenrain tree makes a good urban and street tree.

Try These

'September' is a late-flowering variety that blooms in late summer. However, it's not as hardy as the true species. 'Fastigiata' grows to 25 feet tall in a columnar shape, but doesn't flower as well as other selections and is less cold hardy. 'Beachmaster' is a dwarf version that grows into a large shrub 10 feet tall. 'Rose Lantern' produces pink seedpods in fall.

Hawthorn

Crataegus spp.

Botanical Pronunciation
kruh-TEE-gus

Other Name
Thorn apple

Bloom Period and Seasonal Color
Spring; white; orange-red berries and red, orange, and purple fall foliage

Mature Height × Spread
15 to 30 feet × 15 to 30 feet

This small, deciduous tree delights with its bright white flowers in spring, colorful berries in summer, and attractive fall foliage color. It's a slow-growing tree in the apple family that has a rounded habit and sometimes multiple stems. It makes a nice addition to a wildlife planting in a meadow or a hedgerow with other fruiting trees. Birds, especially cedar waxwings, enjoy the berries, and they also can be harvested and made into jams. Because of its size and three seasons of interest, hawthorn makes a great plant for small space yards. However, the tree can have sizable thorns that make it difficult to work around. There are some thornless varieties on the market.

When, Where, and How to Plant
Hawthorn trees are hardy throughout New England. Purchase trees from a local nursery and plant from spring to early fall in well-drained, humus-rich soil. They produce the most flowers and fruit in full sun locations. Space trees 20 to 30 feet apart. Grow them closer if planted as a hedgerow.

Growing Tips
Keep the trees well watered; hawthorns grow best in a moist soil. Create a mulch ring covered with wood chips or bark mulch around individual trees planted in lawns to keep the soil moist, prevent weed growth, and protect the trunks from damage due to lawn mowers or string trimmers. Fertilize in spring with a tree plant food.

Regional Advice and Care
Hawthorn trees should be carefully pruned (because of the thorns) in spring to remove dead, diseased, and broken branches and to shape the tree. Remove competing branches, suckers, and water sprouts. Hawthorns can be susceptible to similar diseases as apples, such as rust, fireblight, and apple scab. Select resistant varieties and spray in spring with an organic fungicide to control some of these diseases.

Companion Planting and Design
Plant hawthorn trees as a small tree in the landscape in the lawn or mixed with other fruiting trees, such as crabapples and serviceberry, in a mixed island planting. Hawthorn trees can be grown and pruned into an informal hedge to block a view or provide protection from wildlife. You can also plant hawthorns in meadows or pastures to provide food for birds and other wildlife.

Try These
'Winter King' hawthorn (C. *viridis*) is probably the most common hawthorn on the market. It grows 20 feet tall with white flowers and abundant red fruits in fall that persist into winter. It has good fall foliage color and disease resistance. 'Crimson Cloud' is an English hawthorn (C. *laevigata*) with red flowers and fruits and which has good disease resistance. It has fewer thorns than other selections. 'Princeton' Sentry' is a Washington type hawthorn (C. *phaenopyrum*) that grows in a columnar shape with almost thornless branches.

Honeylocust

Gleditsia triacanthos

Botanical Pronunciation
gled-IT-see-ah try-ah-KAN-thos

Other Name
Sweet locust

Bloom Period and Seasonal Color
Spring; yellow flowers; yellow fall foliage; mostly grown for its shape and open canopy

Mature Height × Spread
30 to 50 feet × 50 feet

Honeylocust is a perfect deciduous tree in a yard where you don't want heavy shade. The small green leaflets and open branch structure allows enough light to penetrate to the ground to allow lawn grass to grow. But it provides enough shade to sit under on your patio or deck. Some selections start out with light yellow leaves that turn green and then yellow again in fall. Honeylocust are tolerant of urban conditions, including air pollution and salt spray, so they make great street trees. However, older selections produce brown seedpods that drop in fall and can become messy. They also may have thorns that can be dangerous when working around the tree. Newer varieties that mostly dominate the market don't produce viable seeds or thorns.

When, Where, and How to Plant
Honeylocust trees are hardy in New England. Purchase plants from your local nursery and plant from spring to early fall in well-drained, deep, fertile soil. However, honeylocust are also tolerant of various soil types. Space trees 20 to 30 feet apart.

Growing Tips
Keep trees well watered. Create a mulch ring covered with wood chips or bark mulch around individual trees planted in lawns. The mulch ring keeps the soil evenly moist and prevents trunk damage due to lawn mowers and sting trimmers. Damaged honeylocust trees are stressed and more likely to have problems with insects and diseases. Fertilize in spring with a tree plant food.

Regional Advice and Care
Honeylocust can be late to leaf out in spring, so don't be concerned if other trees have leaves and your honeylocust does not. Prune in spring to remove small shoots along the trunk, suckers, watersprouts, and competing branches. Prune out dead, diseased, or broken branches anytime. Honeylocust trees can have myriad insects and diseases attacking them. The most prolific are spider mites, gall midges, and webworms. Control these with organic sprays and by keeping the trees stress-free. Select newer varieties that don't have troublesome thorns.

Companion Planting and Design
Honeylocust is a common street tree throughout our region and probably overplanted. However, it is a great tree as a specimen in the lawn or shading a patio or deck. Some shorter growing versions make good small space trees as well.

Try These
'Shademaster' is the most common selection of honeylocust on the market. It grows 40 feet tall with deep green foliage and some seedpods. It also has good drought tolerance once established. 'Suncole' and 'Sunburst' are popular newer selections for their yellow-green spring foliage that turns medium green in summer and yellow again in fall. They grow 35 feet tall and don't produce seedpods. 'Moraine' is an older selection that grows 40 feet tall with a wide top. It doesn't have seedpods and has good pest resistance.

Hornbeam

Carpinus spp.

Botanical Pronunciation
kar-PY-nus

Other Name
Ironwood

Bloom Period and Seasonal Color
Grown for its shape and fall color

Mature Height × Spread
20 to 40 feet × 20 to 30 feet

There are two types of hornbeams generally available to grow in our region. The American hornbeam (*C. caroliniana*) is native, hardy, tolerant of sun or shade, and grows into a multistemmed large shrub or small tree with good fall foliage color. The European hornbeam (*C. betulus*) is more refined. It can grow quite large (40 feet). It isn't as hardy as the American version, but has a beautiful structure, good fall foliage, and is versatile. It grows well as a street tree because it tolerates many different types of soil conditions, air pollution, and heavy pruning. Both trees produce characteristic nutlets that look like hops and turn brown in fall. Both trees are long-lived and good choices in a naturalized or formal setting.

When, Where, and How to Plant

American hornbeams are hardy throughout New England. European hornbeams are hardy to zone 5 and best for warmer sections of our region. Select young trees (older trees are harder to transplant successfully) from a local nursery and plant from spring to early fall in well-drained, moist soil. They will also handle a wide range of soil types. Space trees 20 to 30 feet apart unless you're growing trees as a hedge.

Growing Tips

Keep hornbeam trees well watered and mulched. For formal plantings in lawns, build a mulch ring covered with bark mulch or wood chips around the tree to keep the soil moist and its trunk protected from damage due to lawn mowers and string trimmers. Feed trees in spring with a fertilizer made for trees.

Regional Advice and Care

Hornbeam trees are carefree with few pest problems. They generally don't need much pruning other than removing dead, diseased, and broken branches. European hornbeams may develop narrow branch crotch angles that will cause the tree to split during ice or snowstorms. Prune young trees in summer to prevent sap from bleeding and to develop wide crotch angles. Hornbeams can be more severely pruned into informal hedges.

Companion Planting and Design

Plant American hornbeam trees so that they naturalize along woodlands, in meadows, or in a mixed small tree planting with other natives, such as serviceberries. European hornbeams make good street trees and grow well in urban locations. They have a more formal look. Because of their tall growth, they shouldn't be planted under power lines or too close to buildings. Both hornbeams can be pruned into an informal, deciduous hedge to provide screening from a view or building.

Try These

There are only a few selections of American hornbeam other than the original species. 'Ball O Fire' is a newer selection that has orange-red fall foliage. For European hornbeams, try growing 'Fastigiata'. This commonly grown hornbeam grows in a dense, formal, pyramidal shape. 'Pendula' is a weeping form that still grows up to 50 feet tall.

Horse Chestnut

Aesculus spp.

Botanical Pronunciation
ES-ku-lus

Other Name
Buckeye

Bloom Period and Seasonal Color
Mid- to late spring; white, pink, yellow, and red

Mature Height × Spread
40 to 60 feet × 30 to 40 feet

The name of this large, deciduous tree is actually a bit of a misnomer. The horse chestnut is only distantly related to the European or American chestnut and doesn't produce edible nuts. And horses don't really like eating them. However, this tree does have noteworthy large, colorful flowers blooming from mid- to late spring. Because of its size, vertical growing shape, and flowering characteristics, horse chestnuts make good shade trees in parks, college campuses, large lawn areas, and other open spaces. The flowers are by far the showiest part of this tree. The erect clusters can reach up to 12 inches long and make a beautiful statement when the whole tree is in bloom. There are even some dwarf types.

When, Where, and How to Plant

Horse chestnuts are hardy throughout New England depending on the selection. Purchase trees from a local garden center and plant from spring to early fall in full to part sun in moist, well-drained fertile soil. They are adaptable to many soil types. Space trees 20 to 30 feet apart, closer for dwarf versions.

Growing Tips

Keep trees well watered, especially when they're young; older trees are drought tolerant. Create a mulch ring around trees planted in lawns to keep the soil evenly moist and protect the trunk from damage due to mowers and string trimmers. Fertilize in spring with a product made specifically for trees.

Regional Advice and Care

Horse chestnuts are commonly used as street trees and in parks. Although they have beautiful flowers and generally are a tough tree, they can get a number of leaf diseases. Most selections will get some form of leaf scorch during the summer making the leaves dry up prematurely. Plant trees in protected areas and avoid hot, dry locations. Horse chestnuts should only be pruned to remove dead, diseased, or broken branches. The seeds can be messy when they drop; look for seedless selections.

Companion Planting and Design

Horse chestnuts grow best in a large open area. Consider planting them at the edge of your property or in an open meadow that is mowed periodically. Avoid planting them in small spaces where they may be stressed and have more problems with diseases.

Try These

Red horse chestnut (*A. carnea*) grows 30 to 40 feet tall and wide and produces beautiful red flowers. 'Briotti' is a good selection that has fewer leaf diseases and has good drought tolerance. 'Baumannii' is a European horse chestnut (*A. hippocastanum*) that grows more than 50 feet tall and wide with seedless, double white flowers. Ohio buckeye (*A. glabra*) is a hardy, large tree with greenish yellow flowers, but it can be messy with twigs and seeds dropping to the ground. Bottlebrush buckeye (*A. parviflora*) stands only 12 feet tall, grows well part shade or on a slope, and has showy white flowers.

Japanese Maple

Acer palmatum

Botanical Pronunciation
AY-sur pal-MAY-tum

Other Name
Smooth Japanese maple

Bloom Period and Seasonal Color
Fall; red foliage; grown mostly for its shape and colorful leaves

Mature Height × Spread
6 to 20 feet × 6 to 15 feet

While bigger maples are quite bold in their stature and fall leaf color, Japanese maples are more elegant and delicate in their appearance. These small-sized trees grow slowly and can be pricey, but they have many delicate features that give them year-round interest. The leaves can be purple, red, or green and sometimes are deeply serrated giving the tree a mysterious look. The seeds can also have a reddish color that combines well with the colorful fall foliage color. The bark has a shiny, gray appearance that contrasts well with winter snow. When you find the right spot for your Japanese maple away from winter winds and a bit protected in colder areas, it will provide pleasures for you for many years.

When, Where, and How to Plant

Japanese maples are generally hardy to zone 5, some only to zone 6, so choose your tree depending on your location. Purchase trees from a local nursery and plant from spring to summer in a protected location in full to part sun. Leaf color is often more vibrant in part sun. Plant trees in well-drained, humus-rich, slightly acidic soils. Space trees 10 to 20 feet apart.

Growing Tips

Water young trees well and deeply water in subsequent years, especially during droughts. Provide a layer of wood chips, pine needles, or bark mulch under the trees to keep the soil evenly moist and reduce competition from weeds. Create a mulch ring when it's being grown in lawns to protect the trunk from damage due to lawn mowers and string trimmers. Fertilize in spring with a plant food made for trees.

Regional Advice and Care

Japanese maples have a fussy reputation, but as long as the soil is well drained and moist and they are protected from winter's cold winds, they are relatively maintenance free. They require little pruning other than removing dead, diseased, or broken branches. In exposed areas they might have more twig and small branches dying in winter. Late spring frosts may damage young leaves.

Companion Planting and Design

Plant larger Japanese maples as a specimen in the yard and smaller selections in a mixed-shrub border or perennial flower garden near a house or garage. Ideally, plant on the east side of buildings to protect them from winter winds. Plant dwarf trees in rock gardens, or train them as bonsai plants in containers (though this requires special root pruning).

Try These

'Bloodgood' is one of the hardiest and most popular varieties for us. Its red leaves turn burgundy in fall, and trees have a good upright growth habit. 'Tamukeyama' is a dwarf (4 feet tall) with finely dissected, crimson leaves that turn scarlet in fall. 'Crimson Queen' features 12-foot-wide weeping branches, and it reaches 8 feet tall with dissected red leaves. 'Flying Cloud' features unusual green-and-white variegated leaves on a 6-foot-tall tree.

Japanese Zelkova

Zelkova serrata

Botanical Pronunciation
zel -KO-vuh ser-RAY-tuh

Other Name
Sawleaf zelkova

Bloom Period and Seasonal Color
Fall; reddish purple foliage; mostly grown for its size, fall leaf color, and colorful bark

Mature Height × Spread
60 to 70 feet × 50 to 60 feet

As shade trees go, Japanese zelkova is one that is often overlooked. This large tree has a shape similar to elm trees with a broad crown that produces bountiful shade in a yard. The leaves turn an attractive yellow, red, or purple, depending on the selection, in fall. The bark exfoliates to reveal orange inner patches that contrast well with the outer gray color. It's not a messy tree, and it tolerates air pollution, drought, and a wide variety of soils. It's probably not grown more just due to a lack of awareness. It can have some dieback in colder areas, and Japanese beetles seem attracted to the leaves, but overall, it's a nice tree for a large lawn area.

When, Where, and How to Plant
Japanese zelkova is hardy to zone 5, so it wouldn't be a good choice in colder parts of New England. Purchase trees from a local nursery or through the mail for rare varieties and plant from spring to early fall in well-drained, moist, fertile soils. Space trees 50 feet apart in the landscape.

Growing Tips
Water young trees well. Once established, Japanese zelkovas are drought tolerant. Mulch trees with bark mulch or wood chips in the lawn to maintain soil moisture and protect the trunk from damage due to lawn mowers or string trimmers. Feed young trees with a tree fertilizer. Older trees don't need fertilizer.

Regional Advice and Care
Japanese zelkova only need a little pruning on young trees to create a central leader system and remove competing branches. Remove dead, diseased and broken branches at any time. Although it's resistant to Dutch elm disease, don't plant where dead elm trees are located to avoid any chance of this disease affecting the trees. Also, control Japanese beetles by handpicking beetles, with traps, and with organic sprays when the tree is young. Controlling beetles on large trees isn't practical or necessary.

Companion Planting and Design
Plant Japanese zelkova as a street tree or in a large lawn or meadow area to eventually be a shade tree. Don't plant large trees near power lines or buildings where they will have to eventually be pruned and their shape will be deformed. Plant where you can enjoy the colorful bark in winter from the house.

Try These
'Green Vase' is a popular form that has a vase-shape with burgundy-red fall foliage. 'Village Green' is another popular selection that's fast growing into a wide vase shape, has red fall leaves, and has good insect and disease resistance. 'Wireless' grows more broad than it does tall; with a height between 20 to 25 feet tall, it's a good selection to grow under power lines. 'Wireless' has bronze fall foliage color. 'Goshiki' is a new 20-foot-tall variegated selection with white-and-green leaves.

Katsura Tree

Cercidiphyllum japonicum

Botanical Pronunciation
ser-si-di-FIL-um ja-PON-i-kum

Other Name
Candy floss tree

Bloom Period and Seasonal Color
Fall; yellow, orange, red, and purple

Mature Height × Spread
40 to 60 feet × 20 to 30 feet, with some
dwarf versions

This ancient tree has been on the earth for millions of years, but many have yet to discover it as a landscape tree. It's distantly related to the tulip tree. While it grows into a large, pyramidal-shaped, handsome specimen, katsura trees are mostly grown for their outstanding heart-shaped leaves that have excellent fall foliage color. Depending on the selection, leaves turn yellow, orange, red, or purple. An added benefit is in the fall trees give off a spicy, brown sugar aroma as the leaves decompose. Hence the other common name of candy floss tree. Yum! The tree bark is shaggy and sinewy, making it an attractive visual in winter. These trees are long-lived and start off growing quickly, but their growth rate slows with age.

When, Where, and How to Plant
Katsura trees are hardy to zone 5, so they should be grown in warmer parts of New England. Purchase trees from a local nursery (or through the mail for rarer selections). Katsura trees can be hard to transplant successfully, so prepare the site well. Grow katsura trees in a full to part sun location in moist, well-drained, slightly acidic soil. Space trees 30 to 40 feet apart; plant more closely for weeping versions.

Growing Tips
Katsura trees need constant moisture when young to survive transplanting, but the soil still needs to stay well drained. Keep trees well watered and mulched with a mulch ring of pine needles, bark mulch, or wood chips especially in a lawn area to maintain the soil moisture and protect the trunk from damage due to lawn mowers and string trimmers. Katsura trees also have shallow roots and flairs at the trunk base, so the mulch ring is important to protect the roots from damage due to machinery. Older trees are drought tolerant, but benefit from occasional deep watering during hot, dry periods. Feed young trees with a tree plant food. Older trees don't need fertilization.

Regional Advice and Care
Katsura trees are uncommon landscape trees that require little care once established. Prune to remove dead, diseased, or broken branches in spring. Plant where it can be protected from strong winds.

Companion Planting and Design
Plant katsura trees in a large lawn area or in a meadow. They can grow in part sun so they make a nice edge of the woods tree as well. There are weeping versions that serve as excellent specimen landscape plants in the yard. Plant them where the attractive bark can be seen from the house.

Try These
'Strawberry' is a newer selection that features strawberry-colored fall foliage. 'Ruby' only grows 30 feet tall and features purplish fall leaves. The weeping katsura tree is a nice plant for a smaller space. It grows 15 to 25 feet tall with blue-green leaves on branches that sweep to the ground. In fall the leaves turn gold and apricot colors.

Linden

Tilia cordata

Botanical Pronunciation
TILL-ee-uh kor-DAY-tuh

Other Name
Littleleaf linden

Bloom Period and Seasonal Color
Midsummer; creamy yellow

Mature Height × Spread
50 to 60 feet × 20 to 40 feet with some dwarf versions

 ☀ ☀

There is something hopelessly romantic about the linden tree. Maybe it's the dark green, heart-shaped leaves with light green undersides that flutter in the breeze. Perhaps it's the fragrant flowers in early summer that perfume a street. Maybe it's because you can make a sweet tea from those flowers. This widely grown tree is a favorite for roadsides, yards, and wide-open spaces. While it's a large tree growing to 50 feet tall, it also is manageable in the landscape. The shape tends to be pyramidal or oval and it has a naturally well-kept appearance. It's a hardy, tough tree that tolerates air pollution, poor soils, and other factors commonly found in urban settings.

When, Where, and How to Plant

Linden trees are hardy throughout New England. Purchase trees from your local nursery and plant from spring to early fall in a full to part sun location. Linden trees grow best in well-drained, moist, fertile soils, but are very adaptable to less-than-favorable conditions. Space trees 20 to 30 feet apart.

Growing Tips

Older trees are drought tolerant but water young trees well. Mulch around the base of trees, especially those growing in lawns, with wood chips or bark mulch to maintain consistent soil moistures levels and protect the trunk for damage due to lawn mowers and string trimmers. Fertilize young trees in spring with a tree plant food. Older trees don't need fertilization.

Regional Advice and Care

Linden trees only need pruning to remove dead, diseased, and broken branches in spring. They can be pruned into an informal hedge, shearing the branches in spring and early summer to keep the tree size manageable. On young trees handpick, trap, and apply organic sprays to control Japanese beetles. Spray to control aphids, whose feeding causes sooty mold disease. On older trees the damage isn't life threatening and there's little need for controls.

Companion Planting and Design

Linden trees are classic street trees in urban areas. But they also are a good choice as a shade tree in a large lawn. By keeping lindens sheared, they make a good, large-sized hedge. Because of their tolerance of a variety of soil conditions and drought, they make good trees for areas with lots of pavement, such as islands in parking lots. Dwarf versions can even be grow in large planter boxes.

Try These

'Greenspire' is a popular selection for its narrow, oval shape; uniform branching; and tolerance of poor soil conditions. 'Shamrock' is a newer selection that's similar to 'Greenspire' but it grows faster, with a more open crown. 'Chancellor' is a narrow tree, only reaching 20 feet wide, with wide branch angles that are less likely to break in storms. 'Green Globe' is a dwarf version that only grows 15 feet tall.

Maple

Acer spp., cultivars, and hybrids

Botanical Pronunciation
AY-sur

Bloom Period and Seasonal Color
Fall; yellow, orange, and red foliage

Mature Height × Spread
30 to 70 feet × 30 to 50 feet

People travel from around the world to see the fall foliage colors of New England and the maple is one of the primary trees making this display so amazing. This native tree has many variations. The smaller growing Japanese maple was profiled in a separate entry (see page XXX). Here I'll talk about the large maples that make great shade trees, add country charm to a residence, and produce the highly desired fall foliage show. But maples aren't just about the fall foliage. The seldom used paperbark maple (*A. griseum*) has attractive peeling bark that gives the tree winter interest as well. Throughout New England, and especially where I live in Vermont, the sugar maple (*A. saccharum*) is famous for yielding the sweet sap used to make maple syrup.

When, Where, and How to Plant
Maples are generally hardy throughout New England, but some hybrids may vary in their hardiness. Purchase trees from a local nursery and plant from spring to early fall in well-drained, moist, fertile soil in a full to part sun location. Avoid alkaline soils because they can cause nutrient deficiencies. Sugar maples do not tolerate salt spray, heat, or air pollution. Silver maples (*A. saccharinum*) are tolerant of seasonal flooding. Space trees 30 to 50 feet apart.

Growing Tips
Keep young trees well watered. Once established, older trees are drought tolerant. When it's being grown as a lawn tree, create a mulch ring around the tree to keep the soil evenly moist and protect the tree trunk from damage due to lawn mowers and string trimmers. Fertilize young trees in spring with a tree fertilizer. Older trees don't need fertilization.

Regional Advice and Care
Maples require little care and pruning once established. Remove dead, diseased, and broken limbs as needed. Silver maples have weak wood that often breaks in storms. Trees may get black tar spot blotches on their leaves during wet summers or leaf scorch during hot, dry conditions. Neither condition is a concern.

Companion Planting and Design
For shade trees, grow red maples (*A. rubrum*) and sugar maples. In wet areas near ponds or streams, select silver maples. But don't plant silver maples near a sidewalk or driveway. Their shallow roots will buckle the pavement. For a more ornamental tree, try the paperbark maple for its shorter stature (30 feet tall) and exfoliating cinnamon-brown bark. Avoid planting invasive maples, such as Norway maple (*A. platanoides*) and amur maple (*A. ginnala*).

Try These
'Armstrong', 'October Glory', and 'Red Sunset' are some of the red maples with particularly good fall foliage color. 'Green Mountain' is a good sugar maple selection. 'Cinnamon Flake' is a newer paperbark maple hybrid that's hardy to zone 5. 'Silver Queen' is a good silver maple selection. 'Autumn Blaze' is a newer hybrid cross between a red and silver maple with fast growth rate, brilliant fall color, and good drought tolerance.

Magnolia

Magnolia spp. and hybrids

Botanical Pronunciation
mag-NOH-li-a

Other Name
Many types

Bloom Period and Seasonal Color
Early spring; white, pink, or yellow

Mature Height × Spread
15 to 35 feet × 10 to 30 feet

When you say "magnolias," you normally think of movies like *Gone with the Wind* and the classic, evergreen, southern magnolias. But magnolias are a diverse group of trees, and there are some that grow well in New England. The most popular magnolias for our climate are the star magnolia (*M. stellata*) and the saucer magnolia (*M. soulangiana*). These are deciduous trees that aren't as majestic as the southern magnolias, but still produce the richly fragrant flowers that we all love, especially in spring after a winter of scent deprivation. Magnolias are beautiful trees in the landscape and produce attractive red fruits in fall. The smooth, gray bark adds a nice touch to winter as well.

When, Where, and How to Plant
Star magnolias are hardy to zone 4, while saucer magnolias are hardy to zone 5. Purchase trees from a local nursery and plant in spring in moist, slightly acidic, well-drained soil high in organic matter. Plant where the trees will stay cool in spring to delay flowering and reduce the chance of losing blooms to frost. Space trees 10 to 20 feet apart.

Growing Tips
Keep young trees well watered. Mulch the base of trees in the lawn with wood chips, pine needles, or bark mulch to create a mulch ring that will keep the soil consistently moist and prevent damage to the trunk from lawn mowers and string trimmers. Fertilize trees in spring with fertilizer for acid-loving plants.

Regional Advice and Care
One of the biggest problems with magnolias in New England is their early blooming habit. Flowers and buds are often killed by late spring frosts. To delay flowering, plant them on the east sides of buildings and mulch the trees well to keep the ground cool. Magnolia scale and the resulting sooty mold fungus are often a problem. Spray trees with horticultural oil to control scale insects.

Companion Planting and Design
Plant large trees in the lawn as a specimen or on the side of a garage protected from the cold winds. Plant small trees in a mixed-shrub border with other early bloomers, such as forsythia.

Try These
'Alexandrina' is a popular saucer magnolia with 10-inch-diameter white flowers tinged with rose-purple coloring. 'Brozzoni' has 8-inch-wide white flowers that bloom 2 weeks later than other saucer magnolias. For star magnolias, 'Centennial' is one of the most popular with white flowers touched with pink on a 25-foot-tall tree. 'Royal Star' only grows 10 feet tall and the white flowers open a little later than other star magnolias. 'Jane' features dark pink flower buds. 'Leonard Messel' grows to 15 feet tall with dark purple flower buds that open to white. 'Elizabeth' is a cross that features unusual yellow flowers on a 20-foot-tall tree.

Mountain Ash

Sorbus spp.

Botanical Pronunciation
SOR-bus

Other Name
Rowan

Bloom Period and Seasonal Color
Spring; white; orange, red, or yellow fall berries and good fall foliage

Mature Height × Spread
20 to 40 feet × 20 to 30 feet

This native deciduous tree always surprises me when I take walks in the forest in late summer. All of a sudden I come upon a medium-sized tree with clusters of brilliant red berries. The American mountain ash (*S. americana*) grows throughout New England, but there are many other species that are better landscape trees. Most mountain ash trees have dark green leaves and white flowers in spring. The tree is not as long-lived as other native deciduous trees. However, the berries make this tree worth growing. The fruits can be yellow, orange, or red, depending on the tree selection, and are a main attraction for birds. The berries sometimes last into winter. Some selections will have attractive fall foliage color as well.

When, Where, and How to Plant
Mountain ash is hardy throughout New England. Purchase trees from a local garden center or through the mail and plant in spring in well-drained, slightly acidic moist soil. Trees flower and fruit best in full sun. Space plants 10 to 20 feet apart.

Growing Tips
Keep young trees well watered, especially during a drought. Create a mulch ring around trees planted in the lawn, covering the soil with a layer of wood chips or bark mulch to reduce damage to the trunks due to string trimmers or lawn mowers. Fertilize in spring with a tree plant food.

Regional Advice and Care
Mountain ash trees should be pruned in late winter to remove dead, diseased, and broken branches. Many insects and diseases can attack the trees, such as fireblight and borers. The best protection for your trees is to grow them in the right site on good soil and keep them healthy. Prune out diseased branches.

Companion Planting and Design
Find a spot for mountain ash trees in the lawn as a shade tree or along the edge of a forest as a wildlife tree. Plant trees in a mixed shrub and tree hedgerow with other berry producing plants, such as viburnum and serviceberry. Plant them where you can enjoy viewing the fall berries and the birds from a window in the house.

Try These
'Asplenifolia' has attractive, deeply cut leaves with red fall fruits. 'Cardinal Royal' has a narrow, oval, upright form that fits well in small spaces. It produces bright red berries in fall. 'Coral Fire' is aptly named. It has red stems and bark that contrasts nicely with its white flowers. It produces red fruits in fall with good red foliage color. This showy mountain ash only grows 15 feet tall. 'Brilliant Yellow' grows to 30 feet with beautiful yellow fruits.

Oak

Quercus spp.

Botanical Pronunciation
KWER-kus

Other Name
Common oak

Bloom Period and Seasonal Color
Fall; reddish purple foliage; grown for its stature also

Mature Height × Spread
40 to 90 feet × 40 to 60 feet

Like the maple tree, the oak defines our forest and landscape. These huge, stately trees are long-lived and much desired as shade trees and for wildlife. Like many, I remember hanging a swing from the lower large limbs of a white oak tree when I was young. Most oak trees grow slowly into large trees. The classic leaves turn an attractive reddish purple to bronze in fall depending on the selection, and the leaves often hang on the tree well into winter. The acorns were a major food source for Native Americans and still are prized by squirrels and other wildlife. The wood is often used for cabinets and flooring. Every home that has the space deserves an oak.

When, Where, and How to Plant
Oak trees are hardy throughout New England. Purchase trees from a local nursery. Plant trees in spring in a full sun location in moist, well-drained, loamy, slightly acidic soil. Oaks have taproots so they are best planted when they're young to avoid disturbing the root system. Space trees 30 to 50 feet apart.

Growing Tips
Keep young trees well watered. Mulch around the base of trees planted in lawns with wood chips or bark mulch. Create a mulch ring around the drip line to protect the tree trunk from damage due to lawn mowers or string trimmers. Fertilize young trees in spring with a plant food made for trees. Keep the soil slightly acidic to avoid diseases and nutrient deficiencies. Older trees don't need fertilization.

Regional Advice and Care
Avoid planting oaks close to buildings or power lines so they won't have to be severely pruned in the future. They need little pruning other than removing the occasional dead, diseased, or broken branch. Some oaks, such as red oak (*Q. rubrum*), are periodically attacked by caterpillars, such as the gypsy moth. Older trees can withstand the damage. Protect younger trees with sprays of *Bacillus thuriengiensis* to kill the caterpillars.

Companion Planting and Design
You'll need some room to grow oaks in your yard. Plant them in a large lawn area or create a grove in a meadow. The red oak (Northern red oak) and pin oak (*Q. palustris*) are faster growing than white oak (*Q. alba*) and English oak (*Q. robar*).

Try These
'Crownright' is an upward-growing pin oak that doesn't have branches that droop to the ground as with other oaks. 'Green Pillar' is a narrow, columnar-shaped pin oak that only grows 15 feet wide and has red foliage in fall. 'Skyrocket' is a columnar-shaped English oak that can be used as a street tree. 'Westminster Globe' is a rounded English oak. 'Pendula' is a weeping English oak that only grows 30 feet tall.

Poplar

Populus spp.

Botanical Pronunciation
POP-you-lus

Other Name
Aspen

Bloom Period and Seasonal Color
Fall; golden foliage; also grown for its tall stature

Mature Height × Spread
40 to 80 feet × 10 to 60 feet

Few trees capture the imagination like a grove of quaking aspens (*P. tremuloides*) in fall. The golden leaves tremble peacefully in the breeze against their attractive bark. But there is more to poplars than this classic backdrop to a Western cowboy movie. For an Italian look, try the Lombardy poplar (*P. nigra*) with its tall, lean growth. Cottonwoods (*P. deltoides*) are poplars too. They are huge, native trees that dominate a landscape and have the most unusual trait of sending off fluffy seeds in early summer that can cover a lawn making it look like snow. Poplars are fast-growing, sometimes short-lived trees, that can sucker and create a forest quickly. They make good hedges, specimen trees, or attractive groves depending on your selection.

When, Where, and How to Plant

Poplars are hardy throughout New England. Purchase trees from a local nursery and plant in spring, after all danger of frost has passed, to early fall. Plant trees in full sun on well-drained soil. Poplars are salt-spray and drought tolerant. Space trees 30 to 40 feet apart.

Growing Tips

You should keep young trees well watered, but established trees are drought tolerant. Mulch when the trees are in the lawn with wood chips or bark mulch to create a ring around the drip line of the tree. This will keep the soil evenly moist and protect the tree trunks from damage due to lawn mowers and string trimmers. Fertilize young trees in spring with a tree plant food. Older trees don't need fertilization.

Regional Advice and Care

Poplars are fast growing, but they have weak wood. They often suffer damage during storms. Prune out dead, diseased, or broken branches at any time. Poplars also sucker freely so don't plant near sidewalks, walkways, or septic systems for fear of these suckers clogging your septic field or disrupting your walkway. Poplars also can be subject to a number of diseases and insects. Select resistant varieties and keep the trees.

Companion Planting and Design

Plant cottonwood trees in a large yard to act as shade trees. They tolerate wet soils so they can be planted to stabilize a bank along a stream or in a wet area. Plant aspens in groves in a field or in a forest as wildlife trees. Plant where you can enjoy the view of the fall color and attractive bark. Plant tall thin Lombardy poplars as hedgerows or windbreaks along the boundary of your property. Birds love to nest in the branches. Avoid planting poplars close to buildings or power lines so that they won't have to be severely pruned later.

Try These

'Majestic' is a disease-tolerant version of the Lombardy poplar. 'Siouxland' is a male cottonwood tree variety that doesn't produce seedpods, grows quickly into a good shade tree, and has good disease tolerance. It has interesting, gray-white, diamond-patterned bark.

Serviceberry

Amelanchier spp.

Botanical Pronunciation
am-ul-LANK-ee-ur

Other Name
Juneberry

Bloom Period and Seasonal Color
Early spring; white; blue fruits in summer;
orange and red fall foliage

Mature Height × Spread
15 to 30 feet × 8 to 15 feet

Serviceberry is one of my favorite underappreciated small trees. But I'm happy to see many are realizing the beauty and multiple benefits this tree offers. This small, multistemmed native is one of the first trees to bloom in the forest in spring. Its white flowers contrast well with the new coppery-colored foliage. They give way to blue-black berries that are edible, and birds love them too! In fall the foliage turns a combination of yellow, orange, and red colors. In winter the smooth, light gray bark is a nice contrast with the red stems of native dogwood bushes. This tree handles some shade, poor soils, and wet conditions. Newer selections feature shorter more shrublike plants with large, blueberry-sized fruits.

When, Where, and How to Plant
Serviceberry is hardy throughout New England. Purchase plants from a local nursery and plant from spring to early fall in moist, well-drained soils. It will tolerate wet sites and transplants easily. Serviceberry trees flower and fruit best in full sun, but tolerate some shade. Space plants 12 to 15 feet apart, or group trees closer together to form a thicket.

Growing Tips
Serviceberry trees like moist soils. Water young trees well and mulch around the base of trees planted in lawns with bark mulch or wood chips to keep the soil moist. Fertilize young plants in spring with compost or a tree plant food. Older trees generally don't need fertilization.

Regional Advice and Care
Serviceberry can be pruned into a small tree on a single trunk or allowed to grow multiple trunks as a large shrub. Prune in early winter to reduce sap loss and to shape the tree into the form you like. Remove dead, diseased, and broken branches anytime. Protect the tree from birds with netting if you intend on harvesting the berries in summer. Serviceberry has few major insect and disease problems.

Companion Planting and Design
Plant serviceberry trees in naturalized groups with other spring-flowering trees and shrubs, such as Cornelian cherry and forsythia, or with other berry-producing plants that attract birds, such as viburnum and dogwoods. Serviceberry can be planted at the corner of a home as a foundation shrub and in wet areas where other trees and shrubs can't grow. Locate serviceberry trees where you can see their white flowers and attractive fall foliage from the house.

Try These
'Autumn Brilliance' is a popular selection for its fast growth rate and heavy branching. 'Robin Hill Pink' features pink flower buds that turn white once they open. 'Regent' is a Western serviceberry (*A. alnifolia*) that only grows 6 feet tall, but produces larger and better tasting berries than the Eastern native species. 'Obelisk' and 'Snowcloud' are more narrow, fastigiate forms that grow to 15 to 25 feet tall.

Sour Gum

Nyssa sylvatica

Botanical Pronunciation
NIS-a sil-VAT-i-ka

Other Name Black tupelo

Bloom Period and Seasonal Color
Fall; orange, red, and purple foliage; mostly grown for its stature

Mature Height × Spread
30 to 50 feet × 20 to 30 feet with some dwarf versions

If you're looking for an attractive, low-maintenance, deciduous shade tree for your street or yard with amazing fall foliage color, add sour gum to your list. This native is an underutilized tree. It has many of the qualities we look for in a good shade tree. Sour gum has a pyramidal shape that grows slowly up to 50 feet tall when mature. The flowers are insignificant, but a good source of pollen for bees in spring. It has small, blue-black fruits that birds enjoy. It grows well in wet sites and can even grow in areas with standing water. It is also drought tolerant. *And* it has consistently beautiful scarlet red fall foliage color that makes this tree glow in autumn. Wow!

When, Where, and How to Plant
Sour gum is hardy throughout New England. Purchase trees from your local nurseries or through the mail. Plant trees in spring in well-drained, slightly acidic, moist soils. Sour gum produces the best growth and fall color in a full sun location. It has a taproot, so it's difficult to transplant successfully once it's established. Space trees 20 to 30 feet apart.

Growing Tips
Keep young trees well watered. Mulch trees with pine needles, bark mulch, or wood chips. Create a mulch ring around the trees grown in the yard to keep the soil moist and prevent damage to the trunk due to string trimmers and lawn mowers. Once established, sour gum trees are drought tolerant. Fertilize young trees in spring with an acid-based tree plant food. It's not necessary to feed older trees.

Regional Advice and Care
Sour gum is a carefree tree. Prune in autumn (to reduce sap loss) to remove competing branches or dead, diseased, or broken limbs. Although it's slow growing, plant the tree where it won't eventually interfere with buildings and overhead power lines. Sour gum has few major pest problems.

Companion Planting and Design
Plant sour gum trees as street trees away from power lines or in the yard as a shade tree. Protect them from winter winds in colder parts of our region. Because they tolerate wet conditions, it's fine to plant them in boggy or seasonally flooded areas of your yard. They can naturalize in a woodland setting along a stream or pond. Sour gums are salt tolerant, making them good choices near the coast.

Try These
'Miss Scarlet' is known for its deep green summer foliage that turns brilliant red in fall. 'Forum' is a standard selection with a more upright habit that looks more like a pear or linden than sour gum; its fall leaves are red with yellow veins. 'Autumn Cascades' is a weeping form that only grows 15 feet tall, but still has the beautiful fall foliage color. It's only hardy to zone 5.

Sweet Gum

Liquidamber styraciflua

Botanical Pronunciation
li-kwid-am-BAR sty-RAS-i-FLU-a

Other Name
American sweet gum

Bloom Period and Seasonal Color
Fall; yellow, orange, red, and purple foliage; grown mostly for its tall stature

Mature Height × Spread
50 to 80 feet × 40 to 60 feet

If you're looking for something similar to, but different from, your usual red or sugar maple trees for fall foliage color and shade, try the sweet gum. This deciduous tree grows up to 80 feet tall in a pyramidal shape, though there are some dwarf forms. It has maplelike, star-shaped leaves that smell like camphor oil when they're crushed. The flowers and fruits are not significant, but the fall foliage is *outstanding*. Depending on the individual tree, leaf colors can include yellow, orange, purple, and red. The only downside for New Englanders is that sweet gum is only hardy to zone 5, so not all locations in our region can grow this tree.

When, Where, and How to Plant

Select varieties hardy for your area from a local nursery. Plant in spring to early fall in an open, full to part sun area, avoiding power lines or buildings nearby. Sweet gum grows best in deep, moist, river bottom soils. Space trees 40 to 50 feet apart, closer for dwarf and narrow versions.

Growing Tips

Although older trees are drought tolerant, you should keep young trees well watered. Create a mulch ring around the base of young trees grown in lawns covered with bark mulch and wood chips to help keep the shallow roots moist and reduce damage to the trunk due to lawn mowers and string trimmers. Fertilize young trees with a tree plant food; older trees usually don't need fertilizer.

Regional Advice and Care

Prune dead, diseased, or broken branches in late winter. Otherwise, sweet gum needs little pruning and has few troublesome pests. Avoid high pH soils that may cause a nutrient imbalance. Its spiny fruits eventually fall to the ground and can become a litter problem depending on where the tree is planted (unless you plant a non-fruiting variety).

Companion Planting and Design

Plant sweet gums in a large backyard, meadow, or parklike setting. Older trees develop interesting, corky textured bark. Give it plenty of room to grow tall and wide to get the full effect of its glory. Plant multistemmed selections that grow less than 20 feet tall among other native trees, such as serviceberry and hawthorn. Sweet gums can also be planted as street trees when given enough room.

Try These

'Moraine' is the most popular selection and most cold hardy, surviving temperatures in the minus 25 degrees Fahrenheit range. 'Gumball' is a multistemmed dwarf selection that grows only 15 feet tall and still has good fall color. 'Slender Silhouette' grows 50 feet tall, but only 4 feet wide, making it a good choice for narrow spaces. 'Golden Treasure' has unique yellow and green leaves, but may not be as hardy as other selections. 'Silver King' has white-and-green variegated leaves.

Sycamore

Platanus spp.

Botanical Pronunciation
PLA-tah-nus

Other Name
Plane tree

Bloom Period and Seasonal Color
Year-round; many-colored bark; grown mostly
for its large stature

Mature Height × Spread
70 to 90 feet × 60 to 70 feet

This is a magnificent deciduous tree in the landscape. Not only is it tall, wide, and has beautiful branches, the exfoliating bark leaves the trunk and older branches with colors of yellow, red, and tan depending on the selection. You just can't miss this tree in the landscape. There is a large sycamore growing near a stream close to my house that I marvel at each morning as I drive by. The leaves are large and maplelike in appearance, but lack fall coloring. The fruit balls can hang onto the tree into winter. This tree is salt, drought, and air pollution tolerant, but it's generally too large for use as a street tree unless it's given ample space. Newer selections have good disease resistance.

When, Where, and How to Plant
Sycamore trees are hardy to zone 5, so they are best grown in warmer parts of New England. Purchase trees from local nurseries and garden centers, and plant in spring to early fall in full to part sun in well-drained, humus-rich, consistently moist soils. Space them 50 or more feet apart.

Growing Tips
Keep young trees well watered, but older trees are drought tolerant. Build a mulch ring around the base of young trees planted in lawns, and cover with bark mulch or wood chips to maintain soil moisture and to help reduce damage to the trunk due to lawn mowers and string trimmers. Although older trees don't need extra food, you should fertilize young trees with a plant food formulated for trees.

Regional Advice and Care
American sycamore (*P. occidentalis*) trees are more cold hardy than the London plane tree (*P. × acerifolia*). However, London plane trees are preferred for their tolerance to various diseases, particularly anthracnose. They also are more adaptable to being heavily pruned to fit in a landscape. Otherwise, prune trees only to remove dead, diseased, or broken branches.

Companion Planting and Design
Plant sycamore trees along a streambed, the edge of woodlands, in a parklike setting, or in a meadow. These large trees need room to grow to look their best. Their roots can lift up sidewalks and pavement, so they're generally not used along streets. However, because of their tolerance to pollution, they are good city trees as long as they have enough root and top space. Dropping fruits can cause a litter problem depending on where the tree is planted.

Try These
Most of the selections available are of the London plane tree. 'Bloodgood' has good tolerance to anthracnose disease and tolerates heat, drought, and soil compaction once it's established. 'Columbia' and 'Liberty' tolerate anthracnose and powdery mildew diseases and are tolerant of heavy pruning. 'Yarwood' is a recent new introduction that has good disease resistance, fast growth, and colorful bark that starts exfoliating at a younger age than other introductions.

Tulip Tree

Liriodendron tulipifera

Botanical Pronunciation
lir-i-o-DEN-dron too-li-PIF-er-a

Other Name
Tulip poplar

Bloom Period and Seasonal Color
Late spring; yellow-green flowers; brilliant golden fall foliage

Mature Height × Spread
70 to 90 feet × 35 to 50 feet

This large deciduous tree of the magnolia family can be massive in the landscape. But it's unusual and noted for its large tulip-shaped flowers in late spring. Even the leaves look tulip-shaped. Unfortunately, the flowers on older trees tend to be too high in the canopy to really be appreciated. But their golden fall foliage color stands out. It often turns color later than other deciduous trees, giving a golden glow to the end of autumn. I often forget about my neighbor's tulip tree until fall, when the leaves shine. It also produces conelike fruits that hang on the tree into winter. There are some dwarf selections that are one-third the size of the standard species and that are better choices for a regular-sized yard.

When, Where, and How to Plant
Tulip trees are hardy to zone 5 and perhaps to zone 4 in a protected spot. Purchase trees from local nurseries or garden centers and plant from spring to early fall, in a full sun location in moist, well-drained, compost-amended soil. Avoid hot, dry sites. Space trees at least 40 feet apart, closer for dwarf selections.

Growing Tips
They will drop leaves if drought stressed so keep young trees well watered. Mulch trees with bark mulch or wood chips to protect the shallow roots. Build a mulch ring around the drip line of trees planted in lawns to keep the soil consistently moist and reduce damage to the trunk due to lawn mowers and string trimmers. Fertilize young trees

with a tree plant food, but established trees generally don't need fertilization.

Regional Advice and Care
Prune tulip trees in late winter to remove dead, diseased, or broken branches. Tulip tree branches are brittle and can break easily during winter storms. Tulip trees don't have many significant pest problems. Aphids may attack leaves, causing damage and sooty mold disease to occur. It's only practical to control aphids with sprays of insecticidal soap on young trees; mature trees are too large.

Companion Planting and Design
Most selections of tulips trees grow quickly to a large size. Care should be given where they are planted. Generally, planting in an open, parklike setting, large yard, or at the edge of a forest is best. Avoid areas close to power lines or buildings. Because the flowers attract bees and hummingbirds, it's a good tree to plant if you're growing flowers and fruits and trying to attract pollinators to your landscape. Tulip trees are also hosts for the larval form of the swallowtail butterfly.

Try These
'Majestic Beauty' is an unusual tulip tree introduction with variegated yellow-and-green leaves. 'Arnold' and 'Little Volunteer' are dwarf selections that grow 30 to 50 feet tall and 8 to 15 feet wide in a columnar shape. These are good choices for smaller yards and for along streets.

White Fir

Abies concolor

Botanical Pronunciation
AY-beez KAWN-kull-er

Other Name
Concolor fir

Bloom Period and Seasonal Color
Year-round; blue-green needles; grown for its size

Mature Height × Spread
40 to 70 feet × 20 to 30 feet with some
dwarf versions

If you're looking for an easy-to-grow evergreen tree in your landscape that has attractive coloring and is long lived, consider the white fir. Of all the fir trees that you could grow, the white fir is most tolerant of less-than-ideal soils and conditions and the easiest to grow in your landscape. White fir grows in the classic, Christmas-tree pyramidal shape. The short needles have a blue cast to them giving the tree an attractive appearance. Cones are eventually produced on older trees, but it may be many years before you'll see any. Although this evergreen grows large, there are some compact and weeping forms that may fit well in smaller landscapes.

When, Where, and How to Plant

White fir is hardy throughout New England. Purchase trees from a local nursery and plant from spring to summer in well-drained, moist soil in a full or part sun location. White fir is less fussy about moist soils than other evergreens. Space trees 20 to 30 feet apart, closer for dwarf selections.

Growing Tips

Keep young trees well watered. Mulch young trees with pine needles, creating a mulch ring around the tree to maintain soil moisture levels. Once established, older white fir trees are drought tolerant. Fertilize young trees with an evergreen tree plant food. Older trees generally don't need extra fertilization.

Regional Advice and Care

Great news! White fir trees generally don't need pruning. They can be sheared to increase the pyramidal shape, especially if you're intending on growing these as Christmas trees. Shear trees in spring and early summer to shape and remove errant branches. Protect young trees from deer with fencing and repellent sprays. White fir can be attacked by a wide variety of insects and diseases, though rarely severely.

Companion Planting and Design

Plant white fir along a property boundary, edge of the forest, or in an open meadow. This evergreen can be grown with other large evergreens, such as hemlock and cedar, to create an informal hedge to block a view. Be aware, although they're slow growing, white firs can eventually grow large and block a vista that you treasure. Pruning older trees can deform them.

Try These

'Candicans' has intense silver-blue needles and perhaps the bluest needle color. 'Compacta' is a dwarf white fir that only grows 8 feet tall at maturity. This is a good selection for small yards and for locations under power lines. 'Gable's Weeping' is an unusual introduction with cascading branches. It only grows 6 feet tall in 10 years. 'Wintergold' is a dwarf, only growing 5 feet tall and wide. In spring, its needles are chartreuse. They change to light green in summer and then to a buttery gold in winter.

TIPS FOR PLANTING ANNUALS

IN NEW ENGLAND

To remove annual seedlings, gently pop the young plants from their cell-packs by squeezing the bottom and pushing up. Do not grab plants by their tender stems or leaves.

When planting annuals, plant at the same depth they were growing in the containers. If your growing medium is properly prepared, it will be loose enough that you can easily dig shallow planting holes with your fingers. For gallon pots, use a trowel, spade, or cultivator.

Plants growing in peat pots can be planted pot and all, but remove the upper edges of peat pots so that the pot will not act as a wick, pulling water away from the roots.

Pinch off any flowers or buds so the plant can focus its energy on getting its roots established rather than flowering, then water well.

TIPS FOR PLANTING A TREE

IN NEW ENGLAND

Trees are available bare-root, in containers, and balled-and-burlapped. A fourth way to plant a tree is to employ a professional nursery to come in with a tree spade, which allows you to plant a larger tree faster, but it usually is much more expensive.

Bare-root trees must be planted in spring as soon as the soil can be worked. Balled-and-burlapped, container-grown, and tree-spade trees can be planted anytime but the hottest days of summer. Spring is still the best time for planting, however. The fewer or smaller the leaves are, the faster the tree will recover from transplanting. Plant the tree at the same depth at which it was growing in the container or burlap wrap. Bare-root trees should be planted so that the crown is at ground level.

Above: Dig a hole no deeper than the depth of the rootball but at least twice as wide, preferably three or four times wider.
Below: Amend the soil, if needed, to create a well-drained soil in the correct pH range. To do this, mix the planting soil with organic matter, such as well-rotted compost or manure.

If the wrapping is real burlap, you simply have to cut and remove the fabric on top of the ball and peel the burlap down the sides so it stays below the soil line. It will eventually decompose. Synthetic burlap must be removed completely. Remove the wire basket that surrounds the rootball and burlap, if present.

Place the plant in the hole and adjust the hole depth so that the plant is about 1 inch higher than it was planted in the nursery to allow for settling of soil. Use a shovel handle laid across the hole to help determine the proper depth.

Shovel in the amended soil around the rootball, stopping to tamp down the soil when the hole is half full.

Fill the rest of the hole with loose soil and tamp down again to ensure good contact between the soil and the roots.

Soak the planting area with water. Once the soil has settled, build up a 2- to 3-inch basin around the plant to catch rainfall and irrigation water. However, do not build a basin if your soil is very heavy and doesn't drain well.

Apply 2 to 3 inches of organic mulch, such as shredded bark or wood chips, keeping the mulch a few inches away from the trunk.

NEW ENGLAND RESOURCES

Once you catch the gardening bug, you'll invariably want to know more. Luckily, New England is loaded with great gardens and gardeners who can help. The listings in this section will help you further your gardening education and offer some inspiration and ideas on what to grow in your landscape. By no means is this list complete, but it's a great starting place to make you a better gardener. I divided the listings by state, but since the climate and growing conditions are similar throughout much of New England, feel free to look at other states in our region for information. This is particularly true of soil-testing laboratories and display gardens. Each state has a Cooperative Extension Office operated through the state land grant university where home gardening information is readily available. The first listing under each state gives you a link to that information online. The next listing is that state's Master Gardener Association. Let's start with those.

Master Gardener Associations

Master Gardeners are home gardeners who have attended a series of workshops, often taught by university professors, to increase their knowledge of gardening and horticulture. In exchange for having participated in these workshops, they volunteer their time back to the community answering home gardener's questions (often through a phone hotline) and working on special gardening projects with kids, seniors, and others in their community. They are a great resource for a novice gardener. You might get inspired to take the class and become a Master Gardener yourself.

Soil Testing Laboratories

I mention soil testing as a good first step to determine the health of your soil before you plant. You can purchase home soil-test kits from garden centers. For a more scientific analysis, you can send soil samples to private laboratories to be tested. Some of these labs are located at state land grant universities, and the basic test often costs less than $30.

Public Display Gardens

Public display gardens are great ways to get inspiration and ideas for growing your own flowers, shrubs, and trees. There's nothing like seeing the true color of a flower in bloom or knowing that a certain shrub or trees is hardy in your area.

We are blessed in New England with some great gardens that you can explore. One type is demonstration gardens for the All-American Selection Program. For eighty years this program has been trialing annual flowers and vegetables around the country and bestowing the best varieties with their award—AAS winner. The display gardens feature many of the present and past winners and often are located in a public area. Sometimes the display garden will be associated with a nursery or garden center.

There are many public botanical gardens and private gardens that are open to the public to offer ideas and inspirations.

State Resources

Here is a short list of state-by-state resources to help make you a better gardener. I list the addresses, a brief description, and website (when available) for each.

Connecticut

Home and Garden Education Center
www.ladybug.uconn.edu/

Master Gardener Program
University of Connecticut
Leslie Alexander
State Master Gardener & Education
Program Coordinator
leslie.alexander@uconn.edu
www.ladybug.uconn.edu/mastergardener/
index.html

Bartlett Arboretum and Gardens
151 Brookdale Rd.
Stamford, CT 06903
www.bartlettarboretum.org/
This garden has 91-acres of gardens, greenhouses, trees, and shrubs in a park-like setting.

Bushnell Park Arboretum
Hartford, CT 06123
www.bushnellpark.org/attractions/
tree-walk-in-bushnell-park/

Drew Park Community Garden
280 Warde Terrace
Fairfield, CT 06825
AAS Display Garden

Elizabeth Park Gardens
Corner of Prospect and Asylum Avenues
West Hartford, CT 06117
www.elizabethpark.org/
The park includes 800 varieties of roses and 15,000 rose plants. It also has flower gardens and a greenhouse.

Hollister House Garden
PO Box 1454
Washington, CT 06793
www.hollisterhousegarden.org/
This is a classic English garden on a 25-acre estate with garden rooms filled with flowers, shrubs, and trees.

Soil Nutrient Analysis Laboratory
6 Sherman Place, U-102
University of Connecticut
Storrs, CT 06269-5102
http://soiltest.uconn.edu/
Soil-testing lab.

White Flower Farm
Rt. 63
Litchfield, CT 06759
www.whiteflowerfarm.com/
A famous mail order and display garden with a garden center. It features a broad range of perennial flowers, shrubs, and trees.

Maine

Home Gardening News
http://umaine.edu/gardening/
maine-home-garden-news/

Master Gardener Program
University of Maine Cooperative Extension
extension@maine.edu
5741 Libby Hall
Orono, ME 04469
(207) 581-3188
http://umaine.edu/gardening/master-gardeners/

Analytical Laboratory and Maine Soil
Testing Service
5722 Deering Hall
Orono, ME 04469
(207) 581-3591
http://anlab.umesci.maine.edu
Soil-testing lab.

Asticou Azalea Garden
Peabody Drive, Northeast Harbor
Mount Desert Island, ME 04662
http://gardenpreserve.org/asticou-azalea-
garden/index.html
This 1.5-acre display garden features perennial
flower borders and natural woodlands.

Coastal Maine Botanical Garden
Barters Island Road
Boothbay, ME 04537
www.mainegardens.org/
A relatively new botanical garden, this sits
on 128 acres of land with flower, shrub, and
tree gardens along the ocean.

Ecotat Gardens and Arboretum
Route 2 and Annis Road
Hermon, ME 04401
www.ecotat.org/
This 91-acre display garden features 55
gardens, 280 varieties of trees, and 1,500
varieties of perennials.

Lyle Littlefield Ornamentals Trial Garden
and Research Center
University of Maine
5772 Deering Hall
Orono, ME 04469
www.umaine.edu/enh/
This woody plant display garden features
varieties of crab apples, lilacs, rhododendrons,
and magnolias.

Penobscot County Master Gardener
Demonstration at Rogers Farm
491 Bennoch Road
Stillwater, ME 04489
http://umaine.edu/penobscot/programs/
gardening/rogers-farm/
AAS Display Garden

Massachusetts
Home and Garden Information Center
http://ag.umass.edu/
home-lawn-garden-information

Master Gardener Program
Sonja Johanson
Training Course Coordinator
sonjajohanson@gmail.com
900 Washington Street
Wellesley, MA 02482
(617) 933-4929
www.masshort.org/
Master-Gardener-Program

Western Massachusetts Master Gardeners
wmmga10@yahoo.com
66 Rural Lane
East Longmeadow, MA 01028
(413) 525-6742
http://wmmga.org/
Master Gardener Program

Arnold Arboretum
128 Arborway
Jamaica Plain, MA 02130
www.arboretum.harvard.edu/
This magnificent 265-acre arboretum hosts
one of the largest collections of woody
plants in the world.

Berkshire Botanic Garden
5 West Stockbridge Road
Stockbridge, MA 01262
www.berkshirebotanical.org/
This 15-acre garden has annual and
perennial flower beds, an herb garden,
spring bulb gardens, daylilies, vegetable
gardens, greenhouses, and an AAS winner
display garden.

Leo Levi All American Selections
Display Garden
Langley Rd., Centre St., Beacon St.
Newton Center, MA 02459
AAS Display Garden

Massachusetts Horticultural Society at
Elm Bank
Route 16, Dover, MA 02030
www.masshort.org/
Massachusetts Horticultural Society
headquarters features 36 acres of display
and educational gardens.

New England Wildflower Farm
180 Hemenway Road,
North Framingham, MA 01701
http://newfs.org/
This garden contains more than 1,600
wildflower plants including rare and
endangered species.

Soil and Plant Tissue Testing Lab
West Experiment Station
682 North Pleasant Street
University of Massachusetts
Amherst, MA 01003
(413) 545-2311
http://soiltest.umass.edu/
Soil-testing lab.

Tower Hill Botanic Garden
11 French Drive, Box 598
Boylston, MA 01505
www.towerhillbg.org/
This relatively new 132-acre garden is
still growing. It includes cottage gardens,
greenhouses, tree and shrub gardens, and
wildlife gardens.

Weston Nursery
93 East Main Street, Route 135
Hopkinton, MA 01748
http://westonnurseries.com/
This 650-acre nursery includes an amazing
array of trees, shrubs, and flowers. It also
has a garden center.

New Hampshire
Education Center and Information Line
http://extension.unh.edu/Gardens-Landscapes/
Education-Center-Information-Line

Master Gardener Program
University of New Hampshire Cooperative
Extension
Rachel Maccini
Statewide Program Coordinator
rachel.maccini@unh.edu
200 Bedford Street
Manchester, NH 03101
(603) 629-9494
http://extension.unh.edu/Master-Gardeners/
How-do-I-become-Master-Gardener-Volunteer

Cole Gardens
430 Loudon Rd.
Concord, NH 03301
http://www.colegardens.com/
AAS Display Garden

The Fells
456 Route 103A North
Newbury, NH 03255
http://thefells.org/
This historic summer cottage and gardens
feature alpine plants, rock gardens, and heaths
and heathers.

Meredith Public Library
91 Main Street
Meredith, NH 03253
AAS Display Garden

Pleasant View Greenhouses
7316 Pleasant St.
Loudon, NH 03307
www.pvg.com/info/aboutus.cfm
This annual and perennial flower production
facility grows the Proven Winners™ line of
plants and has a 2-acre display garden at
their greenhouse location. Plants aren't for
sale on-site.

St. Gaudens National Historic Site
139 St.Gaudens Road, Off Route 12A
Cornish, NH 03745
www.nps.gov/saga/index.htm
This historic site features terraced
perennial flower gardens, a birch grove,
and a cutting garden.

University of New Hampshire
Cooperative Extension
Soil Testing Program
Spaulding Life Science Center, Room G28
38 Academic Way
Durham, NH 03824
https://extension.unh.edu/Problem-
Diagnosis-and-Testing-Services/
Soil-Testing
Soil-testing lab.

University of New Hampshire Trial Gardens,
Prescott Park
Prescott Park, Marcy Street
Portsmouth, NH 03801
AAS Display Garden

Rhode Island
Gardening RI Information Center
www.gardeningri.com/

Master Gardener Program
University of Rhode Island
Vanessa Venturini & Kate Venturini
Cooperative Extension Master Gardener
Coordinators
vanessa@uri.edu
kate@uri.edu
3 East Alumni Avenue
Kingston, RI 02881
(401) 874-7142
www.uri.edu/cels/ceoc/

Blithewood Mansion, Gardens, and
Arboretum
101 Ferry Road (Rt. 114)
Bristol, Rhode Island 02809
www.blithewold.org/
This garden consists of 33 acres of trees,
shrubs, roses, and flower gardens surrounding
a great lawn.

Green Animals Topiary Garden
380 Cory's Lane
Portsmouth, RI 02871
On 7 acres, more than eighty life-sized
topiaries or various animals sculpted from
yew, privet, and boxwood.

Roger Williams Park and Botanical Center
950 Elmwood Avenue
Providence, RI 02900
www.providenceri.com/botanical-center/
This site encompasses a Japanese garden, a
rose garden, and two greenhouses.

University of Rhode Island Botanic Gardens
3 East Alumni Ave
Kingston, RI 02881
http://cels.uri.edu/uribg/
AAS Display Garden

Vermont
Information Fact Sheets
www.uvm.edu/mastergardener/?Page=Vermo
ntResources.htm

Master Gardener Program
University of Vermont
Heather Carrington
Master Gardener State Coordinator
heather.carrington@uvm.edu
63 Carrigan Drive
Burlington, VT 05405
(802) 656-9562
www.uvm.edu/mastergardener/

Equinox Valley Nursery
Historic Route 7A
Manchester, VT 05254
www.equinoxvalleynursery.com/
An extensive retail garden center and
nursery featuring display gardens.

Gardeners Supply Company
472 Marshall Avenue
Williston, VT 05495
www.gardeners.com
A mail-order company with retail garden
centers in two locations, featuring
greenhouses and display gardens.

Gardens at Hildene
Historic Route 7A
Manchester, VT 05254
www.hildene.org/
Historic Robert Todd Lincoln summer home
featuring peony, roses, lilies, and other flowers.

Shelburne Museum
Route 7
Shelburne, VT 05482
http://shelburnemuseum.org/
An Americana museum in a parklike setting
featuring annual flowers, roses, daylilys,
peonies, and lilac gardens.

University of Vermont
Agricultural and Environmental Testing Lab
219 Hills Building, UVM
Burlington, VT 05405
802-656-0285
www.uvm.edu/pss/ag_testing
Soil-testing lab.

Vermont Garden Park
1100 Dorset St.
South Burlington, VT 05403
AAS Display Garden

Waterfront Park
College St
Burlington, VT 05401
AAS Display Garden

GLOSSARY

Acidic soil: On a soil pH scale of 0 to 14, acidic soil has a pH lower than 7.0. Most garden plants prefer a soil a bit on the acidic side.

Afternoon sun: A garden receiving afternoon sun typically has full sun from 1:00 to 5:00 p.m. daily, with more shade during the morning hours.

Alkaline soil: On a soil pH scale of 0 to 14, alkaline soil has a pH higher than 7.0. Many desert plants thrive in slightly alkaline soils.

Annual: A plant that germinates (sprouts), flowers, and dies within one year or season (spring, summer, winter, or fall) is an annual.

***Bacillus thuringiensis* (B.t.):** B.t. is an organic pest control based on naturally occurring soil bacteria, often used to control harmful caterpillars, such as cutworms, leaf rollers, and webworms.

Balled-and-burlapped (B&B): This phrase describes plants that have been grown in field nursery rows, dug up with their soil intact, wrapped with burlap, and tied with twine. Most of the plants sold balled and burlapped are large evergreen plants and deciduous trees.

Bare root: Bare-root plants are those that are shipped dormant, without being planted in soil or having soil around their roots. Roses are often shipped bare root.

Beneficial insects: These insects perform valuable services, such as pollination and pest control. Ladybugs, soldier beetles, and some bees are examples.

Biennial: A plant that blooms during its second year and then dies is a biennial.

Bolting: This is a process when a plant switches from leaf growth to producing flowers and seeds. Bolting often occurs quite suddenly and is usually undesirable, because the plant usually dies shortly after bolting.

Branch crotch angles: The angle of branches coming off the main tree trunk. Narrow branch crotch angles can lead to limbs prematurely breaking off the trunk as they get older.

Brown materials: Part of a well-balanced compost pile, brown materials include high-carbon materials, such as brown leaves and grass, woody plant stems, dryer lint, and sawdust.

Bud: The bud is an undeveloped shoot nestled between the leaf and the stem that will eventually produce a flower or branch.

Bulb: A bulb is a plant with a large, rounded, underground storage organ formed by the plant stem and leaves. Examples are tulips, daffodils, and hyacinths. Bulbs that flower in spring are typically planted in fall. Other similar terms often used for bulbs include corms and tubers.

Bulblet: Small bulbs that form around the main bulb. They can be separated from the main bulb and grown as an individual plant, but it may take a few years for them to grow to the flowering stage.

Bush: See Shrub.

Cane: Stems on a fruit shrub; usually blackberry or raspberry stems, are called canes, but blueberry stems can also be referred to as canes.

Central leader: The term for the center trunk of a fruit tree.

Common name: A name that is generally used to identify a plant in a particular region, as opposed to its botanical name that is standard throughout the world. For example, the common name for Echinacea purpurea is "purple coneflower."

Contact herbicide: This type of herbicide kills only the part of the plant it touches, such as the leaves or the stems.

Container: Any pot or vessel that is used for planting; containers can be ceramic, clay, steel, or plastic—or a teacup, bucket, or barrel.

Container garden: This describes a garden that is created primarily by growing plants in containers instead of in the ground.

Container grown: This describes a plant that is grown, sold, and shipped while in a pot.

Cool-season annual: This is a flowering plant, such as snapdragon or pansy, that thrives during cooler months.

Cover crop: These plants are grown specifically to enrich the soil, prevent erosion, suppress weeds, and control pests and diseases.

Cross-pollinate: This describes the transfer of pollen from one plant to another plant.

Dappled shade: This is bright shade created by high tree branches or tree foliage, where patches of sunlight and shade intermingle.

Day-neutral plant: A plant that flowers when it reaches a certain size, regardless of the day length, is a day-neutral plant.

Deadhead: To remove dead flowers in order to encourage further bloom and prevent the plant from going to seed.

Deciduous plant: A plant that loses its leaves seasonally, typically in fall or early winter.

Diatomaceous earth: A natural control for snails, slugs, flea beetles, and other garden pests, diatomaceous earth consists of ground-up fossilized remains of sea creatures.

Dibber: A tool consisting of a pointed wooden stick with a handle. Used for poking holes in the ground so seedlings, seeds, and small bulbs can be planted.

Direct seed: To plant the seed directly into the ground to grow to flower. Some flowers can be directly sown, such as cosmos, while others will need to be started indoors and transplanted, such as geraniums, because they require a longer period to flower.

Divide: Technique consisting of digging up clumping perennials, separating the roots, and replanting. Dividing plants encourages vigorous growth and is typically performed in the spring or fall.

Dormancy: The period when plants stop growing in order to conserve energy; this happens naturally and seasonally, usually in winter.

Drip line: The ground area under the outer circumference of tree branches; this is where most of the tree's roots that absorb water and nutrients are found.

Dwarf: In the context of ornamental gardening, a dwarf tree is a tree that grows shorter than the original species either by grafting onto a dwarfing rootstock or natural selection.

Evergreen: A plant that keeps its leaves year-round, instead of dropping them seasonally.

Exfoliating bark: Bark on a tree or shrub that naturally peels off, revealing various inner bark textures and colors.

Floating row covers: Lightweight fabric that can be used to protect plants from pests. Usually white in color.

Flower stalk: The stem that supports the flower and elevates it so that insects can reach the flower and pollinate it.

Foundation plant: A shrub grown in front or along a house to block the view of the concrete foundation.

Four-inch pot: The 4-inch by 4-inch pots that many annuals and small perennials are sold in. Four-inch pots can also be sold in flats of 18 or 20.

Four-tine claw: Also called a cultivator, this hand tool typically has three to four curved tines and is used to break up soil clods or lumps before planting and to rake soil amendments into garden beds.

Frost: Ice crystals that form when the temperature falls below freezing (32°F) create frost.

Full sun: Areas of the garden that receive direct sunlight for six to eight hours a day or more, with no shade.

Fungicide: This describes a chemical compound used to control fungal diseases.

Gallon container: A standard nursery-sized container for plants, a gallon container is roughly equivalent to a gallon container of milk.

Garden fork: A garden implement with a long handle and short tines; use a garden fork for loosening and turning soil.

Garden lime: This soil amendment lowers soil acidity and raises the pH.

Garden soil: The existing soil in a garden bed; it is generally evaluated by its nutrient content and texture. Garden soil is also sold as a bagged item at garden centers and home-improvement stores.

Germination: This is the process by which a plant emerges from a seed or a spore.

Graft union: This is the place on a fruit tree trunk where the rootstock and the scion have been joined.

Grafted tree: This is a tree composed of two parts: the top, or scion, which bears fruit, and the bottom, or rootstock.

Granular fertilizer: This type of fertilizer comes in a dry, pellet-like form rather than a liquid or powder.

Grass clippings: The parts of grass that are removed when mowing; clippings are a valuable source of nitrogen for the lawn or the compost pile.

Green materials: An essential element in composting that includes grass clippings, kitchen scraps, and manure and provides valuable nitrogen in the pile. Green materials are high in nitrogen.

Hand pruners: An important hand tool that consists of two sharp blades that perform a scissoring motion; these are used for light pruning, clipping, and cutting.

Hardening off: This is the process of slowly acclimating seedlings and young plants grown in an indoor environment to the outdoors.

Hardiness zone map: This map lists average annual minimum temperature ranges of a particular area. This information is helpful in determining appropriate plants for the garden. North America is divided into thirteen separate hardiness zones.

Hard rake: This tool has a long handle and rigid tines at the bottom. It is great for moving a variety of garden debris, such as soil, mulch, leaves, and pebbles.

Hedging: This is the practice of trimming a line of plants to create a solid mass for privacy or garden definition.

Heirloom: A plant that was developed and was available (and more commonly grown) pre-World War II.

Hoe: A long-handled garden tool with a short, narrow, flat steel blade, it is used for breaking up hard soil and removing weeds.

Holdfast: Suction cup like plant parts on vines that attach themselves to walls, masonry, wooden fences, and any solid objects to enable the vine to climb.

Host plant: A plant grown to feed caterpillars that will eventually morph into butterflies.

Humus: Organic compounds present in compost and well-decomposed organic matter that aid plants in water and nutrient uptake.

Hybrid: Plants produced by crossing two genetically different plants; hybrids often have desirable characteristics, such as disease resistance.

Insecticide: This substance is used for destroying or controlling insects that are harmful to plants. Insecticides are available in organic and synthetic forms.

Invasive plant: Any plant that is not native and has spread so that it crowds out native plants and has an adverse impact on the ecosystem.

Irrigation: A system of watering the landscape; irrigation can be an in-ground automatic system, soaker or drip hoses, or handheld hoses with nozzles.

Jute twine: A natural-fiber twine, jute is used for gently staking plants or tying them to plant supports.

Kneeling pad: A padded, weather-resistant cushion used for protecting knees while performing garden tasks, such as weeding and planting.

Landscape fabric: A synthetic material that is laid on the soil surface to control weeds and prevent erosion.

Larva: The immature stage of an insect that goes through complete metamorphosis; caterpillars are butterfly or moth larvae.

Larvae: This is the plural of larva.

Leaf rake: A long-handled rake with flexible tines on the head; a leaf rake is used for easily and efficiently raking leaves into piles.

Liquid fertilizer: Plant fertilizer in a liquid form; some types need to be mixed with water, and some types are ready to use from the bottle.

Long-day plant: Plants that flower when the days are longer than their critical photoperiod, long-day plants typically flower in early summer when the days are still getting longer.

Loppers: One of the largest manual gardening tools, use loppers for pruning branches of 1 to 3 inches in diameter with a scissoring motion.

Morning sun: Areas of the garden that have an eastern exposure and receive direct sun in the morning hours.

Mulch: Any type of material that is spread over the soil surface around the base of plants to suppress weeds and retain soil moisture.

Naturalized: Plants that are introduced into an area, as opposed to being native to it, and have become established in that ecosystem.

Nectar plant: Flowers that produce nectar that attract and feed butterflies, encouraging a succession of blooms throughout the season.

Nematode: Microscopic, wormlike organisms that live in the soil, some nematodes are beneficial, while others are harmful.

New wood (new growth): The new growth on plants characterized by a greener, more tender form than older, woodier growth.

Nozzle: A device that attaches to the end of a hose and disperses water through a number of small holes; the resulting spray covers a wider area.

Old wood: Old wood is growth that is more than one year old. Some shrubs produce flowers on old wood. If you prune these plants in spring before they flower and fruit, you will cut off the wood that will produce flowers.

Organic: This term describes products derived from naturally occurring materials instead of materials synthesized in a lab.

Part shade: Areas of the garden that receive two to four hours of sun a day. Plants requiring part shade will often require protection from the more intense afternoon sun, either from tree leaves or from a building.

Part sun: Areas of the garden that receive four to six hours of sun a day. Although the term is often used interchangeably with "part shade," a "part sun" designation places greater emphasis on the minimal sun requirements.

Perennial: A plant that lives for more than two years. Examples include trees, shrubs, and some flowering plants.

Pesticide: A substance used for destroying or controlling insects that are harmful to plants. Pesticides are available in organic and synthetic forms.

pH: A figure designating the acidity or the alkalinity of garden soil, pH is measured on a scale of 1 to 14, with 7.0 being neutral.

Pinch: This is a method to remove unwanted plant growth with your fingers, promoting bushier growth and increased blooming.

Pitchfork: A hand tool with a long handle and sharp metal prongs, a pitchfork is typically used for moving loose material, such as mulch or hay.

Plant label: This label or sticker on a plant container provides a description of the plant and information on its care and growth habits.

Pollination: The transfer of pollen for fertilization from the male pollen-bearing structure (stamen) to the female structure (pistil), usually by wind, bees, butterflies, moths, or hummingbirds; this process is required for fruit production.

Potting soil: A mixture used to grow flowers, herbs, and vegetables in containers. Potting soil provides proper drainage and extra nutrients for healthy growth.

Powdery mildew: A fungal disease characterized by white powdery spots on plant leaves and stems, this disease is worse during times of drought or when plants have poor air circulation.

Power edger: This electric or gasoline-powered edger removes grass along flowerbeds and walkways for a neat appearance.

Pre-emergent herbicide: This weed killer works by preventing weed seeds from sprouting.

Pruning: This is a garden task in which a variety of hand tools are used to remove dead or overgrown branches to increase plant fullness and health.

Pruning saw: This hand tool for pruning smaller branches and limbs features a long, serrated blade with an elongated handle.

Push mower: A lawn mower that is propelled by the user rather than a motor, typically having between 5 to 8 steel blades that turn and cut as the mower is pushed.

Reel mower: A mower in which the blades spin vertically with a scissoring motion to cut grass blades.

Rhizome: An underground horizontal stem that grows side shoots, a rhizome is similar to a bulb.

Rootball: The network of roots and soil clinging to a plant when it is lifted out of the ground.

Rootstock: The bottom part of a grafted tree, rootstocks are often used to create dwarf trees, impart pest or disease resistance, or make a plant more cold hardy.

Rotary spreader: A garden tool that distributes seed and herbicides in a pattern wider than the base of the spreader.

Scaffold branch: This horizontal branch emerges almost perpendicular to the trunk.

Scientific name: This two-word identification system consists of the genus and species of a plant, such as Ilex opaca.

Scissors: A two-bladed hand tool great for cutting cloth, paper, twine, and other lightweight materials; scissors are a basic garden tool.

Seed packet: The package in which vegetable and flower seeds are sold, it typically includes growing instructions, a planting chart, and harvesting information.

Seed-starting mix: Typically a soilless blend of perlite, vermiculite, peat moss, and other ingredients, seed-starting mix is specifically formulated for growing plants from seed.

Self-fertile: A plant that does not require cross-pollination from another plant in order to produce fruit is self-fertile.

Self-sow: A flower that forms seeds that drop to the ground to create more plants the following spring. Some examples of self-sowing annual flowers include California poppies and cleome.

Shade: Garden shade is the absence of any direct sunlight in a given area, usually due to tree foliage or building shadows.

Shearing: To prune off the tips of a shrub to promote dense thick growth. Shearing is usually done with mechanical or electric pruners on hedge plants, such as privet and cedar.

Shop broom: A long-handled broom with a wide base used for efficiently sweeping a variety of fine to medium debris.

Short-day plant: Flowering when the length of day is shorter than its critical photoperiod, short-day plants typically bloom during fall, winter, or early spring.

Shovel: A handled tool with a broad, flat blade and slightly upturned sides, used for moving soil and other garden materials; this is a basic garden tool.

Shredded evergreen mulch: A mulch consisting of shredded wood from evergreen trees. This mulch suppresses weed growth and keeps the pH of the soil acidic.

Shredded hardwood mulch: A mulch consisting of shredded wood that interlocks, resisting washout and suppressing weeds.

Shrub: This woody plant is distinguished from a tree by its multiple trunks and branches and its shorter height of less than 15 feet tall.

Shrub rake: This long-handled rake with a narrow head fits easily into tight spaces between plants.

Sidedress: To sprinkle slow-release fertilizer along the side of a plant row or plant stem.

Slow-release fertilizer: This form of fertilizer releases nutrients at a slower rate throughout the season, requiring less-frequent applications.

Snips: This hand tool, used for snipping small plants and flowers, is perfect for harvesting fruits, vegetables, and flowers.

Soaker hose: This is an efficient watering system in which a porous hose, usually made from recycled rubber, allows water to seep out around plant roots.

Soil knife: This garden knife with a sharp, serrated edge is used for cutting twine, plant roots, turf, and other garden materials.

Soil test: An analysis of a soil sample, this determines the level of nutrients (to identify deficiencies) and detects pH levels.

Spade: This short-handled tool with a sharp, rectangular metal blade is used for cutting and digging soil or turf.

Specimen: A shrub or tree planted in a prominent spot in the yard, usually by itself, to act as a focal point in your landscape.

String trimmer: A hand-held tool that uses monofilament line instead of a blade to trim grass.

Succulent: A type of plant that stores water in its leaves, stems, and roots, and is acclimated for arid climates and soil conditions.

Sucker: The shoot growth from the base of a tree or a woody plant, often caused by stress, this also refers to sprouts from below the graft of a rose or grafted tree. Suckers divert energy away from the desirable tree growth and should be removed unless you want the plant to sucker to fill in a hedgerow.

Summer annual: Annuals that thrive during the warmer months of the growing season.

Taproot: This is an enlarged, tapered plant root that grows vertically downward.

Thinning: This is the practice of removing excess annual flowers or vegetables (root crops) to leave more room for the remaining annual flowers and vegetables to grow.

Topdress: To spread fertilizer on top of the soil (such has spreading compost around a lawn).

Topiary: The art of pruning shrubs in geometric or animal-like shapes.

Transplants: Plants that are grown in one location and then moved to and replanted in another; seeds started indoors and nursery plants are two examples.

Tree: This woody perennial plant typically consists of a single trunk with multiple lateral branches.

Tree canopy: This is the upper layer of growth, consisting of the tree's branches and leaves.

Tropical plant: This is a plant that is native to a tropical region of the world, and thus, is acclimated to a warm, humid climate and not hardy to frost.

Trowel: This shovel-like hand tool is used for digging or moving small amounts of soil.

Turf: Grass and the surface layer of soil that is held together by its roots.

Variegated: The appearance of differently colored areas on plant leaves, usually white, yellow, or a brighter green.

Water sprout: This vertical shoot emerges from a scaffold branch. It is usually nonfruiting or flowering and undesirable.

Watering wand: This hose attachment features a longer handle for watering plants beyond reach.

Weed and feed: A product containing both an herbicide for weed control and a fertilizer for grass growth.

Weeping: A growth habit in plants that features drooping or downward curving branches.

Well-drained soil: Soil that drains water fast enough so as not to create overly wet conditions that might lead to root rot.

Wheat straw: These dry stalks of wheat, which are used for mulch, retain soil moisture and suppress weeds.

Wood chips: Small pieces of wood made by cutting or chipping, wood chips are used as mulch in the garden.

INDEX

PHOTO CREDITS

MEET CHARLIE NARDOZZI

Charlie Nardozzi is a nationally recognized garden writer, speaker, and radio and television personality. He has worked for more than twenty years bringing expert gardening information to home gardeners through radio, television, talks, online, and the printed page. Charlie delights in making gardening information simple, easy, fun, and accessible to everyone.

He is the author of *Vegetable Gardening for Dummies*, *Urban Gardening for Dummies*, and *Northeast Fruit and Vegetable Gardening*. He also contributed to the cookbook *Vegetables from an Italian Garden*.

Charlie lives and gardens in Vermont where his gardening talents translate into other media as well. Charlie writes and produces the *Vermont Garden Journal* on public radio, hosts gardening tips on the local CBS-TV affiliate in Vermont, and is the former host of the nationally broadcast PBS *Garden Smart* television show.

Charlie also knows the value of teaching kids about gardening. He has partnered with companies and organizations such as Gardener's Supply Company, Cabot Cheese, Stonyfield Yogurt, Northeast Organic Farmers Association, and Shelburne Farms on kids' gardening projects. Charlie is also a widely sought-after public speaker for presentations to flower shows, master gardener groups, and garden clubs across the country.

See his website (www.gardeningwithcharlie.com) for more information.